Furniture Making
Plain & Simple

Furniture Making Plain & Simple

BY Aldren A. Watson AND Theodora A. Poulos

Illustrations by Aldren A. Watson

W. W. Norton & Company

NEW YORK   LONDON

BY ALDREN A. WATSON
Hand Tools: Their Ways and Workings
Country Furniture
The Village Blacksmith
The Watson Drawing Book (with Ernest W. Watson)
Hand Bookbinding

Furniture Making Plain & Simple
was conceived, edited, and designed by
T & A Foxe Ltd, Brattleboro, Vermont

Published simultaneously in Canada
by Stoddart, a subsidiary of General
Publishing Co. Ltd., Don Mills, Ontario
Printed in the United States of America

The text of this book is composed in Primer
with display set in Friz Quadrata and Helvetica.
Composition by Vail-Ballou Press, Inc.
Printing and binding by The Murray Printing Company

First edition

Library of Congress Cataloging in Publication Data

Watson, Aldren A.
    Furniture Making Plain & Simple

    Includes index.
1. Furniture making—Amateurs' manuals.   I. Poulos,
Theodora A.   II. Title.
TT195.W38 1984   684.1'042   84-4197

ISBN 0-393-01812-1

W. W. Norton & Company, Inc.
500 Fifth Avenue, New York, N.Y. 10110
W. W. Norton & Company Ltd
37 Great Russell Street, London WC1B 3NU

1 2 3 4 5 6 7 8 9 0

for Angelikee

Contents

Foreword 9

Wood 11

Buying Lumber 20

Woodworking Practices 27

Fasteners 42

Making Joints 46

   Butt 46

   Dovetail 52

   Groove 60

   Halved 62

   Housed 66

   Mitered 69

   Mortise and Tenon 72

   Notch 80

   Rabbet 83

   Tongue and Groove 88

Turned Legs 95

Drawer Construction 112

Hanging Doors 123

Finishing Wood 130

Furniture Projects 153

   New York Hutch 155

   Armoire 169

   Corner Cupboard 183

   Slant-back Dresser 201

   Pine Dressing Table 219

   One-drawer Stand 235

   Breadboard-top Table 247

   Pencil-post Bed 257

   Writing Table 273

   Blanket Chest 291

   Sideboard 303

Index 327

Foreword

I feel an affinity with all woodworkers before me undertaking for the first time
to build a good and useful piece of furniture; who began at the same place with similar
tools and equal trepidation; who I see now were obliged to make the very mistakes
that are mine; and who no less frequently despaired of ever getting things right.
For, whereas they succeeded in this course of trial and error with patience and practice,
my determination is revived and my belief reaffirmed that I will also.

Making furniture with hand tools is nei-ther easy nor hopelessly complicated. It involves rather a small set of woodworking practices that are repeated over and over again. It begins with joinery—the heart of furniture making. Cutting and fitting joints does indeed demand more time and patience than most other procedures, yet it is by no means the labyrinth of confusing tech-niques you may imagine.

The more experienced you are with wood-working in general, the easier the work will be and the more professional the results. But those starting new have only to begin. Lay out and cut a few trial joints in scrap wood. The first one will probably be clumsier than you like, and

the second attempt may still not be the best fit. Stay with it. Skills are not acquired overnight but through doing, redoing, and even starting all over again. Then suddenly, the unsettling feeling that it is beyond you will vanish.

Take your time. Set realistic work goals that are consistent with what time you have avail-able. Make one part of the furniture and carry out each operation on it as though it were the only one. Take the attitude that if it cannot be finished today, all the more pleasure for tomor-row. And ask yourself if it really matters if a single mortise and tenon joint takes an entire weekend. Enjoy the work, and you will all the more enjoy the furniture.

slabbing off the first cut on a 42-inch band saw

Wood

Trees are converted into lumber in a set series of operations, the basic ones taking place in the woods. A tree is cut down, and once felled its branches are lopped off even with the trunk. It is then sawn into logs conforming to the standard lumber lengths of 8, 10, 12, 14, or 16 feet, each log being cut a few inches over the length to allow trimming the ends square at the sawmill.

The logs are next taken to the mill, where one at a time they are mechanically kicked onto the saw carriage and locked in place with movable dogs. Running on tracks, the carriage rolls forward and back past the saw, which slices off a board on each trip. After each cut, the carriage rolls back and the log is moved out on the carriage—again in the way of the saw—ready for the next slice. The exact thickness of the cut is set by an adjustable device at the hand of the sawyer, who can vary the thickness of the lumber from 1 inch on up. Depending on the size and shape of the particular log, therefore, the first cut may be thick, just to slab off the bark and any irregularities, while subsequent ones may be a series of 1-inch boards, or a combination of dimension lumber and a heavy timber taken out of the center.

Coming from this headsaw, the lumber goes through edger saws that remove the bark and trim the boards to uniform width, and then passes down the line to a cutoff saw that trims it to standard length and square on the ends.

At this stage, lumber is green: it is sap-wet, heavy, and unfit for anything but the roughest construction work. All wood in its natural state, whether in a standing tree, in the log, or in freshly sawn lumber, contains a large amount of moisture, both sap and water. This moisture content must be drastically reduced to the point where the wood will not shrink, check, warp, or change shape, either while it is being worked or after it has been manufactured.

To eliminate most of the moisture, lumber

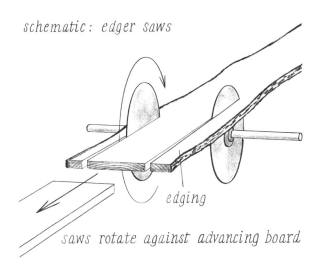

schematic: edger saws

edging

saws rotate against advancing board

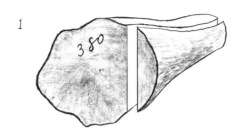

1

first slab cutoff

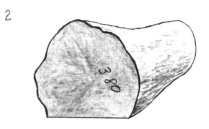

2

log turned on saw carriage

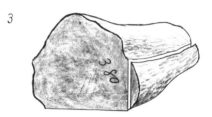

3

second slab cutoff

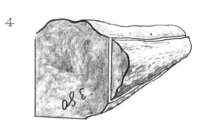

4

log turned, third slab cutoff

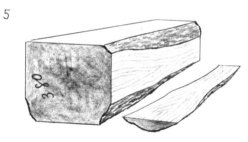

5

fourth slab cutoff

6

sawn into 1" boards and a 2" plank

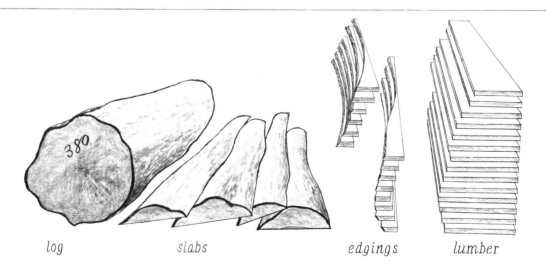

log *slabs* *edgings* *lumber*

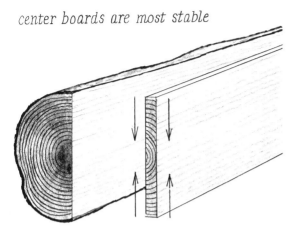

center boards are most stable

nearly equal pull on both sides

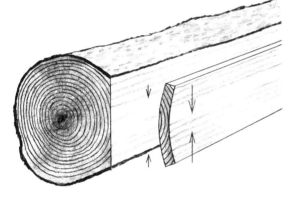

outside boards most liable to warp

least pull   greatest pull

is stacked either outdoors in open sheds for a period of months or in a dry kiln with controlled heat and humidity where the moisture content can be reduced at a much faster rate. Where the best quality lumber is wanted, both methods may be used: several months of air drying followed by a shorter period in the kiln, the object being to bring the moisture content to equilibrium with the conditions in which the wood will be fashioned and used.

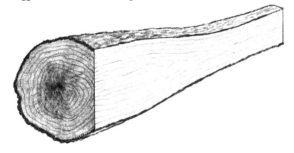

log with a pronounced taper, showing typical cathedral grain pattern

The final step in making lumber is to plane all four sides of boards smooth and to uniform thickness and width, as well as to square both edges. Various terms are used to designate lumber that is ready for the customer. Planed, surfaced, and dressed are all terms that mean the same thing, and are abbreviated by various symbols to denote the particular type of finish. For example, P4S means planed four sides, S2S indicates lumber surfaced two sides only with the edges left rough, while D4S designates stuff dressed four sides. In the average lumberyard selling to the building trades, softwood lumber is sized and planed to standard dimensions. Hardwoods, on the other hand, are frequently sold as rough-sawn lumber either as flitch-sawn stuff (with the bark edges untrimmed) or trimmed to random widths and lengths. In both cases, the customer must have it finished on his own account.

Wood

BOARD FEET

The term board foot (BF) is the standard unit of measure for calculating the amount of lumber in a log, a board, or a timber of any size, and is defined as a board 1 inch thick and 12 inches square. In a standing tree, the amount of lumber it will yield is also estimated in terms of board feet. And the board foot is the basis for figuring the cost of lumber, usually stated in dollars per hundred or per thousand board feet as the case may be.

The formula for finding the board-foot content of a stick of lumber is:

$$BF = \frac{\text{thickness (inches)} \times \text{width (inches)} \times \text{length (feet)}}{12}$$

$$\text{Examples:} \quad 1 \times 4 \times 12' = \frac{48}{12} = 4 \text{ BF}$$

$$1 \times 12 \times 10' = \frac{120}{12} = 10 \text{ BF}$$

$$2 \times 8 \times 10' = \frac{160}{12} = 13 \text{ BF } (13.3)$$

In figuring the cost of lumber, when the fraction is .5 or over, it is rounded up to the next whole number. If below .5, it is rounded down.

wood grain affected by growth rate

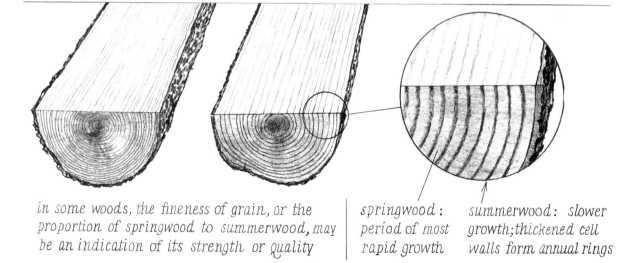

in some woods, the fineness of grain, or the proportion of springwood to summerwood, may be an indication of its strength or quality

springwood: period of most rapid growth

summerwood: slower growth; thickened cell walls form annual rings

In the woods the log scaler uses the diameter of a log at its small top end combined with its length to compute the number of board feet it contains, as well as its dollar value. Applying these factors to a special log stick, or rule, the scaler readily estimates the board foot content. For example, according to the Doyle Log Scale, a 16-inch log 12 feet long theoretically contains 108 board feet. However, if the log shows rot, wind shakes, splits, or other obvious defects, the scaler deducts from the total to arrive at a more realistic figure to account for these imperfections that will be cut out at the sawmill.

NOMINAL AND ACTUAL DIMENSIONS

As lumber comes from the saw, it has been cut to full dimensions. A board sawn 1 inch thick and 12 inches wide will measure a full 1 x 12″. These are the *nominal dimensions*. However, when this same board has been dried and planed, it will be somewhat smaller—approximately 3/4 inch thick and 11 1/2 inches wide. These are the *actual dimensions*. Shrinkage has accounted for some of this loss, and planing off the rough surfaces and edges the rest. In any case, what you order and pay for are the nominal dimensions, while the actual dimensions are what you must work with in the shop. This discrepancy between the two terms must be taken into account when calculating the dimensions and number of pieces of lumber needed for a job. For instance, if you need a full inch of finished thickness in a tabletop, a nominal thickness of 1 1/4 inches (five quarter) will be required. Assuming that this 5/4 stick actually measures 1 1/8 inches thick, the remaining 1/8 inch gives you enough spare wood to plane off the scalloped chatter marks left by the knives of the rotary planing machine and to dress the stick to exact thickness. This handwork usually improves the appearance of a board, giving it a character more agreeable than the mechanical surface imparted by a machine.

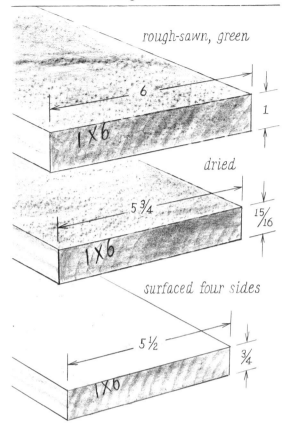

dimensional changes in lumber

rough-sawn, green

1 X 6   6   1

dried

1 X 6   5 3/4   15/16

surfaced four sides

1 X 6   5 1/2   3/4

BOARDS AND FURNITURE SQUARES

The two main types of lumber used in furniture making are boards and furniture squares. Boards of various thicknesses and widths are used for the frames and tops of tables, the sides and shelves of cupboards, and for the construction of doors and drawers. Furniture squares are heavier sticks, 1 1/2 inches or more in thickness and square in section, from which table legs and bedposts are fashioned.

Many pieces of furniture in this book are built of sections of wood wider than 12 inches, the widest normally stocked by most lumberyards. Consequently, the usual practice is followed of edge-joining two or more boards with either an edge-butt or tongue and groove joint, and then trimming the section to the required width.

Single wide boards measuring 12 inches or over are nevertheless available from some lumber dealers and cabinet shops. Finding them may take some time and they may have to be surfaced by hand, as they may be rough-sawn. On the other hand, using wide boards eliminates the time otherwise used in jointing and gluing, and does away with glue lines in the finished work.

PLYWOOD

A third type of lumber in the form of laminated hardwood plywood is specified here for drawer bottoms and the backboards of large pieces such as cupboards. There is a wide selection of plywood on the market, made in various thicknesses from the same species used in solid wood construction, as well as from many of the attractive imported and exotic woods. Plywood is usually made in sheets 4 x 8′ and longer, and

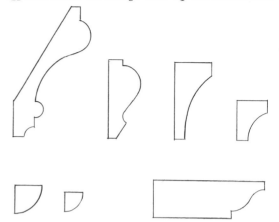

typical stock moldings sold by the linear foot

since most dealers sell full sheets only, you will generally have to cut out what you need and save the surplus for another job.

Wide sections of this kind were formerly covered with thin boards, often planed one side only, rabbeted on both edges and nailed without glue to the back of the furniture. Drawer bottoms were also traditionally made of similar thin stuff milled from thicker boards—in a day and time when big trees and wide boards were common—and then beveled along the edges to wedge tight into grooves cut in the drawer front and sides. This is still a workmanlike method, though obviously entailing more time and labor to find wide stuff and have it milled to thickness.

MOLDINGS AND DOWELS

Moldings are factory-made in a considerable variety of shapes and sizes, and are used to finish the tops and edges of furniture and to conceal end-grain sections. Moldings are made in soft- and hardwoods and are usually sold in standard lengths by the linear foot, rather than by the board foot.

Hardwood dowels for drawbore pins and pintle hinges are made in diameters from 1/8

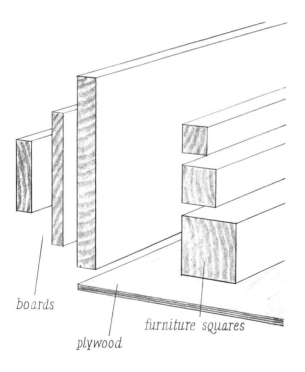

boards

plywood

furniture squares

inch up to 1 inch and larger, in graduations of 1/16 inch. They come in 36-inch lengths and are sold by the piece. The diameters of dowels may vary fractionally from the corresponding size of twist drill and auger bit. It is therefore a good idea to drill a test hole and try the dowel to make sure of a good fit. Depending on the section of wood from which they were made, dowels may be warped or slightly out-of-round, so it is best to pick over and select the best.

hardwood dowels for drawbore pins, pintle hinges, and drawer construction

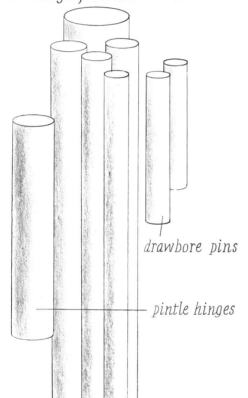

drawbore pins

pintle hinges

KINDS OF WOOD

While there are dozens of domestic and imported woods entirely satisfactory for furniture work, the list here includes a handful of the more commonly available species that can be worked with hand tools alone.

By botanical classification, hardwoods comprise the deciduous species that annually shed their leaves, and the softwoods belong to the coniferous group that keeps its foliage year-round. When you move to the workbench, however, the hardness or softness of wood is more practically measured by the force and energy required to work it with saw, plane, chisel, drill, and auger bit, as well as by its resistance to denting, bruising, and normal wear and tear.

Each tree has individual characteristics, often unique within a specie. Not every piece of maple is equally hard or of exactly the same grain and color. And there is just as much variation in white pine, some boards being much harder than others, some truly white, and others definitely pink or brown. Using this tool-working definition, the following species are arranged in order of their approximate relative hardness, comparatively tested by hand-paring with a sharp chisel.

SUGAR MAPLE

Known also as hard maple and rock maple, it has a creamy color and generally no distinguishable difference between heartwood and sapwood. Heavy, strong, and exceptionally stiff, it has a high resistance to denting and bruising. Maple has a fine, even, closed grain and texture that makes it superior for joinery. In some specimens, freak twists of grain produce variations known as curly maple, bird's-eye, burled, or fiddleback—figures with considerable decorative value. The wood has good tool-working properties but quickly dulls the tools.

RED MAPLE

Also called soft maple, its wood is nearly the same color as sugar maple and has a similar, fine grain. It has good tool-working properties, especially in the better grades, is noticeably softer and may therefore be easier on the tools.

CHERRY

A dark wood, it is colored a soft, reddish tan, often with a narrow band of creamy pink sapwood. With age the wood usually develops a rich purple-red hue and a handsome surface patina. One of the choice cabinet woods, cherry has a dense, closed grain, usually somewhat wavy rather than perfectly straight, and often shows small swirls and attractive darker lines or streaks. It is strong, very stiff, and has superior tool-working properties. Worked with plane, chisel, drawknife, and spokeshave, cherry takes on a high, burnished luster, and holds sharp edges exceptionally well.

WHITE OAK

Usually colored a warm white to pale gray, white oak has long been a first choice among the oaks, not all of which are suitable for furniture work. It is heavy, strong, stiff and resistant to shock, and has an open grain with a pronounced grain pattern. Unlike many of the other oaks—and there are numerous varieties—white oak resists the penetration of water and some liquid finishes. It has good tool-working properties, although in using the plane, isolated areas may tend to be plucked up. Like all the oaks, it splits easily, therefore it is important always to drill pilot holes for nails and screws, and to make tenon joints long enough to avoid the wood breaking out behind the drawbore pin.

NORTHERN RED OAK

Not as heavy as white oak, it has a similar open grain and satisfactory tool-working properties. The color runs from brown heartwood to pinkish-white sapwood.

BEECH

In color the wood of the beech is not unlike maple. A relative of the oak, it is a heavy, hard, and fine-grained wood that works down to a fine surface, has excellent tool-working properties, and is much used for tool handles, workbench tops, and other applications where toughness is required.

BIRCH

Roughly the same color as beech, the wood is moderately heavy, hard, strong, and with a fine, even texture. Birch tends to be somewhat brittle, and care must be used to drill pilot holes when driving nails and screws, especially when located near the ends of boards. The term *mahogany birch* is not a specie variation, but simply refers to birch treated with a dark stain to accentuate its natural similarity to the grain of mahogany.

MAHOGANY

A dark tropical wood, mahogany varies in color from light to dark brown with a pronounced reddish cast. The wood from Honduras is generally considered the choice variety, although much mahogany is also imported from the Caribbean, South America, the Philippine Islands, and Africa. It has a very fine open grain, is easily worked with hand tools—almost as easily as white pine—and can be used for almost any furniture work. It is not as strong as some of the other hardwoods, particularly when worked for mortise and tenon joinery, where additional heft should be allowed.

BLACK WALNUT

Known simply as walnut or American walnut, the wood is dark, ranging from light buckskin or chocolate to the rich, purple-browns, often with darker line streaks. Walnut is a superior furniture wood that has unmatched tool-working properties. Close-grained and moderately hard, it has relatively little tendency to twist or warp and is noted for maintaining its dimensional stability, even when left without any finish whatsoever.

BUTTERNUT

The wood is a light, soft brown which with age and exposure to air and sunlight colors up to a handsome warm gray-brown. Sometimes called white walnut, butternut bears a close resemblance to its relative black walnut, with which it might easily be confused except for the obvious difference in weight—about the same as pine. Neither as strong nor as hard as walnut, its closed grain is similar and the wood has very good tool-working properties.

EASTERN WHITE PINE

Colored a creamy white to pink and a pale, soft brown, pine rapidly darkens with age and exposure to air and sunlight, when it acquires rich variations of warm browns. For generations a prime wood of the furniture maker, white pine, or American pine as it is sometimes called, has an open, straight, and quite uniform grain, is light in weight yet strong enough for all work except the most delicate machine lathe turnings. Pine has excellent tool-working properties, but sharp tools are essential in order to slice cleanly and avoid torn fibers. As new pine boards are easily dented and damaged, they should be handled carefully and protected with scrap wood blocking when put in the vise. Once thoroughly seasoned, however, pine develops a harder, more

resistant skin. *Pumpkin pine* is not a distinct specie variation, but a term used to describe the consistently fine-grained wood from especially fine and large old trees of the white pine, growing to a pumpkin shape as isolated individuals in the open—with room to spread their branches—rather than in a thick forest stand or grove. In some localities, pines of this type and shape are called *cabbage pine*.

IDAHO PINE

Also known as Western white pine, the wood closely resembles Eastern white pine in color, grain, and texture, as well as in its general tool-working properties. When worked with saw and plane, however, the wood fibers may tend to be torn rather than sliced clean; consequently sharp cutting tools and saws of a fine point-size are required.

Buying Lumber

Buy the best lumber you can afford. It should be dry, clear, straight, and without warp, twist, checks, or end splits. While these last two defects can be cut off, there is no cure for a warped board or one that twists from one end to the other. First-class stuff is the easiest and most satisfactory to work, whether sawing, planing, working with the chisel, or boring holes. Tool cuts will be cleaner, smoother, made with less effort, and require less clean-up. Good quality lumber is especially important where joints are concerned, not only for ease of working but also for strength and appearance.

While the best grades of lumber are the most expensive, cost is the least significant factor, considering how little wood goes into any one piece of furniture. The greater investment is always in the amount of manufacturing time, which tends to diminish in direct ratio to the quality of the material used.

Occasionally, less than perfect lumber is acceptable and sometimes even desirable. Furniture that is to be painted need not be built of clear lumber, provided it is dry and stable and that the knots are bound knots rather than the loose kind that shrink and drop out; and provided also that they are properly sealed to accept and hold the paint. Imperfect boards with an especially interesting figure in the grain can often be used to decorative advantage, for example, in a tabletop where there are no joints that would be weakened by the erratic grain. A pair of such boards can be edge-joined in book-matched fashion to give the appearance of mirror images.

two boards book-matched for a tabletop

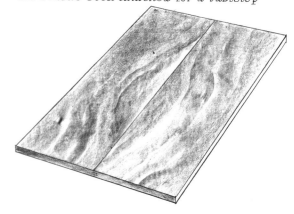

One of the best sources of quality lumber is the dealer who specializes in fine wood for cabinet and furniture work, boat building, and architectural work. There are scores of these companies in all sections of the country, and a great many of them advertise in newspapers and magazines. They stock numerous species of hardwoods and softwoods in standard and special sizes, as well as the better grades and species of hardwood plywood. Many of these companies ship by truck on receipt of payment, and are accustomed to handling small retail orders. Quite a number publish brochures and price lists and maintain a customer service representative to assist in ordering. Others will cut and mill stuff to special dimensions and thicknesses for an extra charge. Included in this category are countless dealers who stock high grade domestic and imported lumber and plywood used in boat building, a branch of woodworking that demands first quality material.

Another practical approach to buying lumber is to locate a small cabinet shop in your vicinity. These shops manufacture custom kitchen cabinets, tables, mantelpieces, cupboards, and other pieces requiring the same sort of material you will need, and many of them are willing to sell small quantities retail. They have the machines to mill stuff to your specifications, and are also likely to have wide boards that are not generally available elsewhere. The proprietors of these shops are usually experienced woodworkers who know their woods and tools and are in a position to give useful help. And there is much to be said for being able to see and select the lumber you need, piece by piece.

A third source of wood is the common lumberyard, better known today as a building supply company. It carries a full range of construction lumber such as 2 x 4s, 2 x 6s, and 2 x 8s for framing, rough lumber for sheathing, subflooring, and roofing, preshaped interior trim for doors and windows, and construction-grade fir plywood. While the stock is complete and adequate, it is not intended for furniture making. Nevertheless, lumberyards carry some lumber that is suitable, notably 1-inch P4S pine boards up to 12 inches wide, in lengths to 12 feet and occasionally longer. This lumber is not always clear, straight, and flat, and generally you will have to take boards as they come, since few yards allow you to pick over a whole stack.

Home centers and self-service building supply companies are in pretty much the same class. The lumber is not generally of furniture quality, and because their range of sizes is more limited, buying by the piece rather than the board foot tends to be wasteful and expensive.

Small lots of wide, dry, or otherwise suitable furniture wood can also be found by scanning the classified advertisements in local newspapers and buyers' guides, examples of which are included at the end of this chapter.

ORDERING AND BUYING

Don't worry. It isn't necessary to know the whole language of lumbering jargon to order and buy lumber. Before you go shopping, study the entire project from beginning to end: the list of materials, lumber required, cutting diagram, and the illustrated directions. Have a thorough grasp of the sequence of the work procedures. Then go in person rather than using the telephone. Take the project plans and the list of materials with you. The clerk at the order desk is experienced with lumber calculations and is usually very efficient at offering help. Ask for it. The main thing is to make clear exactly what you are building.

If the project calls for lumber milled to special thickness, the clerk should be able to tell you how and where it can be done, and give you telephone numbers.

STORING LUMBER

Before bringing home a batch of lumber, plan where to put it and how to take care of it. Even though it may have been kiln-dried, the storage conditions at the lumberyard are quite different from those in the average, overheated home. Boards fresh from the kiln are usually stacked in open sheds where the moisture content of the atmosphere may remain more or less constant at about 20 percent and the air temperature close to 60 degrees. If left undisturbed, such stuff will remain unchanged almost indefinitely. But when suddenly moved into a shop where the humidity is low and the temperature high, the boards come to life immediately and the process of drying and shrinking begins all over again—immediately—in an effort to reach equilibrium with the new environment, which may now be as low as 8 percent. As the moisture content decreases, so too does the size of the board, most noticeably in its width. It is not uncommon for a so-called dry stick of 1 x 12 white pine to shrink in width as much as 1/4 inch in the first four months indoors.

3. Keep away from the furnace, water heater, or hot-air ducts and radiators. Hang a thermometer near the lumber. Slow, cool seasoning allows it to age with the least amount of stress. If the space seems too hot and dry, drape the lumber pile with a sheet of plastic, raised a few inches above the top and hanging down loosely and away from the sides. Leave the bottom open for air circulation.

4. Stack boards flat and level with stickers between each board. A pile of boards laid flat together cannot dry out except on the top and edges, usually causing them to cup or warp. Stickers should be at least as thick as the boards

stacking lumber

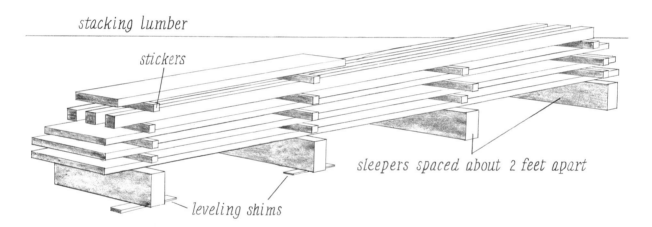

stickers

sleepers spaced about 2 feet apart

leveling shims

There are a few simple measures that will help control the effects of temperature and humidity and allow the lumber to adjust to the new conditions with a minimum of damage.

1. Paint the ends of boards to seal out moisture and prevent end checking—cracks that run back into the board. The ends dry out first and more rapidly than any other part of a board. One coat of any paint will do, well scrubbed into the end grain. Melted paraffin also works very well.

2. Store lumber in a well-ventilated space, away from damp floors and walls. Leave 4 or 5 inches of clear space under it and next to walls to allow good air circulation.

in the stack, all the same thickness, and an inch or two longer than their width. Allow one sticker for every 2 feet of board length, and see that the stickers in each successive layer are placed directly over those below, and directly over the sleepers or foundation blocks, to prevent sagging. Use a carpenter's level and shims as necessary to start the pile flat and level.

5. As you build the stack, mark the edge of each piece with the date, and when new stuff is added, put it on the bottom of the pile. This way, the driest boards will be accessible on top.

All of this points to the advantage of buying lumber as far in advance as possible, to allow additional seasoning before you use it.

WOOD AND LUMBER SOURCES

Typical listings picked at random from newspapers, telephone directories, and woodworking and home workshop magazines.

Dealers

ALABAMA

American Hardwoods
7242 Highway 20 West
Huntsville, 35804

ARIZONA

Austin Hardwoods
3821 East Broadway
Phoenix, 85040

CALIFORNIA

The Cutting Edge
1836 Fourth Street
Berkeley, 94710

Hardwood Center
Fountain Valley, 92708

White Brothers
4801 Tidewater Avenue
Oakland, 94601

Whispering Winds Hardwoods
565 7th Avenue
Santa Cruz, 95062

COLORADO

Austin Hardwoods
2625 South Santa Fe Drive
Denver, 80223

Silverton Victorian Mill Works
Box 877-12
Silverton, 81433

CONNECTICUT

Piper Woodworking
75 Center Street Floor C
Bristol, 06010

Fearon Enterprises, Inc.
Kissman Wood Company
16 West Road
Marlborough, 06447

General Woodcraft
100C Blinman Street
New London, 06320

Woods of Heavenly Valley
38 Harwinton Street
Plymouth, 06782

FLORIDA

F. J. Fitchett
409-411 24th Street
West Palm Beach, 33407

Henegan's Wood Shed
7760 Southern Boulevard
West Palm Beach, 33411

GEORGIA

Atlanta Hardwood Center
5322 South Cobb Drive
Smyrna, 30080

ILLINOIS

Owl Hardwood Lumber Company
1514 East Algonquin Road
Arlington Heights, 60005

Craftsman Wood Service Company
2727 South Mary Street
Chicago, 60608

Windsor Classic Ltd
15937 Washington Street
Gurnee, 60031

INDIANA

Northwest Lumber
5035 Lafayette Street
Indianapolis, 46254

Wood-Crafter's Supply Center
3201 North Shadeland Avenue
Indianapolis, 46226

MAINE

Milk and Silver Hardwoods Company
6 Milk Street
Portland, 04111

MARYLAND

Harbor Sales Company, Inc.
1401 Russell Street
Baltimore, 21230

Craftwoods
10921 York Road
Cockeysville, 21030

Piscataway Company
14514 Main Street
Upper Marlboro, 20772

MASSACHUSETTS

Factory Lumber Outlet
Route 140
Boylston, 01505

Allied Plywood
490 Rutherford Avenue
Charlestown, 02129

Box 1776
Cohasset, 02025

Cohasset Woodcrafters
19A South Main Street
Cohasset, 02025

Amherst Woodworking & Supply Inc.
Hubbard Avenue
Northampton, 01002

Boulter Plywood
24 Broadway
Somerville, 02145

NEVADA

Austin Hardwoods
2901 South Highland #15A
Las Vegas, 89109

NEW HAMPSHIRE

P. J. Currier Lumber Company
Route 122
Amherst, 03031

Mahogany Masterpieces
Suncook, 03275

NEW JERSEY

Mr. Roberts Lumber Center
50 Clements Bridge Road
Barrington, 08007

Paul Bunyan Wood Shop
12 Route 519
Branchville, 07826

Orange Valley House of Hardwoods
606 Freeman Street
Orange, 07050

Willard Brothers Woodcutters
300 Basin Road
Trenton, 08619

NEW YORK

Allied Plywood
1635 Poplar Street
Bronx, 10461

Albert Constantine & Son Inc.
2050 Eastchester Road
Bronx, 10461

John Harra Wood & Supply Company
511 West 25th Street
New York, 10001

Native American Hardwoods Ltd
Route 1
West Valley, 14171

Maurice L. Condon Company
248 Ferris Avenue
White Plains, 10603

Cryder Creek Wood
PO Box 19
Whitesville, 14897

NORTH CAROLINA

Educational Lumber Company, Inc.
PO Box 5373
21 Meadow Road
Asheville, 28803

American Wood Mart
PO Box 1390
Jamestown, 27282

Eastern Carolina Lumber Co., Inc.
PO Drawer 660
Windsor, 27983

OHIO

Denier Brothers
710 East Shepherd Lane
Cincinnati, 45215

American Woodcrafters
1025 South Roosevelt
Piqua, 45356

Willis Lumber Company
545 Millikan Avenue
Washington C. H., 43160

PENNSYLVANIA

Talarico Hardwoods
Box 303 RD 3
Mohnton, 19540

Allied Plywood
East Street and Erie Avenue
Philadelphia, 19134

Austin Hardwoods
5701 Magnolia Street
Philadelphia, 19144

Thompson Mahogany Company
7400 Edmund Street
Philadelphia, 19136

Woodcrafters' Supply
9509 Perry Highway
Pittsburgh, 15237

TENNESSEE

Hardwoods of Memphis
PO Box 12449
Memphis, 38182

TEXAS

Austin Hardwoods
PO Box 3096
Austin, 78764

Interwoven Hardwoods
202 West Park
Fredericksburg, 78624

Wood World
1351 South Floyd Suite 101
Richardson, 75081

VERMONT

Depot Woodworking Inc.
683 Pine Street
Burlington, 05401

Weird Wood
Box 190
Chester, 05143

Smead Lumber Company, Inc.
Stebbins Road
Vernon, 05354

VIRGINIA

Mountain Lumber Company
1327 Carlton Avenue
Charlottesville, 22901

Austin Hardwoods
8930 Telegraph Road
Lorton, 22079

McFeely's
43 Cabell Street
PO Box 3
Lynchburg, 24505

Yukon Lumber Company
520 West 22nd Street
Norfolk, 23517

Buying Lumber

WASHINGTON

Austin Hardwoods
11844 NE 112th Street
Kirkland, 98033

Compton Lumber Company
2315 Western Street
Seattle, 98121

Kaymar Wood Products Inc.
4603 35th Street S. W.
Seattle, 98126

WISCONSIN

Punkin Hollow Wood & Tool
N 34 W 24041 Capitol Drive
Pewaukee, 53072

CANADA

A & M Wood Specialty Inc.
PO Box 3204
Cambridge, Ontario N3H456

Unicorn Universal Woods Ltd
137 John Street
Toronto, M5V 2E4

Classified Advertisements

Typical listings from newspapers and wood-working and home workshop magazines.

Boatbuilding / Cabinet woods. Air or kiln-dried. Honduras mahogany, white pine, white oak, cherry, maple, ash, poplar, birch, basswood. Churchill Forest Products, Inc., 91 Franklin St., Hanson, MA 02341. 617/293-3577.

Teak lumber, first quality, dry. Large selection. By appointment only. B. Axelford & Co., San Francisco, CA. 415/626-4949.

White oak, walnut, cherry, ash, poplar. 150,000 feet, sawed and properly dried for boatbuilding. Best prices, excellent quality, sensible marketing practices, individual attention to your needs. Shrewsbury Farms, Box 150, Princeton, KY 42445. 502/365-6119.

Quarter-sawn—red and white oak, white and pitch Pine, Birch, Beech, Maple, also plain sawn Cherry. Red Hat Woodworking, Box 306, Stow, MA 01775. 617/897-6455.

For Sale: 1″ air-dried pine lumber. Call Tim Hamilton. 802/257-0597.

Bird's-eye and Curly Maple. 4/4 to 10/4, $1.80 to $12 [board foot]. Cornucopia Inc., Harvard, MA 01451. 617/456-3201.

Walnut, AD [air-dried], 4/4 and 8/4 thick up to 10″ wide by 8 ft. long. Rough-sawn, clear and straight. Roy Biddle, Warrendale-Bayne Rd., Warrendale, PA. 412/935-2114.

Wide Walnut Lumber $3 / bd. ft. Quantity discounts apply. Gerry Grant, Gettysburg, PA. 717/334-6020.

KD [kiln-dried] Canadian butternut, 200 bd. ft 8/4, 150 bd. ft. 4/4 AD walnut. Wm. Duckworth, Ridgefield, CT. 203/431-3824.

Wide Pine Flooring and Paneling; approximately 20 inches wide. Carlisle Restoration Lumber. 603/446-3937.

Elliott & Brown Inc. Purveyors of the finest domestic and exotic lumber for cabinetmakers, hobbyists, home craftsmen, boatbuilders, and instrument makers. Stock includes rosewoods, teak, pine, butternut, cedar. All lumber is S & B. 999 Rue du College St. Henri, Montreal, Quebec. 514/935-7697.

We will Custom Plane your lumber—up to 8″ thick and 24″ wide—hard or soft—to your specifications. Call 413/648-9021. Leon L. Andrews, Bernardston, MA.

Woodworking Practices

long dimensions following the grain

Making furniture with hand tools involves a set of fundamental woodworking practices that are repeated over and over again. When they are carried out carefully and consistently on every job, they become second nature and tend to steadily improve the quality of workmanship, and to save time and lumber as well.

LONG DIMENSION FOLLOWING THE GRAIN

Almost without exception, pieces of wood intended for furniture parts should be cut with the long dimension following the wood grain, to take advantage of its natural strength. An obvious example is a narrow board supported at each end by an upright. Despite its crudity, this model "table" with its three parts cut to this rule will support an enormous load. Yet a similar model made of parts with the grain running the other way will collapse under a very slight amount of stress.

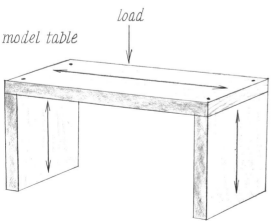

model table *load*

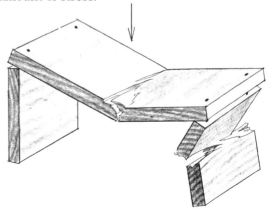

PREPARING LUMBER

Before it is ready for manufacture into furniture, nearly every piece of lumber should be prepared by (1) jointing the edges straight and square, (2) surface planing the flat sides to remove the corrugations left by the machine planer, and (3) marking the good edge and the good side for future reference.

Jointing

This job is best done with a long plane, the longer the better. A 24-inch jointer is ideal, but an 18-inch jack plane or a 13-inch jack rabbet will do entirely satisfactory work. These long planes reach over more of a board's length and do a better job of leveling the high spots than the common 9-inch smoothing plane, which tends to *follow* the hollows and high spots, rather than leveling them.

Put the work on edge in the vise and adjust the plane's cutter iron for a fine cut. Set the plane on the near end of the board and slide it forward until you feel the cutter catch on the wood. Then hold the toe of the plane down firmly on the work and push the plane the full length of the board in a fairly slow but steady, nonstop stroke. Keep the sole of the plane square with the edge of the board. At the end of the stroke, lift the plane clear, go back and repeat the process. Don't drag the plane back along the edge of the board, as this dulls the cutting edge. On the first stroke the plane will probably shave only a little here and there and skip others entirely. With the second and third strokes, however, the shavings will be longer and longer as the high spots are cut down and the hollows eliminated.

Check your work after each stroke or two by holding the try square over the edge of the board and sliding it from one end to the other. If this test shows that the edge is beveled rather than square, tilt the plane toward the high side on the next stroke, then check with the square

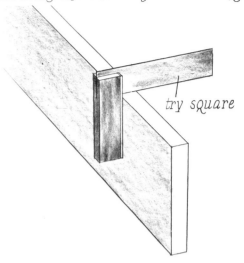

checking a jointed edge with the square

try square

again. When the edge tests square over its full length, make one final pass with the plane, which should produce one continuous shaving equal to the thickness and length of the board.

Surface Planing

Although lumber from the mill has been planed four sides, none of the surfaces are smooth enough for furniture work, typically showing quite visible corrugations made by the knives of the rotary planer. These machine marks must be removed by hand planing.

Lay the board flat on the bench and hold it securely with bench dogs or holddowns at both ends. Use a 9-inch smoothing plane, a jack plane, or a jack rabbet. Set the cutter for a fine cut and test it on a scrap of wood to make sure the cutter is sharp and that it planes flat without one corner cutting deeper than the other. Start planing at the far end. Hold the plane down on the work with a fair amount of pressure, and plane in the direction of the grain rather than across it at an angle. Work from the far end back toward you, planing fairly short patches rather than attempting great long strokes. The object is to take off only enough wood to level the sur-

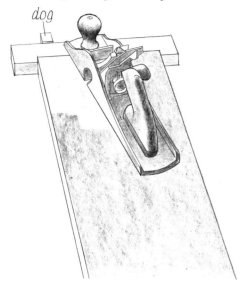

surface planing with a jack rabbet dog

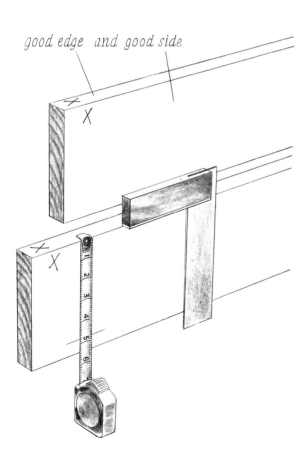

good edge and good side

face without reducing the thickness of the board. After every two or three strokes, check to see that the cutter is cutting level and that the cut is as fine as possible.

Good Edge and Good Side

After jointing and surface planing have been done, mark the best edge and the best side with penciled X's. These marks are used as points of reference for all work to be done on the board. For example, when marking off for a crosscut, always lay the square against the X-marked good edge; when trimming a board to width, measure from this same good edge; and work from the good edge as well when using the marking gauge. This system also makes it a simple matter to keep track of the better surface of a board so that it can be faced out in the finished furniture.

PLANING END GRAIN

After a board has been sawn to length, the rough saw cut must be smoothed and the end made square. The usual difficulty is in holding the plane level and square with the work while at the same time using enough pressure to prevent the plane's chattering and scalloping the wood. Chattering is caused by the cutter iron chopping through the hard parts of the grain and then suddenly skipping over the softer wood in between. And since these end-grain sections are usually quite short (across the end of a board), there is the additional hazard of running the plane off the far corner and splintering the wood. These problems can largely be overcome by clamping the work between pieces of scrap wood to increase the width of the planing surface, or by clamping a wide scrap to the edge of the work to lengthen the surface (see also *Making Joints,* p. 48 and p. 92).

The block plane is the traditional tool for this work, but the heavier smoothing and jack rabbet planes often work just as well, and sometimes even better, not only because their weight minimizes chattering, but also because the hand grips are larger and facilitate exerting more pressure. And pressure is important since the cutter iron must chop directly across the wood grain instead of working parallel to it.

Use a plane that is sharp. A dull cutter simply does not work on the end grain. Set it for a fine cut. With the work held end-up in the vise, hold the plane firmly in both hands and flat on the work. Using as much down pressure as possible, push the plane level across the end grain, sliding it at an angle to get a shearing, slicing action. This takes less force and also makes a cleaner cut, at the same time helping to prevent chatter marks.

MEASURING

A good quality steel tape rule is generally more accurate than the folding wooden extension type, which with age may develop enough slop in the pivot joints to create visible—and later baffling—errors. Whenever practical, hook the end of the tape over the edge of the work and tick off cumulative measurements along the rule without moving it. This maintains a common zero starting point and reduces errors that occur when you make one measurement, then slide the rule along to make the next. In a series of such measurements, the accumulated error may add up to as much as 1/8 inch or more.

For the greatest accuracy, use the same rule throughout a job. Switching from a tape rule to

planing end grain

work

scrap

planing direction

scrap wood

work

a folding one and back again is likely to produce more discrepancies, since not all rules are calibrated with uniform precision. When laying out any work, make it a habit to measure at least twice before cutting. And if the second measurement differs from the first, measure a third time.

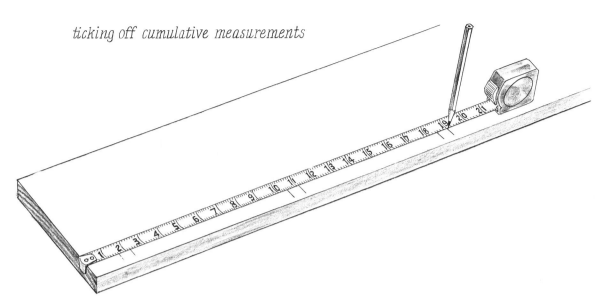

ticking off cumulative measurements

PATTERNS

Lay out tapered or curved work with patterns made of thin wood, stiff cardboard, or hard-finish drawing paper. The best pattern material is 3/32-inch plywood, which can be cut with a coping saw and then faired to exact shape with file and sandpaper. A wooden pattern reproduces identical curves more reliably than a paper one and has the added advantage of rigidity and long wear.

Paper and cardboard patterns are satisfactory for a limited number of uses, although more tedious to cut and smooth up. Lay out the curved or tapered shape with a pencil, drafting templates, and straightedge, or by enlarging from a cross-section diagram. Tape the pattern paper firmly to a cutting board of thick cardboard to keep it from slipping. Cut the pattern with a sharp xacto knife, using enough pressure on the knife to cut clear through the pattern material the first time. This makes the underside of the cut as clean as the top. Try to draw the knife in continuous sweeps. Stopping and starting usually produces uneven curves with flat places. In this respect the knife is preferable to scissors, which also tend to leave ragged edges that are difficult to clean up.

MARKING THE WASTE

When the work has been laid out, X-mark the waste wood to be cut off or removed, in order to avoid confusion and as a reminder always to cut on the *waste side* of the layout lines. This practice is especially important when cutting intricate work such as a series of dovetails.

X-marking the waste

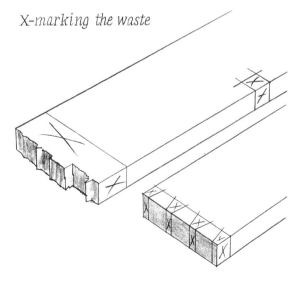

CUT PARTS AS NEEDED

Do not cut out all the parts at once. Cut only those needed for the stage of work at hand. Then use the dimensions given in the list of materials as a reference for cutting the next pieces, first measuring and checking the work so far completed. Fractional discrepancies between the specifications and the actual work can thus be discovered and taken into account to maintain the objective of a good fit.

CUT OVERSIZE

Cut parts at least an inch or two longer than the specified size and trim them to finished length only after all other shaping and machining have been done. This protects the ends of the wood from damage while holding it in the vise, handling it, and working on it with other tools. Cutting the ends last ensures good clean joints. This routine is especially important when shooting rabbets, grooves, bevels, and tongue and groove joints. In the event that the planes used for these jobs dip, or round off the ends of the cut, these imperfections can then simply be cut off with the surplus waste allowance. And this practice is just as useful when simply trimming a board to length. It is impossible to saw accurately to a mark that is only 1/4 inch from the end.

IDENTICAL PARTS

When laying out work on two or more duplicate parts, for example the mortises in a pair of table legs, it is more accurate to clamp the two of them together and lay out both joints at the same time than to do them one at a time. Make sure the ends of both legs are aligned exactly before tightening the clamps.

laying out a pair of table leg mortises

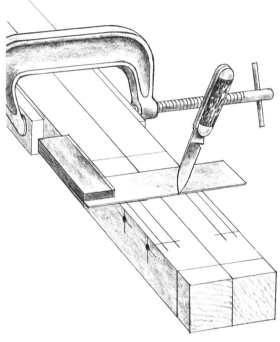

trimming to finished length after machining

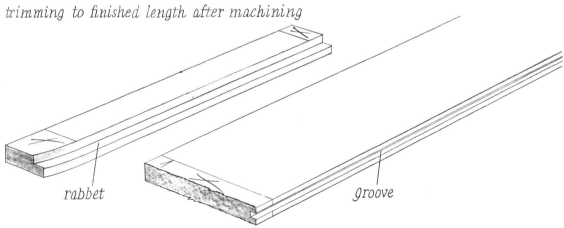

rabbet   *groove*

REPEAT OPERATIONS

When a series of woodworking procedures is involved in making furniture parts, there is much to be gained by doing all of one kind of procedure on all the parts at one session. In building a table, for example, it is better to cut the mortises in all four legs before going on to the next phase. Drill all the drawbores, cut all the mortises, and finally shape all the legs. This system improves skill and accuracy and reduces the number of times you must pick up the same tools over and over again. This is a particular advantage when shooting grooves, rabbets, bevels, and tongue and groove joints, all of which involve exacting adjustments of the planes.

marking joining parts

side rail

drawer rail

NUMBERING JOINTS

Since furniture joints are more often than not cut in multiples of two, the finished parts—for example, four table legs—may look so much alike that when the time comes to assemble everything, they may be mistaken as interchangeable. To avoid the vexation of trying to fit a tenon into the wrong mortise, it is wise to mark both parts of mating joints with the same letter or number. An inconspicuous place can always be found for these marks so that they need not be cleaned off later with sandpaper.

HOLDING WORKPIECES

For almost every job except sawing a long board on a pair of sawhorses, put the work in the vise, protected with scraps of waste wood, or secure it flat on the top of the bench with holddowns or bench dogs. This prevents the wood and the tools from slipping, leaves both hands free to control the tool, and to a large extent reduces the chance of injury to your hands and the work.

SQUARES

Constantly make use of the try square, the combination square, and the carpenter's square—sometimes all three. They are essential tools for marking out and checking saw cuts, for jointing, end-grain planing, laying out joints and nailing lines, and for aligning shelves and other furniture parts at the various stages of construction.

SAWING

Whether using the crosscut, ripsaw, backsaw, or coping saw, always make the cut on the waste side of the line, and leave the line showing. Sawing directly on the line obliterates the very reference mark you need to finish the work. And by the time you have planed the saw cut smooth, the dimension originally marked off will have been shortened.

Every saw leaves torn wood fibers on the exit side of the cut, and this ragged material must be removed with a plane or some other tool in order to get a clean, sharp finish.

With a 10-point crosscut saw, make the cut 1/32 to 1/16 inch outside the mark. With the backsaw, a bare 1/32 inch is enough, as the cut itself is much finer. But allow almost 1/8 inch of extra wood for a ripsaw, whose teeth are coarse and leave a very ragged edge requiring much more planing. When using a coping saw, leave extra wood about equal to the thickness of a pencil line.

NARROW WORKPIECES

In cases where a bevel or some other machining is to be worked on the long edge of a narrow stick less than 2 inches wide, first complete the machining on one edge of a wide board. Then measure and cut off the narrow piece with the ripsaw. Attempting this kind of work in reverse order usually fails because there is no way to securely hold a narrow piece of wood in the vise or flat on the bench, as both of these methods obstruct the use of the plane.

CLAMPS

Furniture clamps, C-clamps, and bar and pipe clamps are all capable of crushing the surfaces of wood, even when tightened only moderately. To protect the work, use commercial clamp pads slipped over the clamp feet, or sandwich the work between lengths of scrap wood blocking.

C-clamps are indispensable in furniture work. Where two parts are to be fastened with nails or screws, clamp the parts together in the proper alignment, drill and countersink the pilot holes, then drive the nails or screws with the clamps left on. Where the pilot holes are drilled through the outside part only, drill the holes first, then clamp the part in place and drive the fasteners with the clamps left on (see also *Fasteners*, p. 44).

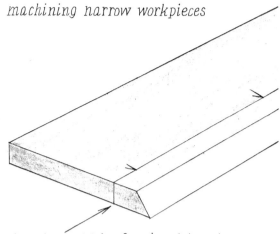

machining narrow workpieces

ripped to width after bevel is cut
[*pilasters of Corner Cupboard*]

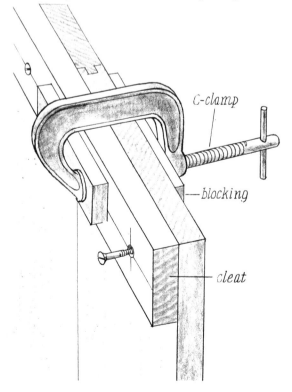

attaching a cleat with clamp in place

C-clamp

blocking

cleat

CLAMP BOARDS

In many situations, simple clamp boards and wedges will do the work of commercial iron clamps and can be made from inexpensive pine or hemlock lumber to fit the particular job. As the stress on a clamp board is in the end-to-end tension, use lumber that is reasonably straight-grained and free of knots.

The opening should be equal to the distance to be clamped plus a little extra space for the wedges, and for blocking at both ends to protect the work, as shown in the illustration. Clamp boards for drawer construction can be made from material as light as 1/2 x 1 1/2″, while those for work as large as the *Armoire* and the *Slant-back Dresser* should be made from 1 x 4 or 1 x 6 lumber. Lay out the opening with a try square and straightedge. Then bore a 3/4-inch hole through the clamp board as shown in the illustration. Start a compass saw in this hole, and saw along the line to both ends of the opening. Then saw out the ends with a crosscut saw. No sanding is necessary, in fact the rough saw cut provides a better purchase against the wedge to prevent its slipping.

It is an advantage to have numerous pieces of blocking of various sizes on hand. For drawer construction, plane a length of 1 x 2 pine down to a thickness of 1/2 inch. Plane and sandpaper both sides smooth, then cut it into 4-inch lengths. The blocking pieces must have no rough spots that might emboss the surface of the work itself. For heavier work where more pressure is needed, cut the blocking pieces 10 or 12 inches long, or simply use scraps of stock 1 x 2 lumber (screen stock). For extra protection, glue smooth cardboard—not corrugated carton material—to one side of the blocking, and lay that side against the work.

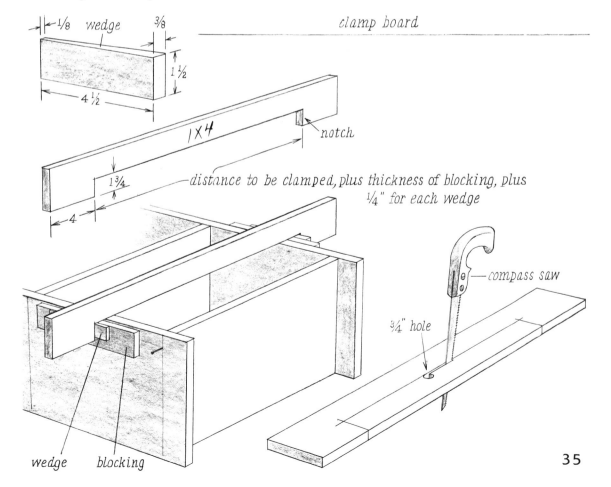

clamp board

1/8 *wedge* 3/8

1 1/2

4 1/2

1 X 4 *notch*

1 3/4

4

distance to be clamped, plus thickness of blocking, plus 1/4″ *for each wedge*

compass saw

3/4″ *hole*

wedge *blocking*

NAILING LINES

Whenever fastening furniture parts with nails or screws, lay off nailing lines on which to drill pilot holes for the fasteners. While the main purpose here is to ensure getting the fasteners in exactly the right place, the use of nailing lines also makes for a neater appearance than haphazard location.

It is especially important to locate the lines to correspond with solid wood underneath, which in many instances will be the edges of cupboard shelves or the narrow rabbets into which backboards are fitted. The narrower the

using a straightedge to lay out nailing lines for locating pilot holes

batten

measured marks

using the carpenter's square to lay out nailing lines on the side of a cupboard

wood underneath, the more carefully the nailing line must be laid off, or the fasteners may stab through on the inside, weakening the construction, splintering the wood, and creating unwanted holes and blemishes that are hard to cover up or eliminate.

Measure accurately and use a square and straightedge, or wooden batten, to extend and keep the lines straight and properly aligned. Use a sharp, soft pencil and draw lightly so that the lines, especially those on surfaces that will be exposed in the finished work, can be cleaned off as easily as possible.

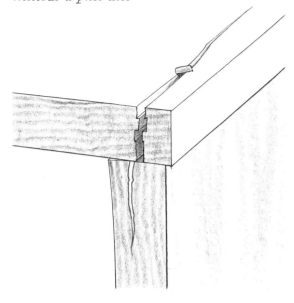

7d old-fashioned fine finish nail driven without a pilot hole

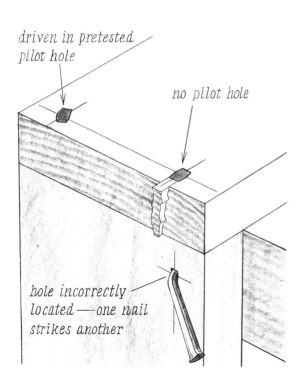

driven in pretested pilot hole

no pilot hole

hole incorrectly located—one nail strikes another

PILOT HOLES

Nails and screws should almost never be driven without first drilling pilot holes. Used in conjunction with nailing lines, they ensure that the fastener drives straight, in the right place, and without splitting the wood or causing failure of the fastener or damage to the work.

Without them, nails may bend over or double up and damage the work, veer off and puncture the wood in a conspicuous place, or even miss the wood underneath. Screws driven without pilot holes turn with difficulty and often break off from the weakening of frictional heat, in which case the screwdriver usually slips and punches a hole in the work. If not this, it may jump out of the screw slot, in the process damaging the screw and the work in one motion.

Pilot Hole Diameter

For common finish nails, drill a hole a fraction smaller than the diameter of the nail shank to allow some compression of the wood fibers, which provides most of the holding power. As an example, a 1/16-inch pilot hole is about right for an 8d finish nail driven into white pine. Holes for old-fashioned cut nails must be gauged by making trials, as their shanks are tapered as well as square, and the diameter of the hole must be determined in conjunction with the length of the nail and the depth of penetration.

Screw pilot holes should be drilled the same diameter as the smooth shank of the screw just under the head to allow it to turn freely. Whether for nails or screws, pilot holes in hardwood are generally made larger in diameter than in softwood. The greater density of the wood limits the degree of compression, makes the fastener drive harder, and therefore increases the chance of its failure. This applies particularly to brass screws and antique finish nails which are softer than steel and therefore more likely to twist, bend, or break.

Pilot Hole Depth

The pilot hole for a nail should generally be one-half to two-thirds the length of the nail in softwood, and slightly deeper in hardwood. This allows the pointed end of the nail to penetrate and establish a solid hold in untapped wood.

For screws driven into softwood, it is usually sufficient to drill a hole the same diameter as the screw shank through the outside piece of wood only, leaving the threaded end to pull its own way into the untapped wood of the piece underneath. In hardwood, however, a secondary pilot hole no larger than the root diameter should be drilled a short distance into the underneath piece, as shown in the illustration.

Trial Pilot Holes

Although pilot hole diameters and depths may be given in the project directions, it is a wise precaution to use them only as references for making trial holes, and testing their accuracy by driving screws or nails in scrap pieces of the same kind of wood.

Pilot Hole Depth Gauge

When a number of pilot holes are to be drilled to the same diameter and depth, make a depth gauge from scrap wood as shown in the illustration. Drill a hole of the correct diameter all the way into the end of the block of wood. Then

countersunk screw pilot hole: softwood

through outside piece only

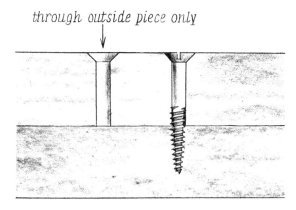

countersunk screw pilot hole: hardwood

through outside piece

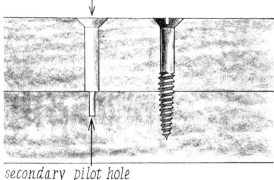

secondary pilot hole

pilot hole depth gauge

hand drill

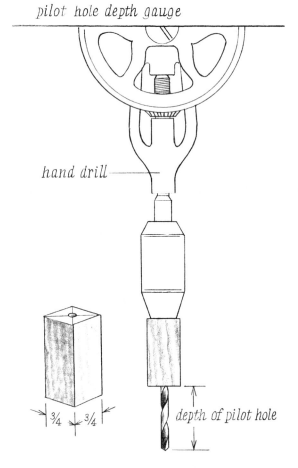

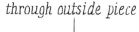

depth of pilot hole

measure and cut it off to the length that will leave the drill point protruding the same distance as the depth of the pilot hole. Sand the ends of the gauge and slip it over the drill point.

COUNTERSINKING

Screw pilot holes should always be countersunk to let the heads of flathead screws into the wood flush with the surface. This is not just for the sake of appearance, but mainly because the beveled rim of the countersunk hole fits the shape of the screw head and provides it with a good seat. It is this congruence of countersink and screw head that gives maximum strength as the screw threads draw the workpieces tight together.

SANDING INSIDE SURFACES

Before assembling furniture parts such as cupboard sides, shelves, backboards, and drawer parts, sand their inside surfaces to final smoothness (see *Sanding,* p. 132). These surfaces are difficult to reach after things have been put together, and almost impossible to properly sand.

Lay the furniture part on a piece of carpet or an old towel on the bench to protect the work. When sanding close to machined edges such as rabbets, grooves, and housed joints, be especially careful not to tip the sanding block at an angle over the edges, or they will be rounded.

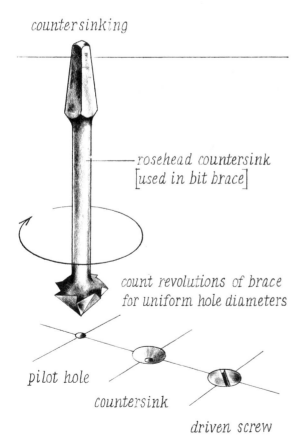

countersinking

rosehead countersink [used in bit brace]

count revolutions of brace for uniform hole diameters

pilot hole

countersink

driven screw

SANDING END GRAIN

To sand short sections of end grain such as the ends of counter shelves *(New York Hutch* and *Slant-back Dresser)*, put the work end-up in the vise. Clamp a piece of scrap wood of the same thickness to one edge of the work, with both end-grain surfaces flush, as shown in the illustration. Use a sanding block and plenty of pressure to keep it flat on the work. Sand the end grain of the work and the scrap as one piece, being careful not to let the sanding block run off the ends or tip over the edges, otherwise they will be rounded. By extending the length of the work surface, the scrap wood makes it easier to sand the end grain square and true.

To sand long sections of end grain such as the ends of tabletops *(Pine Dressing Table, One-drawer Stand, Writing Table,* and *Sideboard)*, stand the tabletop on end against the workbench with one edge held in the vise for support. Use a sanding block with plenty of pressure to keep it flat on the work. Sand with strokes as long as possible, but be careful not to let the block run off the ends or tip over the edges, or they will be rounded (see *Sanding,* p. 132).

sanding short sections of end grain

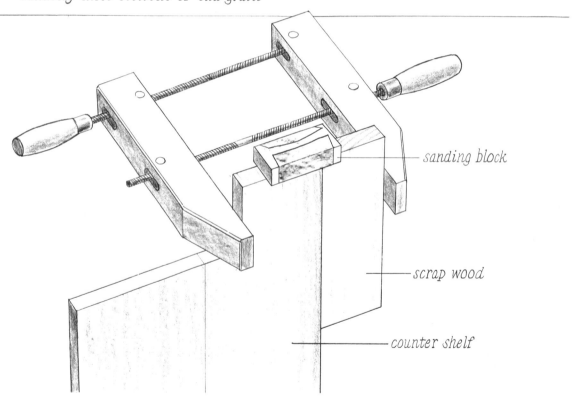

sanding block

scrap wood

counter shelf

sanding long sections of end grain

use plenty of pressure
to keep sanding block flat on the work

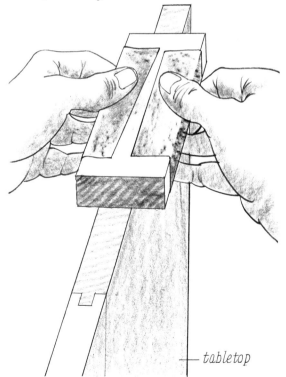

tabletop

Fasteners

As used here, the term *fastener* includes nails, screws, glue, and cleats, all of which are intended to stabilize and hold wooden parts securely in their proper structural alignment. In their various forms they have all been used for generations in simple country furniture as well as in more sophisticated pieces. Many fine old chests and cupboards, for example, were put together with nothing but square-cut nails and a few screws. Nails are still a workmanlike way to a strong joint, much stronger in end grain than screws, and more attractive. Driven into end-grain wood, the nail shank forces the fibers apart, creating a tension which then closes on the nail to hold it. A screw, on the other hand, cuts the wood fibers, virtually destroying its capacity to hold.

FINISH NAIL

In some eyes the modern, polished finish nail is the obvious choice because the small head can be set below the surface and the hole filled with putty, wood filler, or a mixture of sawdust and glue. But a plugged hole will always look like a plugged hole: putty and other compounds rarely accept stains and finishes to match the color of the wood. To put it another way, better to accept nail heads as part of the furniture than to call attention to an unsuccessful attempt to conceal them.

GALVANIZED FINISH NAIL

In terms of holding power, the galvanized finish nail is an improvement over the smooth-shanked version. The zinc coating is rough and provides much greater resistance to pullout.

wood fibers wedged against the nail prevent its loosening and pulling out

7d old-fashioned cut finish nail

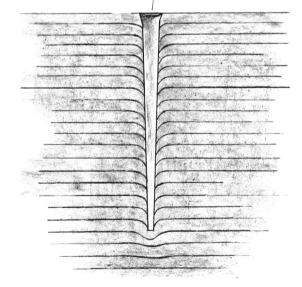

OLD-FASHIONED CUT NAIL

Of the nails used here, the old-fashioned square-cut finish nail—now manufactured by machine as a reproduction—is the most satisfactory. Properly driven into a trial-tested pilot hole of the correct diameter and depth (see *Woodworking Practices*, p. 37), this tapered nail with its greater surface area takes and maintains an extremely tight hold in the wood, while its exposed head has a neat, businesslike appearance quite in keeping with the rectangular character of much furniture.

SCREWS

Broadly speaking, screws make a tougher fastening than nails, and if damaged while driving can be removed and replaced without risk of injury to the work. Their chief drawback is in the less than handsome appearance of their slotted heads, which is why they are generally used only in concealed places. For this kind of work, flathead steel screws are entirely satisfactory and the least expensive. But where screws must be used in exposed locations, as in attaching hinges and door buttons, brass flat-

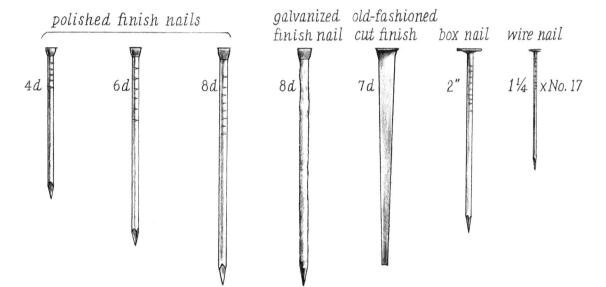

polished finish nails   galvanized   old-fashioned

4d   6d   8d   finish nail   cut finish   box nail   wire nail

8d   7d   2"   1¼ x No. 17

heads are more consistent with good appearance and also have the advantage of being rustproof. Extra care must be used, however, to see that the pilot holes are tried and tested beforehand to prevent the soft brass from overheating and breaking (see *Woodworking Practices*, p. 38).

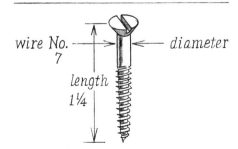

1¼ x No. 7 *flathead screw*

wire No. 7   diameter

length 1¼

GLUE

Of the many adhesives on the market, two that have proven most satisfactory for furniture work are Franklin Titebond Wood Glue and Elmer's

Carpenter's Wood Glue. For all practical purposes they have the same basic characteristics and working properties. Both are nontoxic, develop a strong initial tack, set relatively fast, and resist heat, water, sealers, and solvents. They can easily be cleaned from wood, tools, and hands with warm water, but it must be done without delay, particularly where wood is concerned, as these glues may leave a stain or light spots when the finish is applied. They are packaged in plastic squeeze bottles stoppered with plunger caps, which should be replaced after each use in order to maintain good working consistency. Store the glue at normal room temperature, and keep it from freezing.

GLUING

The wood surfaces should be prepared flat and smooth for maximum contact, dry, clean, and free of oil, grease, dust, and especially sandpaper tailings. The temperature of the room and the work itself should be at least 70 degrees Fahrenheit.

Before starting work, collect everything you'll need and lay it out ready to hand: clamps, blocking, spreader, sponge, and a container of warm water. Have a clean cloth for wiping your hands. Make the clamp board and wedges (see *Woodworking Practices*, p. 35), or if you are using iron clamps, adjust them to within two or three turns of the required opening.

Spread a thin, even coat of glue on both surfaces using a palette knife or an old 1/2-inch chisel, or by wiping with a finger. In many instances, a finger is the best possible tool. Avoid slopping glue over the edges of the work by spreading it from the center toward the outside. Let the glued pieces stand four or five minutes to allow the glue to penetrate the wood surface and to develop a good tack. This helps prevent the pieces from slipping or creeping when clamp pressure is applied.

Then put the pieces together, and put on the clamps or clamp boards, with scrap wood on both sides to protect the work. Check and adjust the alignment of the work, then tighten the clamps. For iron furniture clamps and C-clamps, turn the screw up only until it feels solid. There is no need to go to the limit of the clamp. Extra pressure does not improve the bond, and in squeezing out too much glue it may actually starve and weaken the joint. For clamp boards, tap the wedges with the hammer until all the slack has been taken up and the wood sounds solid.

As soon as the clamps are set and tightened, immediately scrape off any excess glue and wipe the wood clean with a sponge and warm water. Most glues repel sealers, varnishes, and stains, and if not cleaned off promptly will leave areas to which the finish will not adhere. Leave the clamps on and set the work aside to dry overnight. While the directions for both these glues may suggest that a 30-minute drying period is sufficient, complete bonding takes several hours.

Dovetail Joints

While it is the fit between the dovetails and pins that provides the excellent front-to-back strength in a drawer, it is the care with which this joint is glued that keeps it from opening up laterally. Apply glue sparingly *to the sides only* of the dovetails and pins, then put the joint together at once. Don't wait for the glue to get tacky, or the close-fitting parts will not go together easily and may even refuse to close all the way. In the case of a dovetail mortise (the bearer rail of the *Writing Table*), tap the joint together as soon as the parts have been glued, and drive the screws. They act as clamps to draw the parts together and hold them.

Nails and brads should never be used to fasten dovetails. They will almost always split the wood and because of their small size have practically no holding power.

Tongue and Groove Joints

Spread a thin, even coat of glue *on the tongue only*—none in the groove, or it will puddle and prevent the joint from closing tight. Use as many clamps or clamp boards as possible to distribute the pressure uniformly along the entire joint.

Housed Joints

Treat these the same as a tongue and groove joint, gluing *the edges of the shelf only*—none in the housing.

breadboard cleat

tabletop cleats

end cleats also
fastened to
side rails

side rail

CLEATS

The cleat is a simple and effective device for securing and preventing warp in wide sections such as edge-joined tabletops, cupboard sides, counter shelves, and doors. In some instances, as when they are used to attach a tabletop to the frame, cleats do double duty, screws being driven one way into the tabletop to hold it flat, and the other way into the rails of the table to attach it.

Cleats are most efficient when screw-fastened to the work dry—without glue. Since it is a fact that the boards in a wide section will expand and contract according to changes in the humidity, dry-fastened cleats allow them the flexibility to adjust while at the same time maintaining them in a flat configuration. When cleats are glued, however, two opposing forces are at work. The boards continue to expand and contract, but the cleats do not, because their long dimension is virtually unaffected by humidity. The resulting tension creates broken glue joints, or split boards, or both.

When fastening cleats, it is always preferable for the sake of accuracy to clamp them in place, adjusting and checking their exact position with the rule and with a square. Then tighten the clamps and drive the screws. Where clamps cannot be used, or are unavailable, lay the cleats in place, check their positions, and tack them down with a finish nail at each end. Leave the nail heads projecting. Check their positions once again, then drive the screws. Finally, remove the temporary nails.

Making Joints

BUTT

The joints described here are the edge-butt, often used in place of the tongue and groove joint to join boards in making up wide sections; the breadboard butt, to join cleats to the ends of tabletops; and the plain butt, as used to join the rails and legs of the *Breadboard-top Table*.

EDGE-BUTT

This joint is used to join boards edge to edge in making up wide sections such as tabletops, wide shelves, and the sides and doors of cupboards.

Take special care to joint the meeting edges of the boards straight, square, and even—as nearly perfect as you can make them (see *Woodworking Practices*, p. 28). If the edges of the boards are not square to their faces, the pressure of clamping will nonetheless draw them together and create a buckled rather than a flat surface. By the same token, if poorly jointed from end to end, hollows and high spots will show up in the glued joint as cracks that no amount of pressure will close.

After jointing the edges, clamp the boards edge to edge with only moderate pressure for an inspection. The joint should show as an even hairline, when the boards can then be glued up.

Gluing Up

Use at least three furniture, bar, or pipe clamps or clamp boards (see *Woodworking Practices*, p. 35)—more if the work is longer than 3 feet. Place two clamps across the work on the underside, one near each end. Put a third clamp on top in the middle. Opposing the clamps exerts a counterpull that helps to keep the boards flat.

When more than two boards are to be glued up, glue and clamp the first two, let them dry overnight, then glue on the next one. Since some adhesives set up quickly, this method allows you time to align the boards properly before tightening the clamps.

edge-butt joints

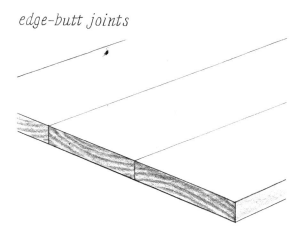

Have blocking pieces and battens ready and the clamps adjusted to approximately the right opening. Check to be sure there are no loose chips or shavings stuck to the jointed edges. Spread a thin coat of glue evenly along the edges of both boards and let stand a few minutes until the glue is tacky.

Lay the glued boards into a pair of clamps or clamp boards which should be protected with

glues repel stains and finishes. Stand the work aside to dry overnight.

Trimming to Width

Remove the clamps from the glued-up work and with a jack or jointer plane smooth one edge, using the same technique as when jointing new lumber (see *Woodworking Practices*, p. 28). Set

gluing up a pair of boards with clamp boards, battens, and C-clamps

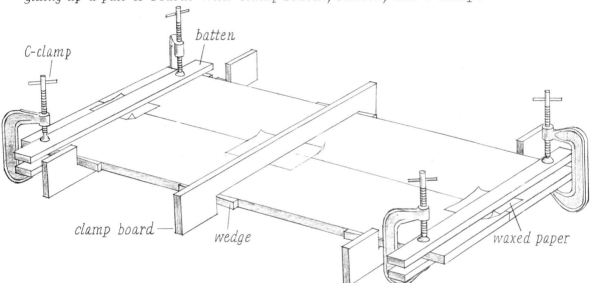

C-clamp
batten
clamp board
wedge
waxed paper

waxed paper. Put the blocking pieces in place and tighten the clamps—just enough to bring the joint together. As quickly as possible, lay waxed paper over the glued joint and clamp a pair of battens across each end of the work to hold the boards in alignment. Put the third clamp across the top of the work and then slowly tighten all three main clamps alternately to draw the joint together evenly. Stop when small beads of glue appear along the joint.

After four or five minutes, when the glue has taken hold, remove the battens, scrape off the excess glue, and wipe the surface clean with a damp sponge. This is important because most

the cutter iron for a fine cut and make one or two full-length passes. Take off no more wood than is necessary to remove any irregularities and to make the edge straight and square. At each end measure across from this good edge and make a pencil mark to the correct width. Lay a straightedge on the marks and connect them by drawing a pencil line the full length. Then hold the work in the vise and use a long plane to trim the edge exactly to the line. After each pass, use the rule to check the width at both ends and in the middle, and the try square to be sure the edge is square to the face of the work. If the amount of wood to be removed is

3/8 inch or more, trim off the bulk of it with the ripsaw and then joint the edge down to the line with the plane.

Squaring the Ends

To trim the glued-up panel to finished length, hold the carpenter's square against one edge of the work and draw a pencil line across one end. Use a fine-toothed crosscut saw (12 pt. or 14 pt.) to trim off the surplus wood to the line. To smooth the end-grain saw cut, clamp a pair of straight battens flush with the end of the work

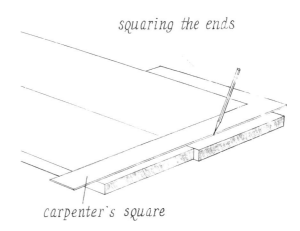

squaring the ends

carpenter's square

squaring the end of a glued-up panel

battens

C-clamp

square

and stand it on end against the workbench with one edge held in the vise for support. Use the block plane set for a fine cut, working from both sides toward the middle. On a very wide panel, the jack or jack rabbet plane works very well. Hold the plane level and check the work frequently with the try square.

Then measure off from this planed end and mark the finished length. Lay the carpenter's square on the mark and draw a line across the unfinished end of the panel. Trim off the surplus wood with the crosscut saw and plane the cut smooth and square in the same way.

BREADBOARD BUTT

This is the joint used to attach the cleats across the ends of the *Breadboard-top Table*. Any such section of wood, whether a single wide board or several narrow ones glued together, tends to warp or cup with changes in the atmosphere. The breadboard cleats help to minimize this distortion, and at the same time they cover and conceal the end grain for better appearance. This joint is best put together dry—without glue—leaving the panel free to expand and contract. Moreover, glue has almost no holding power on

*breadboard cleat
butt-joined to end of tabletop*

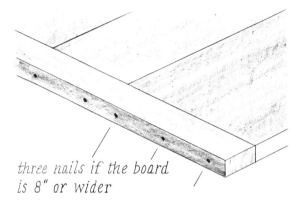

*three nails if the board
is 8" or wider*

nailing breadboard cleat in place

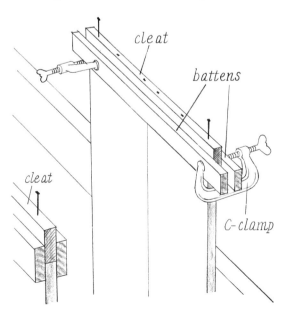

cleat

battens

cleat

C-clamp

end grain, being almost completely absorbed into the wood pores.

After the wide panel has been glued up, trim both ends square as described above in the section "Squaring the Ends."

Cut the breadboard cleat to width and about 2 inches longer than finished length. The extra wood is trimmed flush with the sides of the panel after the cleat has been attached. Then joint both the long edges. Make sure that the edge abutting the end of the panel is square.

Drill pilot holes clear through the cleat, spaced so there will be 2 nails in each board of the glued-up panel. If the boards are wider than 8 or 9 inches, use 3 nails. Since the nails are driven through the thin dimension of the cleat, the nail pilot holes must be gauged large enough to prevent splitting the cleat. It is a good idea to first drill test pilot holes in a scrap of wood.

Before nailing on the cleats, apply one or two coats of sealer (see *Finishing Wood*, p. 136) to the end-grain ends of the panel, to fill the pores and retard the penetration of moisture.

To nail the cleat in place, stand the panel on end against the workbench with one edge in the vise for support. Clamp the cleat sandwiched between two battens straddling the joint, as shown in the illustration. Use a mallet to tap the cleat down tight against the end of the panel, then tighten the clamps. Extend the pilot holes into the end grain of the panel, drilling through the holes in the cleat. Drive a nail at each end of the cleat, then work toward the center driving the other nails. To avoid hammer marks, drive the nails not quite flush, then loosen the clamps and use a sharp-pointed nail set to set the nailheads just flush with the wood surface.

Remove the clamps and trim the waste wood from the ends of the cleat. With a fine-toothed backsaw, saw not quite flush with the sides of the panel. Then carefully shave the ends of the cleat flush, using a sharp block plane set for a very fine cut. Plane from the corners toward the middle of the panel.

PLAIN BUTT

This joint is made with a saw and plane, and when carefully marked out and cut, is strong and serviceable. All meeting surfaces should be flat, smooth, and square to provide full contact, particularly when the joint is to be glued.

Use a combination or try square and jack-knife to mark out the saw cuts. This not only makes an accurate line to which to work, but also leaves a cleaner edge on the finished saw cut. For consistently accurate saw cuts, use a good miter box and a fine-toothed backsaw (12 pt. or 14 pt.). Clean up the end-grain cuts with a block plane set for a fine cut (see *Woodworking Practices,* p. 29) and check to see that the work is square in both directions.

In much old country furniture, butt joints were fastened only with nails, usually of the square-cut variety which hold better then the smooth-shanked modern finish nail. When nailing this joint, always use pilot holes drilled slightly smaller in diameter than the nail shank, but large enough to prevent splitting the wood (see *Woodworking Practices,* p. 37). Drill clear through the thinner piece of wood and a distance into the thicker one. The exact diameter and depth of the pilot hole must first be determined by making trial holes, using the actual nail and scraps of the same wood you will use. If nailing into pine, the pilot hole in the thicker piece need not be very deep. But in hardwood the hole should generally be larger and deeper to prevent the nail from bending or doubling up under the hammer blows.

Screws can be used for extra strength in a butt joint, or to fasten parts that are hidden from view, as when attaching cleats to the underside of a tabletop. But if screws are used in exposed areas, for example to fasten the rails of a table to the legs, the screw head should be set about 1/4 inch below the surface in a counterbored hole and then covered with a glued-in plug. The diameter of the counterbore should be a shade

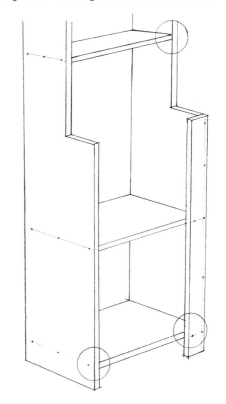

butt joints in cupboard construction

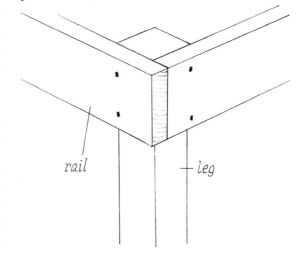

rails joined to table leg with nailed, plain butt joints

rail   leg

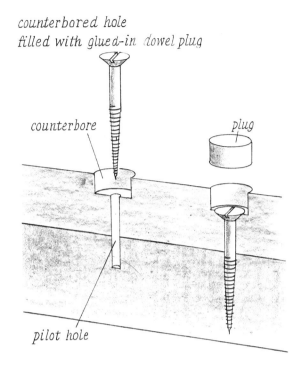

counterbored hole
filled with glued-in dowel plug

counterbore

plug

pilot hole

larger than the screwhead and correspond to a stock-sized dowel from which the plug is made. Bore the counterbore first, then drill the pilot hole for the screw shank, centered in the bottom of the counterbored hole.

After aligning the parts and driving the screws, cut dowel plugs about 1 inch long—to facilitate handling them—and slightly round the entering ends. Then wipe glue around a plug, twist it into the counterbore, and drive it in tight with the hammer. Let the glue dry overnight, then trim the plug flush with the work surface. Use a backsaw laid flat on a piece of cardboard, sliding it on the work surface to saw off the bulk of the plug. Trim the rest flush with a sharp 1-inch chisel laid flat on the work and held bevel-up. Work the chisel with the hands only, slicing round the plug several times and then slicing flat across it to make a smooth, clean cut (see *Mortise and Tenon*, p. 79).

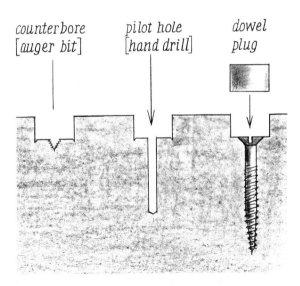

counterbore
[auger bit]

pilot hole
[hand drill]

dowel
plug

DOVETAIL

The dovetail joint, widely used in drawer construction, is one of the strongest ways to join pieces of wood at right angles. Although it may be the most intricate of all joints to cut, satisfactory dovetails can be made with some patience and the help of a simple homemade gauge with which to mark out the work.

DOVETAIL GAUGE

The time used in making a gauge will be more than recovered in the ability to cut accurate dovetails and pins to a uniform rake, or slope, on which depends the strength of this joint. Make a gauge according to the specifications given in the illustration. Use about a .035-gauge galvanzied sheet metal, a scrap of which can be bought at a plumbing and heating shop. Sheet brass or copper of a similar thickness will make a fancier version.

Mark out the blade using a combination square and an awl to score the lines. First lay out and score the center line. Drill and countersink the three holes as shown. Then cut out the blade with a hacksaw—tin shears will deform the metal. Saw a shade outside the layout lines, then carefully file down exactly to the scored lines, keeping the edges straight and smooth. Dull the finished sharp edges with a stroke or two of the file.

The blade must be attached with its center line exactly at right angles (90 degrees) to the stock. Clamp the blade to the stock and use the square to check and adjust the blade's position. Then drill pilot holes in the stock and drive the screws. Since the clamp will cover a good part of the blade and therefore one of the holes, drive 2 screws with the clamp in place, then remove the clamp to drive the third one.

This gauge has a rake of about 1 in 6, which makes a dovetail with good holding power as well as a nice appearance.

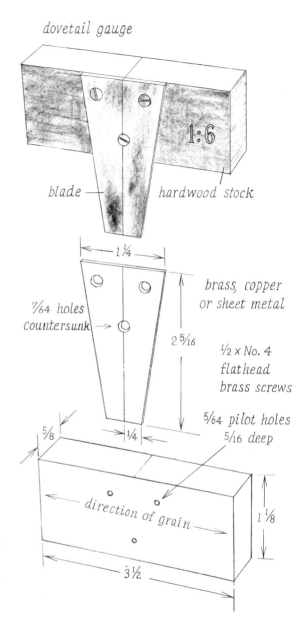

dovetail gauge

blade — *hardwood stock*

1:6

1¼

$\frac{7}{64}$ *holes countersunk* →

brass, copper or sheet metal

2 $\frac{5}{16}$

½ x No. 4 *flathead brass screws*

$\frac{5}{64}$ *pilot holes* $\frac{5}{16}$ *deep*

⅝

¼

direction of grain

1 ⅛

3½

LAP DOVETAIL

There are several versions of the dovetail, one of the most common being the lap dovetail. The dovetail part is cut into the front ends of the drawer sides and locks with corresponding pins cut into the ends of the drawer front. There are

lap dovetail as used in a drawer

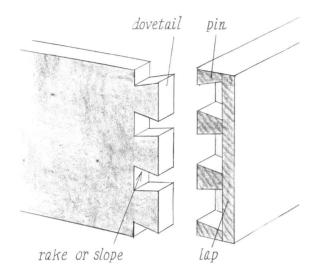

dovetail   pin

rake or slope   lap

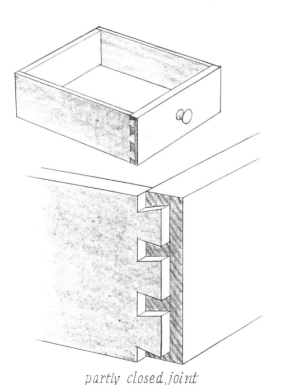

partly closed joint

no set rules as to how many dovetails should be used in a joint, other than the size of the drawer, but there should be at least three to make the joint strong.

Marking Out

A typical drawer is used here as an example of the basic procedures. Use the marking gauge to lightly score lap lines on the ends of the drawer front 1/4 inch in from its face. The rest of the marks are laid out after the tails have been cut on the drawer side, when they are scribed off directly.

scoring the lap line on the end of the drawer front

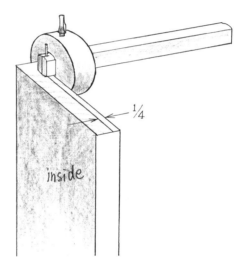

¼

inside

Next, lay out the tails on the drawer side, using the illustration as a guide. First use the square and jackknife to score a line across the drawer side at A, and carry it over onto the top and bottom edges as well. Hook the rule over the top edge of the drawer side and with a sharp pencil tick off on this A line the series of tail measurements given in the particular project directions. Keep some tension on the rule. These marks should be accurate, as the angles of the dovetails are struck off from them.

To lay out the angles, hold the dovetail gauge against the end of the drawer side, lined up with the first tick mark, which represents one side of a dovetail. Score a line. Skip the next mark, slide the gauge to the third one, and score another line. Mark the corresponding sides of all the dovetails in the same way. Then use the opposing slope of the gauge to score their other sides. Carry the scored marks over onto the end grain, using the try square. Although these scored lines cannot be cleaned off, they will show in the finished work only when the drawer is opened. With a pencil, X-mark the waste wood to be removed as shown in the illustration.

laying out the tails

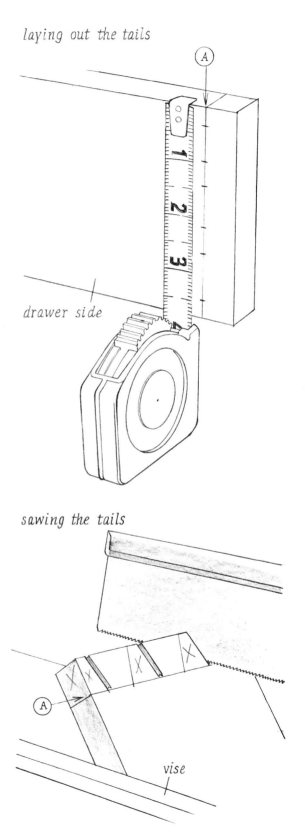

drawer side

scoring the tails with the dovetail gauge and knife

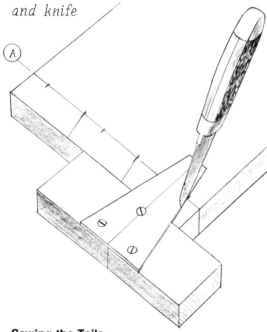

Sawing the Tails

sawing the tails

Put the work in the vise cocked up at an angle so that the marks on the side and on the end grain can both be seen at the same time. Use a tenon saw or a fine-toothed backsaw (12 pt. or 14 pt.) to saw down on the waste side of the marks not quite to the A line. If neither of these saws are available, use a hacksaw. Its wide, flat

vise

sawing from the other side

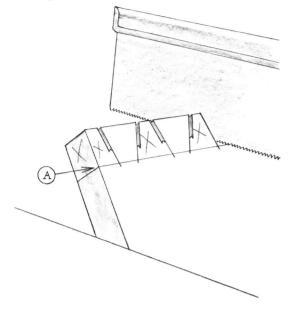

blade and fine teeth make a smooth-faced cut. When these first cuts are done, flop the work over in the vise and make similar cuts from the other side.

To clean out the waste, lay the work flat on the bench on a flat piece of scrap hardwood and hold it immobile with a clamp or bench hold-down. Use a sharp, narrow chisel to make a vertical chop on the A line, as shown in the illustration. Then hold the chisel bevel-up and pare out a bit of wood. Make another vertical chop in the same place and pare out more wood. Continue chopping and paring, taking out the waste about halfway through. Turn the work over and remove wood from the other side in the same way. The last bits of waste can then be cut loose. Finally, use a 1/4-inch chisel to clean out the inside corners just to the layout lines. Leave the sides of the dovetails to be trimmed and fitted later.

chopping out the waste

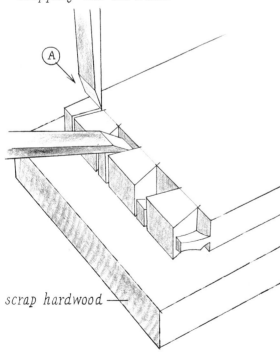

scrap hardwood

cleaning up the inside corners

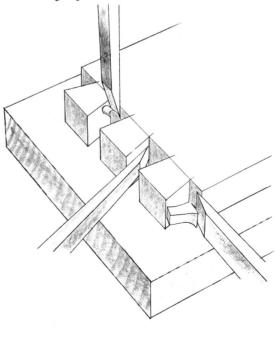

marking out the pins on the drawer front

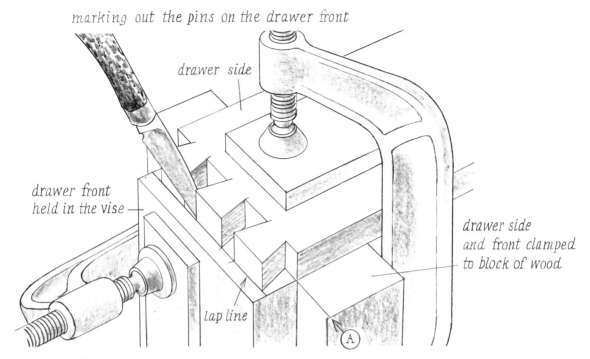

Sawing the Pins

When the dovetails have been cut they are used to mark out the pins on the drawer front. To manage this without the work slipping, clamp the drawer side to the drawer front as shown in the illustration. The ends of the dovetails should just touch the lap line, and the edges of the drawer side should be flush with those of the drawer front.

Use the point of the knife to score lines against both sides of each dovetail, holding the blade flat against them but without shaving off any wood. Let these scored lines run past the lap line to clearly outline the corners of the pins. Mark the waste wood to be removed with X's.

When this is done, remove the clamps and lay the drawer front facedown on the bench.

marking out the pins

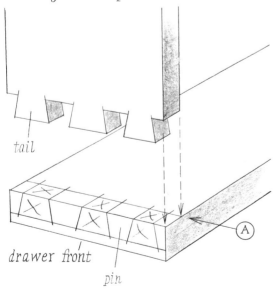

sawing the pins

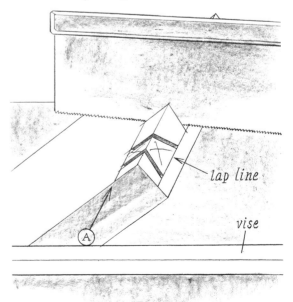

chopping out the waste

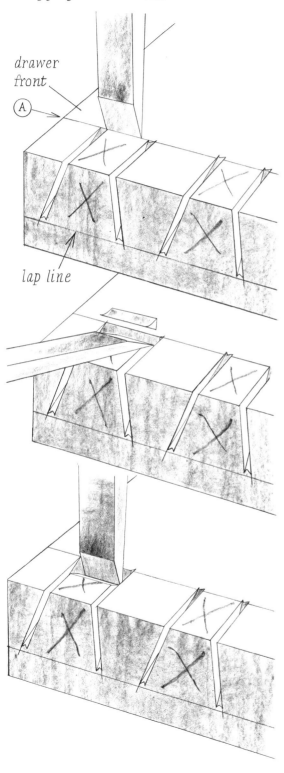

drawer front

(A)

lap line

Use the try square or combination square to lay off an A line across the inside face, measured in from the end of the drawer front the same distance as the thickness of the drawer side. With the square and knife, carry scored lines back to the A line to mark out the sides of the pins. Mark the waste sections with X's.

Put the work in the vise cocked up at an angle—the end of the drawer front facing you—so that the layout lines are clearly visible. Hold the saw level and saw on the waste side of the lines as before down to a point just short of the A line and the lap line. Secure the work flat on the bench again and chop out the waste with a chisel as shown in the series of illustrations. Leave the sides of the pins to be shaved and fitted later.

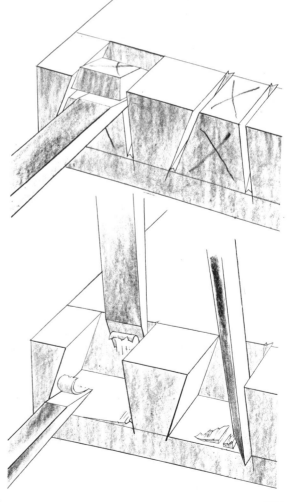

Fitting the Joint

Check each part carefully for flaws, then start the joint together, using a light push in order to inspect the fit. Note where the joint is loose or tight and where cracks are showing. Mark a pencil X where wood needs to be shaved off. With a sharp chisel, pare very gingerly, taking off the thinnest flakes of wood possible. Then start the joint together again and have another look. Do not push or drive the joint all the way shut, or the tails and pins will be damaged enough to prevent a tight fit when finally assembled. When both halves of the joint have been fitted to the best of your ability, mark them with letters or numbers to facilitate final gluing and assembly (see *Woodworking Practices*, p. 33).

dimensions for a trial single dovetail

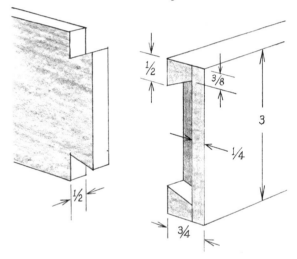

fitting the joint

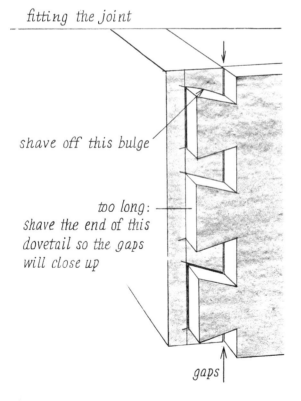

shave off this bulge

too long: shave the end of this dovetail so the gaps will close up

gaps

TRIAL SINGLE DOVETAIL

Before dovetailing an actual piece of work for the first time, cut a trial joint on two pieces of scrap wood. Lay out a large, single dovetail the exaggerated scale of which helps to get the hands accustomed to working with angles and the principles of fitting.

DOVETAIL MORTISE

This variation, which is used to fit the bearer rail of the *Writing Table,* is laid out and cut in the same way as the lap dovetail on a drawer front as described above.

cutting a dovetail mortise

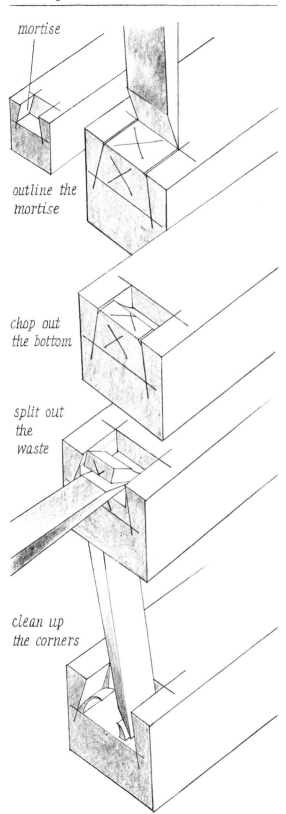

mortise

outline the
mortise

chop out
the bottom

split out
the
waste

clean up
the corners

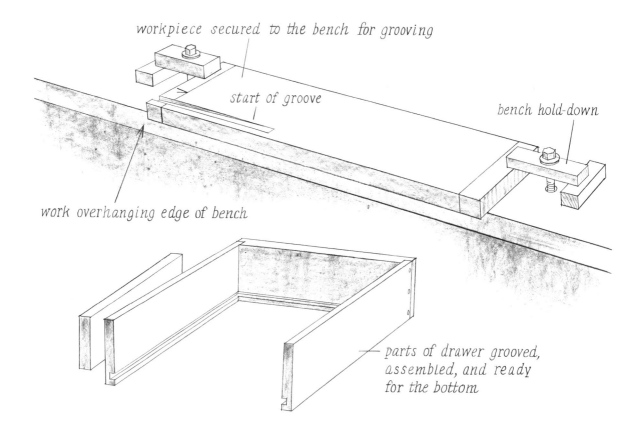

workpiece secured to the bench for grooving

start of groove

bench hold-down

work overhanging edge of bench

parts of drawer grooved, assembled, and ready for the bottom

GROOVE

Worked on the sides and edges of boards, the grooved joint always runs parallel with the wood grain. A groove is relatively simple to make, is strong, and neat in appearance. And preparing the work is just as simple, as there is no marking out to be done. Once the width of the groove and its position on the edge of the board have been determined, the plane is adjusted accordingly and the groove is shot with no further preliminaries.

ADJUSTING THE PLANE

Whether you use a combination plane, or multiplane, or the older single-purpose grooving plane, there are five essential steps in getting it ready for work: (1) check the sharpness of the cutter iron, (2) set it for a fine cut, (3) set the depth gauge to the required depth of groove,

(4) adjust the sliding fence to fix the distance from edge of board to edge of groove, and (5) shoot a trial groove. This is the only way to prove the accuracy of the adjustments. Set up the plane and shoot a trial groove on a scrap piece of lumber about 14 inches long. Then use measurements taken from this trial work to readjust the plane as needed. Make two or three trials if necessary.

SHOOTING A GROOVE

The workpiece must be well secured flat on the bench. Let the working edge overhang the edge of the workbench so that the plane with its fence can slide clear of all obstructions. Clamp the work tightly at both ends.

Start at the far end of the board. Set the plane on the work about 3 inches back from its end, holding the plane's fence firmly against the edge of the board. Make a couple of strokes with

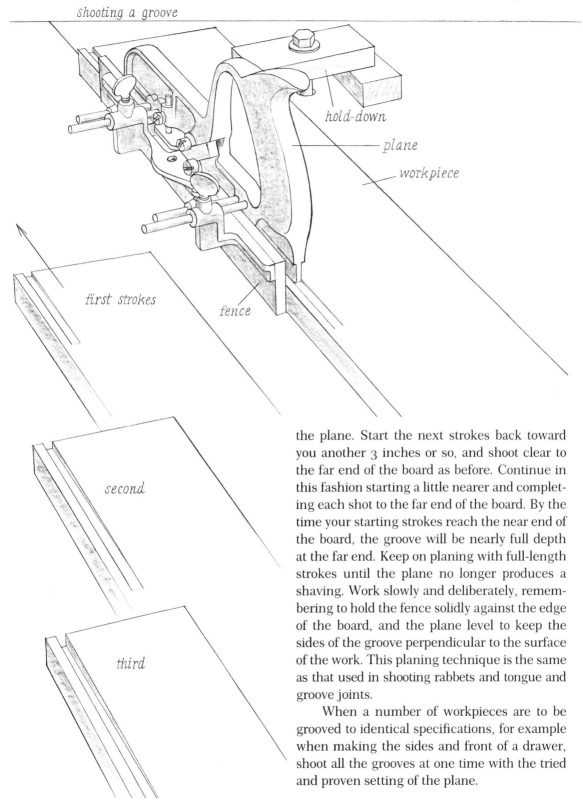

shooting a groove

hold-down

plane

workpiece

first strokes

fence

second

third

the plane. Start the next strokes back toward you another 3 inches or so, and shoot clear to the far end of the board as before. Continue in this fashion starting a little nearer and completing each shot to the far end of the board. By the time your starting strokes reach the near end of the board, the groove will be nearly full depth at the far end. Keep on planing with full-length strokes until the plane no longer produces a shaving. Work slowly and deliberately, remembering to hold the fence solidly against the edge of the board, and the plane level to keep the sides of the groove perpendicular to the surface of the work. This planing technique is the same as that used in shooting rabbets and tongue and groove joints.

When a number of workpieces are to be grooved to identical specifications, for example when making the sides and front of a drawer, shoot all the grooves at one time with the tried and proven setting of the plane.

WIDE GROOVES

To cut a groove wider than the largest standard-sized cutter, adjust the plane and shoot one groove to mark one side of the wide groove. Then readjust the position of the sliding fence and shoot a second groove to mark its other side. The waste in between the two can then be cleaned out by shifting the fence and making several overlapping cuts. Naturally, the adjustment of the depth gauge should not be changed.

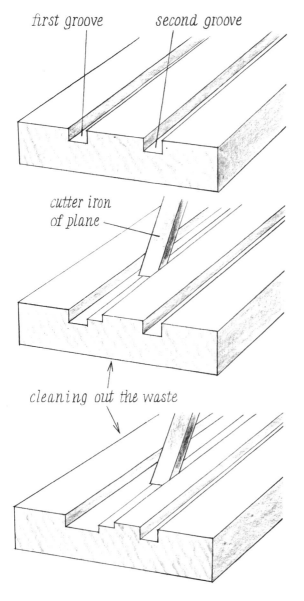

first groove   *second groove*

cutter iron of plane

cleaning out the waste

HALVED

In working a halved joint, an equal amount of wood is removed from both joining members to allow their face sides to come flush when assembled. This joint is often used in place of a mortise and tenon, particularly in stuff as thin as 3/4 inch where accurately cutting a very narrow mortise often presents difficulties. A halved joint is comparatively easy to make since the cuts are open and can be sawn with a backsaw and then cleaned up and fitted with a chisel.

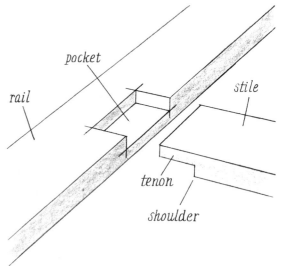

typical halved joint

pocket

rail

stile

tenon

shoulder

LAYING OUT

Mark out the width of the pocket on the rail part of the joint, using the combination or try square and a jackknife. Carry the marks over onto the edge of the rail. Then adjust the marking gauge for the specified depth of the pocket and scribe a line lengthwise on its wide face side. Use the same gauge setting to scribe the shoulder line across the stile part of the joint.

Before laying out the halving lines on the edge of the rail and on the end and sides of the

marking the width of the pocket

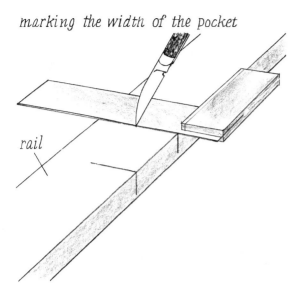

rail

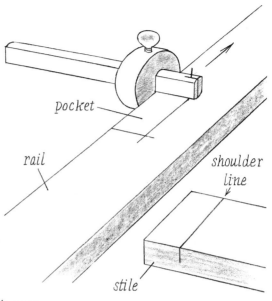

pocket

rail

shoulder line

stile

setting the marking gauge to the half-thickness

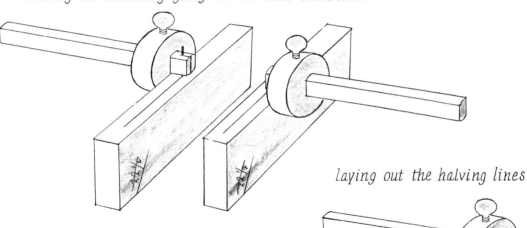

laying out the halving lines

stile, adjust the marking gauge as follows. Use the rule to measure and set the gauge for half the thickness of the lumber, and scribe a trial mark on a scrap of the wood you are using. Then from the other edge of the same piece scribe another mark. The half-thickness setting is correct when the two lines exactly coincide.

Scribe the halving line on the edge of the rail as well as on both edges and the end of the stile. Then X-mark the waste wood to be removed.

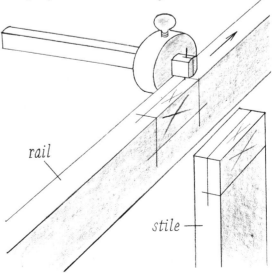

rail

stile

CUTTING THE POCKET

Use a sharp chisel to outline the pocket, making light chops along the layout lines as shown in the illustration. Pare out both ends of the pocket. Then hold the chisel perpendicular and make a series of scoring chops over the full length of the pocket. Clean out the waste chips by pushing the chisel bevel-up into the pocket from the edge of the rail. Continue scoring and cleaning out waste down to the halving line. Then, with the chisel bevel-up, shave thin flakes from the bottom of the pocket to make it smooth and level.

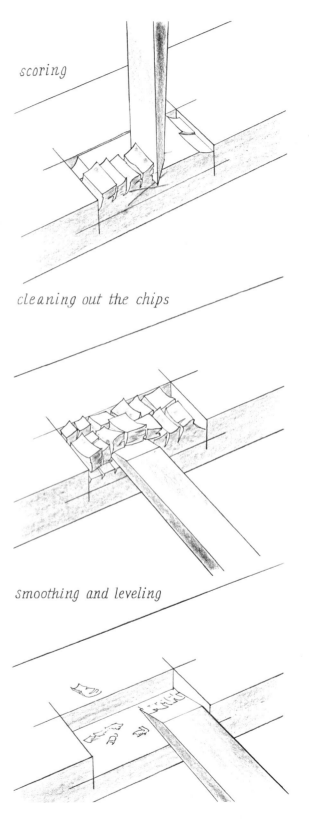

scoring

cleaning out the chips

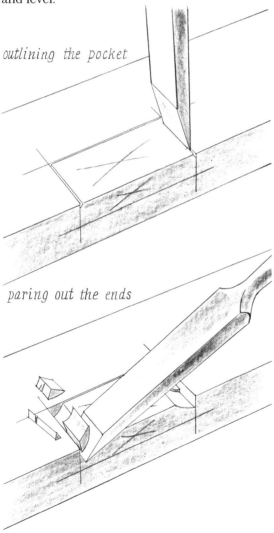

outlining the pocket

paring out the ends

smoothing and leveling

SAWING THE TENON

Clamp the stile end-up in the vise, edge to edge with a piece of scrap wood of the same thickness. Scribe the halving line over onto the scrap wood. This extra length on the work makes it much easier to saw a straight line. Then use the backsaw to saw down on the waste side of the line, not quite to the shoulder line.

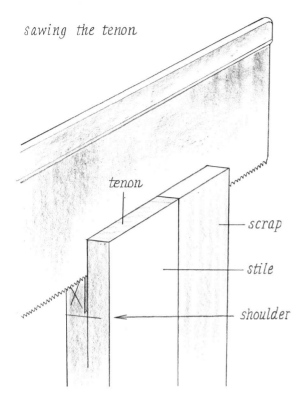

sawing the tenon

tenon

scrap

stile

shoulder

cleaning up the inside corner and fitting the tenon

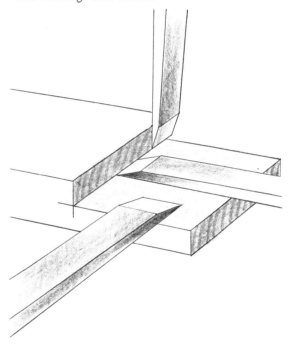

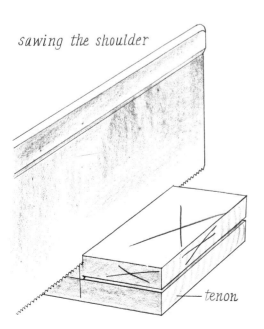

sawing the shoulder

tenon

Lay the stile in the miter box and make the shoulder cut, stopping just short of the marks. Break out the waste wood and clean up the inside corner with the chisel.

If the halved joint is also to be notched, for example in making the drawer runners for the *Pine Dressing Table,* cut the halved joint first, and then cut the notch and remove the waste wood.

FITTING THE JOINT

Try the two halves of the joint together. The tenon of the stile should be a tight-push fit into the pocket of the rail—using hand pressure alone—and the faces of both pieces should be flush. If the fit is too tight, ease the edge of the tenon with a stroke or two with the block plane. And if the faces do not come quite flush, make the adjustment on the tenon part only, shaving its inside surface with a sharp chisel held bevel-up.

fitting the joint

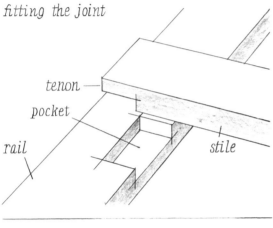

tenon

pocket

rail

stile

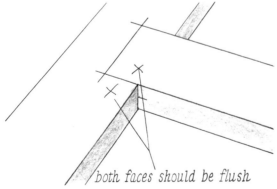

both faces should be flush

HOUSED

The housed joint is a wide groove cut across the grain of one board, into which is fitted the end of another. Extremely strong as well as neat in appearance, it is not difficult to make and is typically used in fitting shelves that must carry heavy loads.

Lay out the width of the housing with the carpenter's square and a sharp knife, scoring two parallel lines spaced apart about 1/32 inch less than the finished thickness of the shelf board. Carry these lines over onto both edges of the board and X-mark the waste to be removed.

Make the depth of the housing no more than one-third the thickness of the lumber. Set the marking gauge for the depth of the housing and scribe a line on both edges of the work *from the inside face.*

Lay the work flat on the bench and secure it with stops tacked on either side as shown in the illustration. If the lumber is 3/4 inch thick and the housing is to be 1/4 inch deep, make stops from 1/2-inch stuff. This way, the stops prevent sawing too deep.

housed joint as used in cupboard construction

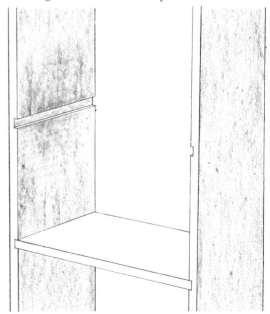

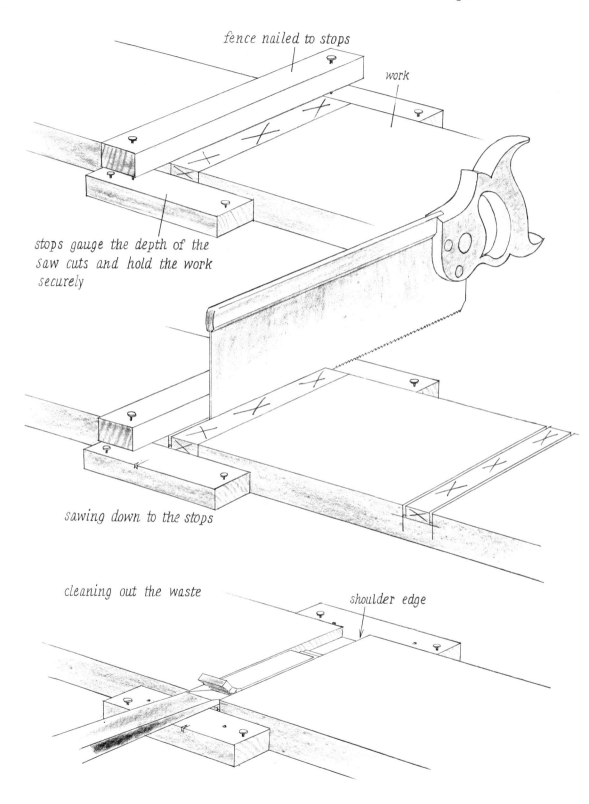

fence nailed to stops

work

stops gauge the depth of the
saw cuts and hold the work
securely

sawing down to the stops

cleaning out the waste

shoulder edge

MAKING THE SAW CUTS

Tack a straight piece of scrap wood across the work aligned exactly with the scored line on one side of the housing, so that the saw cuts into the waste. This acts as a guide fence for the saw. Use either a tenon saw or a fine-toothed backsaw. Hold the saw snug against the waste side of the fence and start the cut with slow, even strokes. Keep the saw perpendicular. When the saw almost touches the stops, tip it up and use the point to saw an extra stroke or two in the middle of the cut. Then finish with another level stroke or two until the saw teeth just nick the stops. Move the guide fence to the other scored line and saw the other side of the housing. Leave the work and the stops in place to clean out the waste wood.

CLEANING OUT THE WASTE

Use a sharp 1/2-inch chisel held bevel-up. Lay it flat on the stop and with a light tap of the mallet split out an inch or so of wood. Do the same on the other end of the housing. This helps avoid splintering the exposed ends of the joint when the chisel is shot clear across. Then clean out the remaining waste, using the chisel bevel-up with hand pressure alone, which gives better control and a feeling of shaving wood level. Work from both ends of the housing toward the middle. Be careful not to bruise the sharp shoulders of the housing with the chisel, as any damage here cannot be repaired. The bottom of the housing should be level or slightly hollowed, to allow the outside corners of the shelf to make tight seams when the joint is assembled.

FITTING THE JOINT

When this work is done, stand the shelf on end over the housing and try it for fit. The shelf should be a trifle too thick to go into the hous-

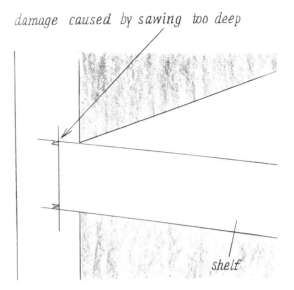

damage caused by sawing too deep

shelf

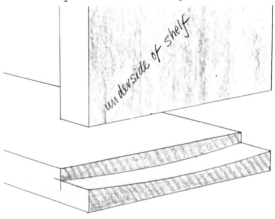

cutaway view of a housed joint

underside of shelf

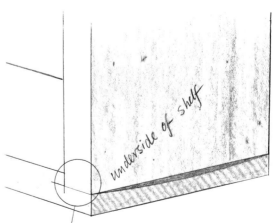

underside of shelf

hollow housing makes a tight seam

ing. To remedy this intentional oversize, strike a pencil line across the underside of the shelf, about 1/2 inch in from its end. With the block plane set for a fine cut, shave a fine bevel across the grain coming back no farther than the pencil line. Shave a very little, then try the shelf again. It should be a slight wedge fit requiring only to be tapped in, not pounded.

The joint is closed by tapping it together with the mallet against a scrap of wood to protect the work, after which nails are driven from the side through the housed part and into the end grain of the shelf. The nails carry none of the load, serving only to hold the shelf into the housing.

fitting shelf to housing

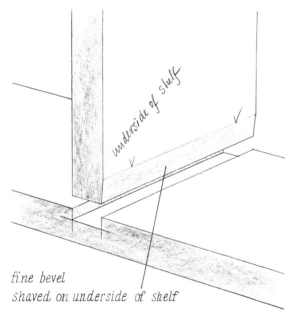

underside of shelf

fine bevel
shaved on underside of shelf

MITERED

The miter is typically used to finish the top of a cupboard with molding run around three sides. While the molding covers otherwise unsightly joints in the furniture, the mitered ends provide the way to turn 90-degree corners without showing any end-grain wood.

The best miters are made with a miter box, either a wooden one or one of the commercial types with locking adjustments for 45 degrees, 90 degrees, and other intermediate angles. Always use a length of scrap wood laid in the miter box under the work to prevent sawing into and damaging the box itself.

It is important to measure accurately and to accurately transfer the measurements to the molding. This can be done in one step. The long front piece of molding should be measured and cut first and the short side pieces last, other-

taking off a measurement
directly onto the molding

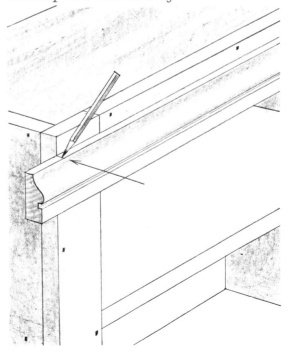

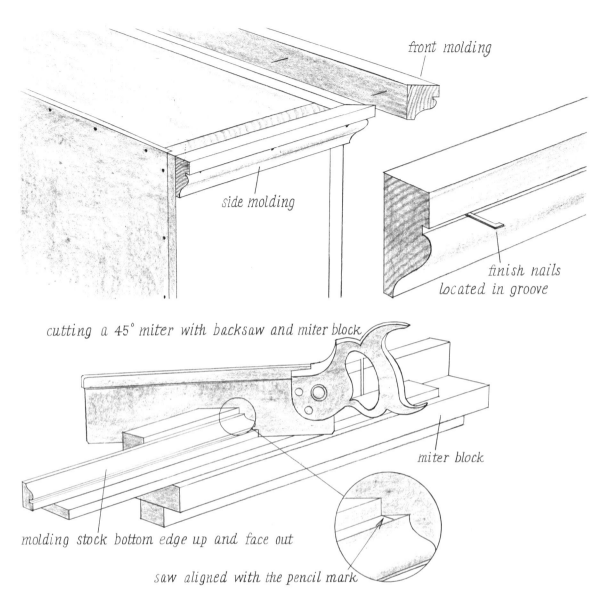

front molding

side molding

finish nails located in groove

cutting a 45° miter with backsaw and miter block

miter block

molding stock bottom edge up and face out

saw aligned with the pencil mark

wise you have the dubious job of cutting two miters to an exact fit at both ends.

Cut a length of molding about 4 inches longer than needed. Turn it bottom edge up and lay it face out across the front of the cupboard, leaving an equal amount of overhang at each side. Hold the molding tight against the cupboard, and with a sharp pencil make a mark on the edge of the molding at each side of the cupboard. Lay the molding into the miter box as shown in the illustration—bottom edge up and face out. This position of the molding is important, as the saw should always cut into the face

of the molding and not out of it, to ensure a clean edge.

Use a tenon or fine-toothed backsaw (12 pt. or 14 pt.). Ease the saw into the 45-degree slot, but hold it up clear of the work. Slide the molding until the pencil mark just meets the left-hand side of the saw. Then with one hand clamp the molding tight against the miter box while you saw slowly with the other. Do not bear down on the saw: the weight of the saw provides enough pressure to cut its own way. Saw lightly and clear through the molding into the scrap wood underneath. To cut the opposing

*paring the back and middle of the miter
to improve the fit*

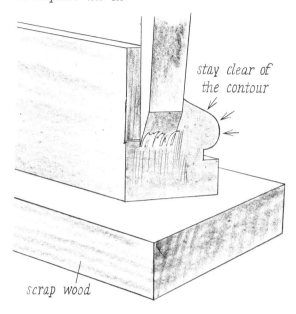

stay clear of
the contour

scrap wood

angle on the other end of the molding, shift the saw to the other 45-degree slot, slide the molding to the other pencil mark, and repeat the process. This may mean switching and sawing with your other hand in order to hold the work firmly into the miter box, but this is not so difficult when the miter box is held in the vise. Do not sandpaper sawn miters, or the joint will not be clean and sharp.

Tack the front molding in place with a nail at each end. Drive the nails only partway in. Cut the side pieces of molding about 3 inches longer than needed, and saw a 45-degree miter on one end of each piece. Then hold one in place to see how it fits with the molding already tacked on. If the joint does not close to your satisfaction, carefully pare the angle of the short molding with a narrow chisel, as shown in the illustration. Then hold the molding in place again and mark its length at the back of the cupboard. Use the 90-degree slot in the miter box to trim it to the mark.

Wide cove moldings must be supported in the miter box in order to hold them square and cut matching 45-degree angles, as shown in the illustration.

mitering a piece of wide cove molding

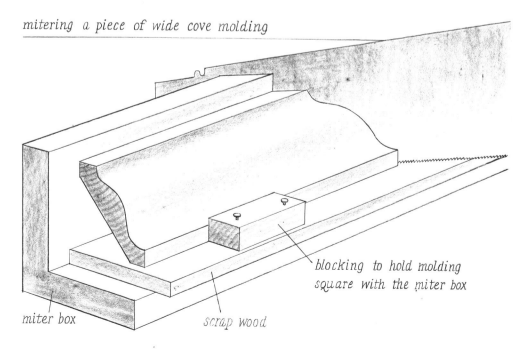

blocking to hold molding
square with the miter box

miter box

scrap wood

MORTISE AND TENON

The mortise and tenon joint is based on the simple mechanical device of a boxed recess in one member into which is fitted the end of another, the two being drawn tight together and secured by wooden pins driven through holes drilled in both pieces.

The joint is made in the following sequence of operations: (1) drill the drawbores, (2) cut the mortise, (3) cut and fit the tenon, (4) locate and drill the tenon drawbores, and (5) cut and drive the drawbore pins. As with all joinery, accuracy is of paramount importance, notwithstanding that a poorly made mortise and tenon will generally be stronger than any other joint meant to do the same job. A good deal of useful experience can be gained by making a few trial joints before commencing the actual work.

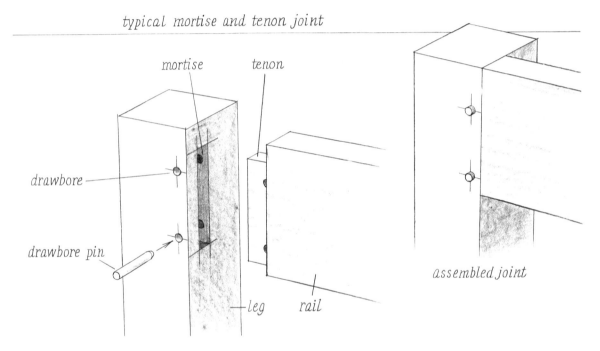

typical mortise and tenon joint

mortise

tenon

drawbore

drawbore pin

leg

rail

assembled joint

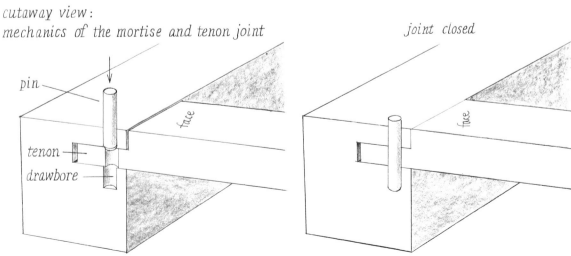

cutaway view:
mechanics of the mortise and tenon joint

joint closed

pin

tenon

drawbore

face

face

DRAWBORES

Lay out the drawbore centers on the leg or post as the case may be, using the marking gauge for the vertical marks and the square and jack-knife for the horizontal ones. Check the setting of the marking gauge on a scrap of wood, then mark all identical workpieces at one time.

Next, mark the drawbore centers with a center punch to make a nonslip indentation in which to start the drill. Set the punch on the cross marks and give it one fair tap with the hammer.

Put the workpiece in the vise to drill the drawbores. Use a wooden depth gauge slid over

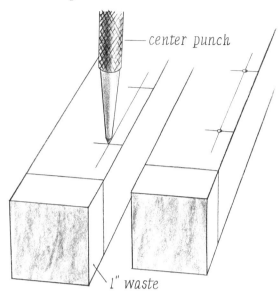

marking the drawbore centers

— center punch

1" waste

the drill point to ensure uniformly deep holes, having first made a trial to get the gauge the right length (see *Woodworking Practices*, p. 38). Drill all the drawbores in all the legs or posts.

MORTISE

Lay out the mortise to the specified dimensions, using the marking gauge for the long vertical marks, and the square and jackknife for the horizontal ones. When four identical mortises are to be laid out, it makes for accuracy to clamp them together and mark all four at one time. Make the width of the mortise (the narrow dimension) to conform to a standard chisel size. This way, the chisel chops the full width of the mortise.

To cut the mortise, put the work in the vise on a piece of hardwood blocking for a solid support. Then chop the mortise as shown in the series of illustrations. When outlining the mortise, hold the chisel straight up and down, and keep it exactly on the layout lines. When mak-

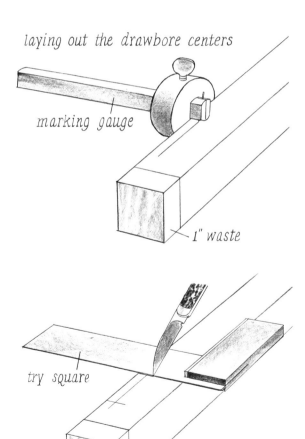

laying out the drawbore centers

marking gauge

1" waste

try square

1" waste

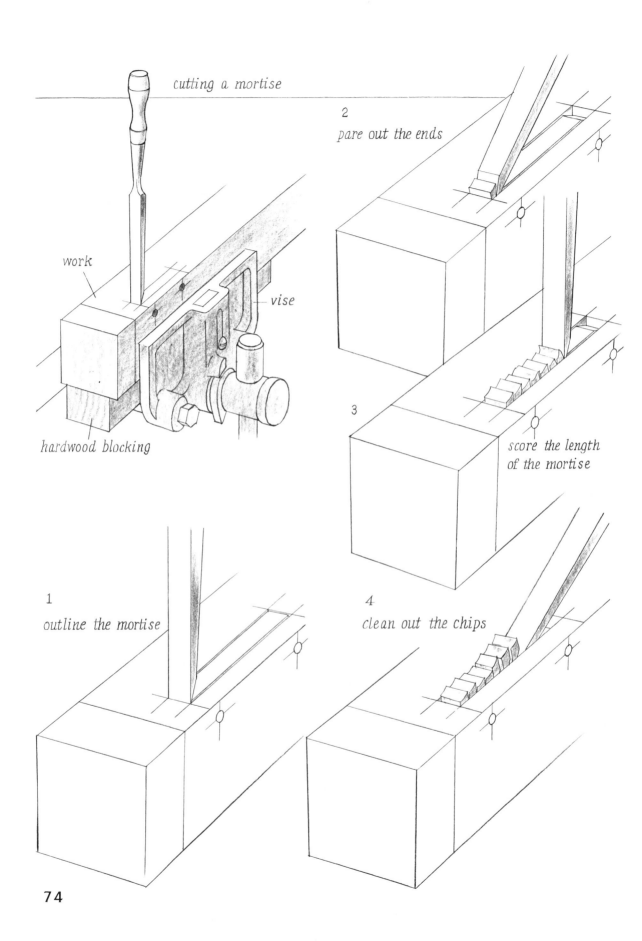

cutting a mortise

work

vise

hardwood blocking

2
pare out the ends

3
score the length
of the mortise

1
outline the mortise

4
clean out the chips

74

ing the scoring strokes, hold the chisel as straight as possible to keep the inside walls of the mortise smooth and even. Check the depth from time to time, and pare the bottom of the mortise another 1/16 inch deeper to provide clearance for the end of the tenon. With this extra depth there is no great need to smooth the bottom of the mortise.

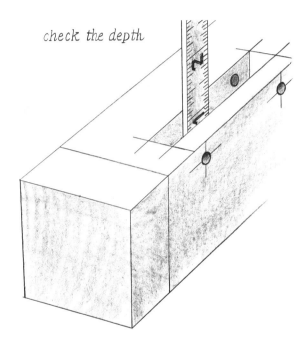

check the depth

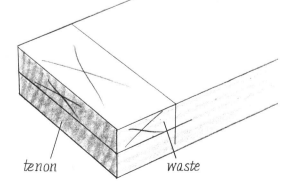

tenon laid out on end of rail

tenon   waste

TENON

Lay out the tenon on the end of the rail to the specified dimensions, using the square and knife, and the marking gauge. Carry the marks over onto the end and the edges. X-mark the wood to be removed.

Put the work in the vise cocked up at an angle so that the end and edge marks are clearly visible, as shown in the illustration. Use a tenon or fine-toothed backsaw (12 pt. or 14 pt.) to start the rip cut. Saw the corner first, on the waste side of the mark. Then turn the work around in the vise and saw the other corner. Straighten the work in the vise and hold the saw level to bring the cut down not quite to the shoulder line.

To make the shoulder cut, put the work in the miter box and use the backsaw to cut down not quite to the tenon. The waste can then be broken out and the inside corner cleaned up with the chisel. Be careful not to bruise the sharp edge of the shoulder. Finally, lay out and cut the haunch with the backsaw and chisel.

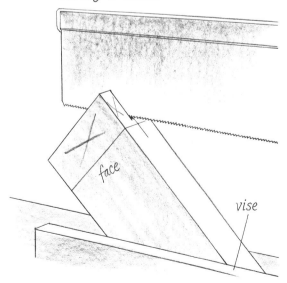

sawing a tenon

face   vise

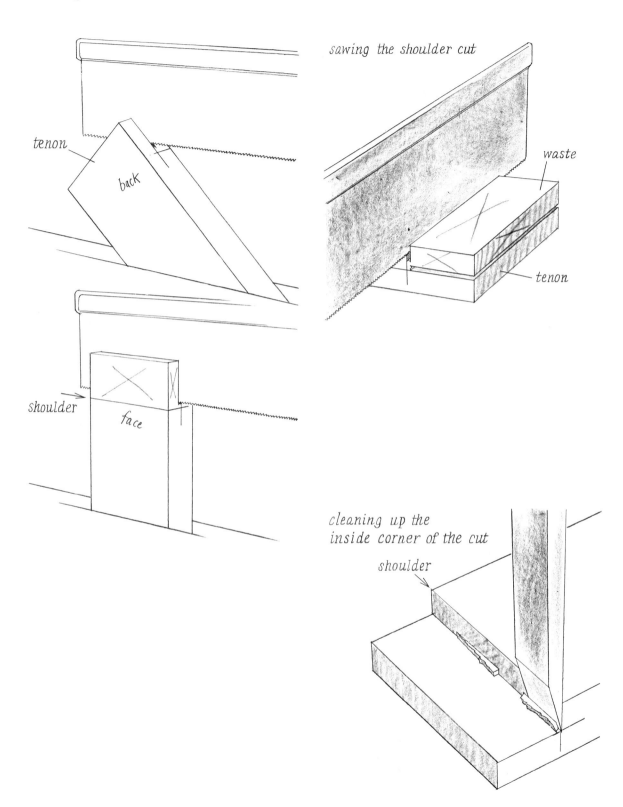

tenon

back

sawing the shoulder cut

waste

tenon

shoulder

face

cleaning up the
inside corner of the cut

shoulder

cutting the haunch

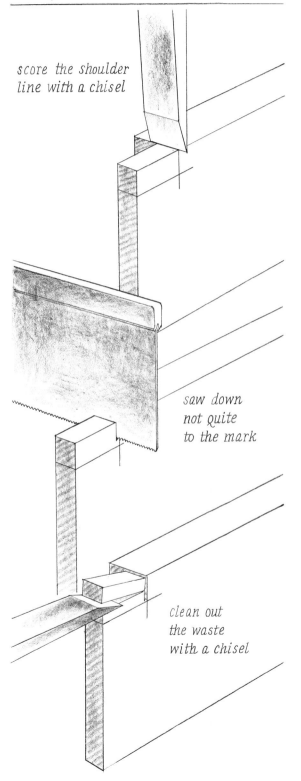

*score the shoulder
line with a chisel*

*saw down
not quite
to the mark*

*clean out
the waste
with a chisel*

FITTING THE JOINT

Most of the fitting should be done on the sawn face of the tenon, as this is simpler and more accurate than attempting to pare the inside walls of the mortise. First round off the sharp edges on the end of the tenon for easier entry, and then try it in the mortise. It should be a shade too thick to go in. With the tenon flat on the bench, use the chisel bevel-up to pare paper-thin slices across the tenon. Do not use sand-

fitting the joint

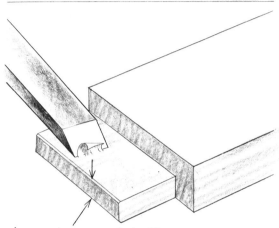

sharp edges rounded off

paper for this job. Then try pushing the tenon into the mortise as far as it will go with hand pressure alone. When it sticks, mark the tenon with a pencil at that point, remove the tenon and shave off the pencil mark with the chisel. Continue paring and trying until hand pressure brings the tenon shoulder tight against the mortise. Never drive the joint together with a mallet: you may never get it out again, or you may split the mortise. As each tenon is fitted, mark it and its mortise with the same letter to facilitate assembly (see *Woodworking Practices*, p. 33).

TENON DRAWBORES

The next step is to locate the position of the tenon drawbores, which is best done with the joint assembled and held together with a clamp or clamp board (see *Woodworking Practices*, p. 35). Use an auger bit—not a twist drill—the same size as the drawbore in the leg or post. Twist the bit by hand into each drawbore until the point of the bit stabs a pinpoint mark in the wood of the tenon. Remove the clamp and pull the tenon out.

Use the awl to shift the pinpoint marks toward the shoulder of the tenon. Set its point at an angle on the pinpoint mark and push it into the wood about 1/16 inch. Then pry the awl up straight and push it into the wood a distance of about 1/8 inch. Set the center punch in this awl hole and enlarge it to an indentation by tapping it once with the hammer. Set the drill in this indentation and drill the drawbore clear through. Locate and drill all the drawbores in the same way.

locating the positions of the tenon drawbores

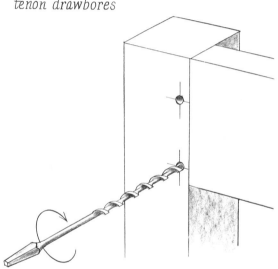

shifting the center marks

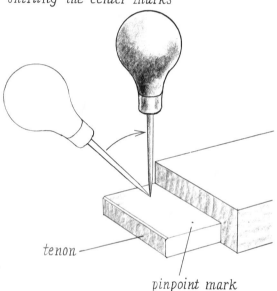

tenon

pinpoint mark

Now comes the fussiest part of the whole joint. The tenon drawbores must be drilled—not exactly on the pinpoint marks—but *a fraction closer to the shoulder* of the tenon. This is so that the drawbore pins, as they are driven through the mortise and into the tenon, will engage the offset holes and draw the joint tight together. The location of these drawbores is therefore most important. If they are too close to the shoulder, the pins may not drive through at all, or what is worse, they may break off halfway in. And when the tenon drawbores are too far the other way, the joint will never close.

DRAWBORE PINS

Cut the drawbore pins about 1/8 inch longer than needed, and slightly taper their entering ends with a file or sandpaper so they will engage the tenon drawbores more readily.

ASSEMBLING THE JOINT

Push the joint together and hold it there with either a clamp or a clamp board. Start both pins into the drawbores of the leg or post, and tap first one and then the other with the hammer until they engage the tenon drawbores. Then drive them alternately all the way in to draw the joint together evenly. As the pins pass through the tenon and engage the other side of the mortise, you may have to use heavier hammer blows. But keep them moving, or they may seize up.

TRIMMING THE PINS FLUSH

Use a sharp 3/4-inch or 1-inch chisel, and have the work clamped to the workbench or otherwise held securely so both hands are free. Lay the chisel flat on the work (leg or post) with the bevel up. Use two hands: one to hold and push the chisel handle, the other to guide and swivel the blade. Work round and round the pin, cutting a bit deeper with each circuit, and cutting mainly with the trailing corner of the chisel, as shown in the illustration. Do not use a mallet to chop the chisel straight across the pin, as this method breaks the wood and leaves a ragged surface on the pin.

trimming the drawbore pins flush

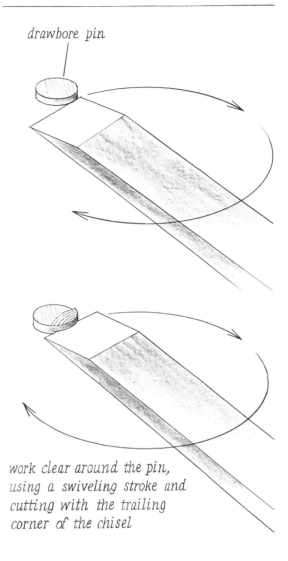

drawbore pin

work clear around the pin, using a swiveling stroke and cutting with the trailing corner of the chisel

making drawbore pins

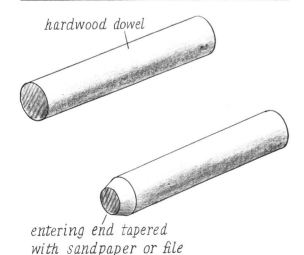

hardwood dowel

entering end tapered with sandpaper or file

If for some reason the pin projects more than 1/8 inch above the surface, use a fine-toothed backsaw (12 pt. or 14 pt.) to cut off the bulk of the pin. Lay the saw blade flat on the work on a piece of cardboard, sliding the saw and the cardboard as one to prevent gouging the finished surrounding wood. After this preliminary step, finish trimming the pin as described above.

NOTCH

The notch is simple to make with nothing more than a backsaw and a chisel. Mark out the notch to the required dimensions with the marking gauge and try square, carrying the marks over onto the edges. Then X-mark the waste wood to be removed.

Make the rip cut first and the crosscut last to avoid having the waste split off prematurely and unpredictably. When the cuts are made in the reverse order, the piece of waste is likely to break out before the saw cut has been completed, leaving much ragged wood to be cleaned out with needless extra chisel work.

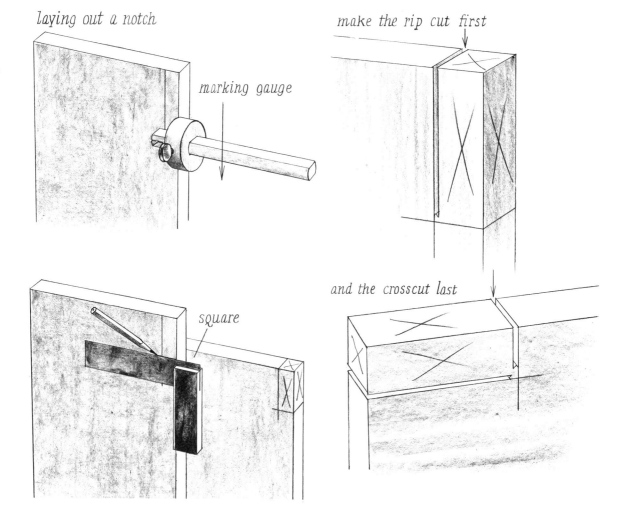

laying out a notch

marking gauge

make the rip cut first

square

and the crosscut last

chop out the remaining waste with the chisel

sawing two workpieces simultaneously

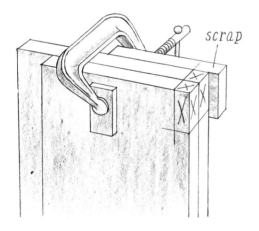

scrap

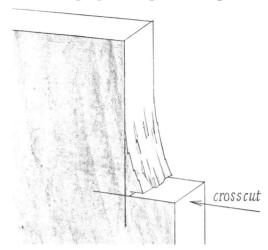

waste may split off prematurely

crosscut

To overcome the usual difficulty of notching a single board, clamp one or two pieces of scrap wood to the back side of the work. Then use the try square to extend the layout lines over onto the scraps. The extra thickness of wood and longer sawing line makes it easier to saw square, while at the same time the exit side of the cut in the work will be much cleaner. When two or more workpieces are to be notched identically, this same principle holds true. Clamp two or more pieces together with scrap wood on the back side, making sure that the top edges of the work and scrap are aligned flush.

With either the ripsaw or crosscut, saw not quite to the bottom mark, leaving a thread of wood to be chopped out with the chisel. This makes a good sharp inside corner, which the saw alone cannot do.

CLOSED NOTCH

Make the two saw cuts with a piece of scrap wood clamped to the work, and saw down not quite to the bottom of the notch. To clean out the waste, lay the work flat on a piece of waste lumber. Use a chisel somewhat narrower than the width of the notch. Set the chisel about halfway down into the notch and split out a small chunk with a mallet tap. Then turn the work over to see the run of the grain before making another chisel cut. Continue chopping small bites from both sides down to a point about 1/16 inch from the bottom layout line. Finally, pare thin shavings from both sides toward the middle to bring the notch exactly to the mark.

cutting a closed notch

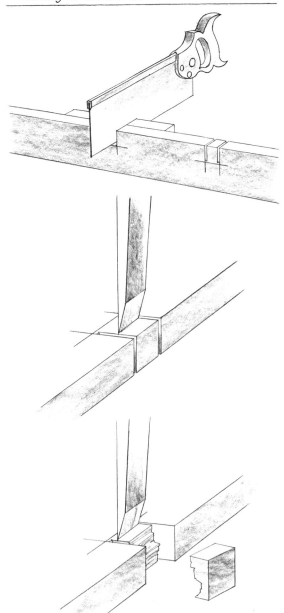

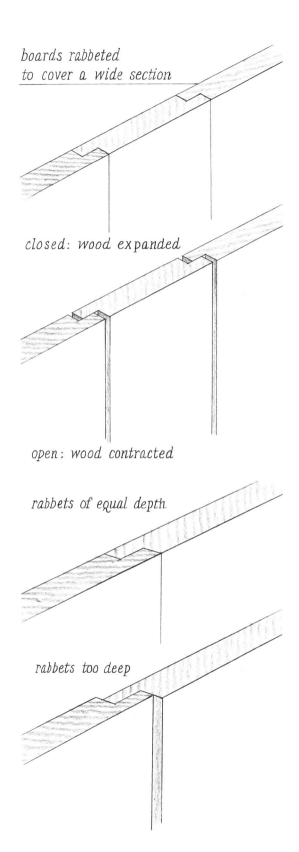

boards rabbeted
to cover a wide section

closed: wood expanded

open: wood contracted

rabbets of equal depth

rabbets too deep

RABBET

PARALLEL RABBET

All rabbets are worked either on the edges of boards running parallel with the grain, or on the ends of boards across the grain. The parallel rabbet is used to fit several boards lapped edge to edge to cover wide sections such as the backs of cupboards, as well as to recess them flush into the cupboard's back edges. Nailed without glue, the rabbeted boards can expand and contract with atmospheric changes while preventing drafts and daylight from getting through. And the parallel rabbet is equally suited to fitting plywood for the same purposes and for providing the necessary bracing.

Before shooting the rabbets, take special care to joint the edges of boards square, straight, and even—as nearly perfect as you can make them (see *Woodworking Practices*, p. 28). Because the rabbet plane rides on the jointed edge, any irregularities will be duplicated in the rabbet as well.

rabbet joint conceals
end grain of top board

top board

side

83

Adjusting the Plane

Whether you use a combination plane, or multiplane, or a rabbet plane, there are five essential steps in getting it ready for work: (1) check the sharpness of the cutter iron, (2) set it for a fine cut, (3) set the depth gauge to the required depth of rabbet, (4) adjust the sliding side fence, and (5) shoot a trial rabbet. This is the only way to prove the accuracy of the adjustments, and to make sure that in the case of rabbeted backboards, their faces will come flush when fastened in place. A grooving plane can also be used, but the board must be held edge-up in the vise and the rabbet cut on the offside, since this plane's depth gauge is to the left of the cutter iron. Set up the plane and shoot a trial rabbet on a scrap of lumber about 14 inches long. Then use measurements taken from the trial to readjust the plane as needed. Make two or three trials if necessary.

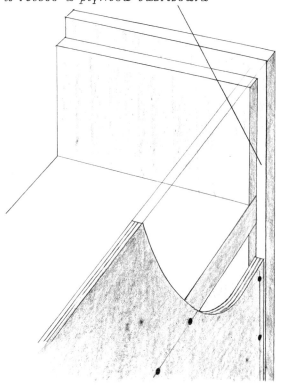

cutaway view:
rabbet shot in back edge of cupboard side
to recess a plywood backboard

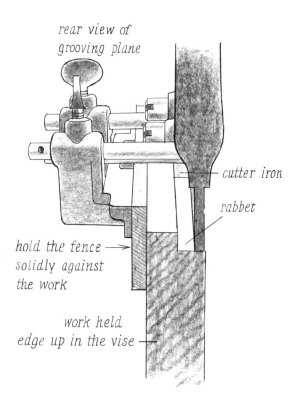

rear view of
grooving plane

cutter iron

rabbet

hold the fence → solidly against the work

work held edge up in the vise →

starting a rabbet at the far end of a board

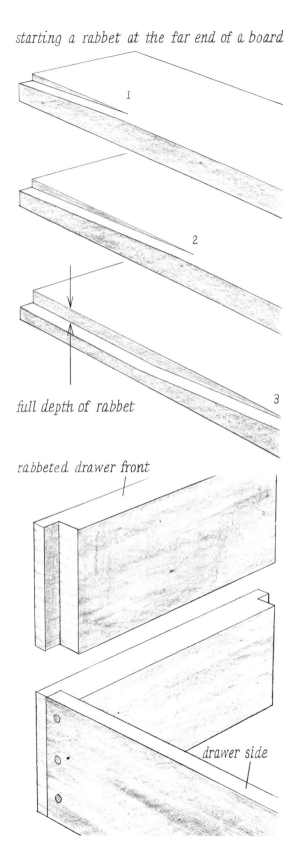

full depth of rabbet

rabbeted drawer front

drawer side

Shooting a Rabbet

The workpiece must be well secured flat on the bench. Let the working edge overhang the edge of the bench so that the plane with its fence can slide clear of all obstructions. Set the plane on the work about 3 inches back from its end, holding the plane's fence firmly against the edge of the board. Make a couple of strokes with the plane to the end of the board. Start the next strokes back toward you another 3 inches or so, and shoot clear to the far end of the board. Continue in this fashion until you are planing at the near end of the board, at which time the rabbet at the far end will be nearly full depth. Keep on planing with full-length strokes until the cutter no longer produces a shaving. Work slowly and deliberately, remembering to hold the fence solidly against the work, and the plane level with its surface. This same planing technique is used in making grooves and tongue and groove joints.

laying out a cross-grained rabbet

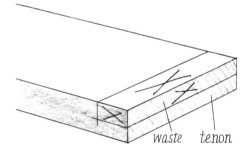

waste   *tenon*

CROSS-GRAIN RABBET

This joint provides a strong and simple means of joining two pieces of wood at right angles while concealing most of the end grain. It is used in one type of drawer construction to join the front and sides, as well as in fitting the top board into a cupboard.

Lay out the rabbet as shown in the illustration, using the square and jackknife to score across the face of the board, and the marking gauge for the end grain and edges. X-mark the waste wood to be removed. Lay the work flat on the workbench with stops tacked on both sides to secure it. If the stops are made of lumber the same thickness as the tenon, they will prevent sawing too deep.

Next, tack a straight piece of scrap wood across the work aligned exactly on the scored shoulder line, to act as a guide fence for the saw. Then use a tenon or fine-toothed backsaw (12 pt. or 14 pt.) to make the cut. Hold the saw snug against the guide fence and saw down not quite to the edge marks. Use slow, steady strokes, and light pressure.

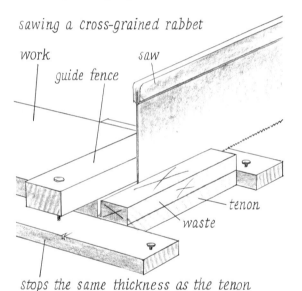

sawing a cross-grained rabbet

work

guide fence

saw

tenon

waste

stops the same thickness as the tenon

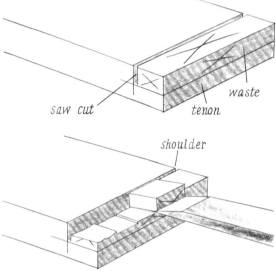

cross-grained rabbet :
cleaning out the waste with the chisel

saw cut

waste

tenon

shoulder

splitting out the waste with the chisel

To clean out the waste, split out small sections of wood with the chisel, using light mallet taps. Do not attempt to chisel right to the mark the first time: the wood grain may run down and cause the waste to split below the mark. Instead, start at a point well above the tenon and work clear across. If the grain is consistently straight you can make the next chisel cuts closer to the mark. Then shave the inside face of the tenon, planing the chisel across the grain as shown in the illustration, using the stops this time as depth guides for the chisel.

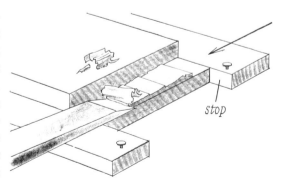

stop

shaving the tenon, using the stops
as depth gauges, and working from both sides

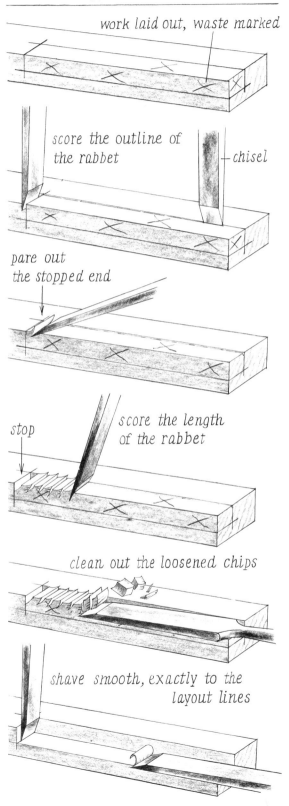

cutting a stopped rabbet

work laid out, waste marked

score the outline of
the rabbet — chisel

pare out
the stopped end

stop   score the length
of the rabbet

clean out the loosened chips

shave smooth, exactly to the
layout lines

STOPPED RABBET

Because only one end of this rabbet is open, it is cut with a chisel rather than a plane, in much the same way as a halved joint pocket.

Lay out the work with the try square and marking gauge, carrying the marks over onto the end and the edge. Proceed as shown in the illustrations, scoring and cleaning out the loosened chips down not quite to the bottom of the rabbet. Then carefully pare exactly to the bottom line, sliding the chisel plane-fashion toward the stop.

TONGUE AND GROOVE

The tongue and groove joint is used to join boards edge to edge in making up wide sections such as tabletops, wide shelves, and the sides and doors of cupboards. Because this joint has more glue surface than the edge-butt joint used for the same purpose, it is often believed to be stronger. But its chief advantage is in the ease with which adjoining boards are aligned with their surfaces flush.

The two mating parts of the joint can be made with a combination, or a multiplane, or the older double-end match plane, all three of which are equipped with matching pairs of cutter irons—one to cut the tongue on one board, another to cut the groove in the other. In any case, take special care to first joint the meeting edges of boards square, straight, and even—as nearly perfect as you can make them (see *Woodworking Practices*, p. 28). Because all these planes ride on the jointed edge of the work, any irregularities in the jointing will be duplicated in the tongues and grooves. After jointing, clamp the boards together lightly for an inspection. If the joint shows as an even hairline, the tongues and grooves can be shot.

ADJUSTING THE PLANE

Whichever plane you are using, there are five essential steps in getting it ready for work: (1) check the sharpness of the cutter iron, (2) set it for a fine cut, (3) set the depth gauge to the required depth of tongue or groove, (4) adjust the fence to center the cutter on the edge of the board, and (5) shoot a trial tongue or groove. This is the only way to prove the accuracy of the adjustments. Set up the plane and shoot a trial tongue and groove on scraps of lumber about 14 inches long. Then use measurements taken from these trials to readjust the plane as needed. Make two or three trials if necessary.

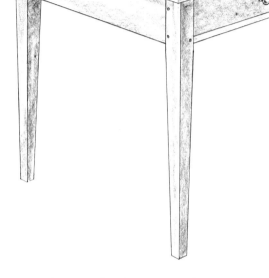

tongue and groove joints in a tabletop

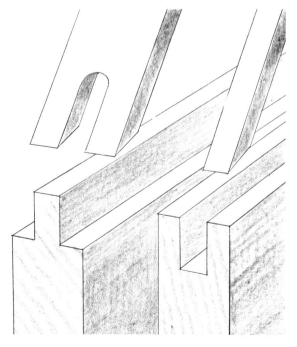

cutter irons of a tongue and groove plane

SHOOTING A TONGUE

Put the board in the vise jointed edge up. Start at the far end of the board. Set the plane on its edge about 3 inches back from the end and hold the plane's fence firmly against the side of the board. Shoot a couple of strokes with the plane to the far end. Then start the next strokes back toward you another 3 inches or so, and shoot clear to the far end. Continue in this fashion, starting a little nearer and completing each shot to the far end. By the time you reach the near end of the board, the tongue will be nearly full height. Keep on planing with full-length strokes until the cutter no longer produces a shaving. Work slowly and deliberately, remembering to hold the fence solidly against the side of the board, and the plane level with its edge. This

same planing technique is used in shooting grooves and rabbets.

Finally, remove the sharp edges along the top of the tongue by planing one or two strokes with the block plane set for a very fine cut. Then mark the good surface of the board with a pencil X. Also mark the good side of the board to be grooved, so that when both halves of the joint are done, all the good surfaces will come on the correct side.

SHOOTING A GROOVE

The groove is shot in the same way as the tongue, and the inner sharp edges of the groove are removed with a light stroke or two of the block plane as before. This allows the joint to close more easily. Before gluing the joint and

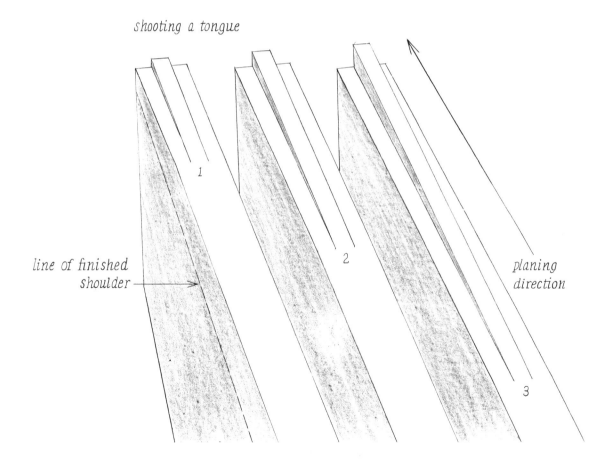

shooting a tongue

1

2

3

line of finished shoulder →

planing direction

clamping it together, push the joint together for one last inspection. When more than one pair of boards are to be tongue and grooved, shoot all the tongues first with one setting of the plane, then shoot the grooves.

GLUING UP

Use at least three furniture, bar, or pipe clamps or clamp boards (see *Woodworking Practices,* p. 35)—more if the work is longer than 3 feet. Place two clamps on the underside of the work, one near each end. Put a third clamp on top of the work in the middle. Opposing the clamps exerts a counterpull that helps prevent buckling the boards.

When more than two boards are to be glued up, glue and clamp the first two, let them dry overnight, then glue on the next one. Since some adhesives set up rather quickly, this method allows you more time to glue up and start the joint together before tightening the clamps.

Check to be sure there are no chips or shavings stuck to the tongue or groove. Spread a thin even coat of glue along the sides and top *of the tongue only.* In this close-fitting joint there is little room for glue, and if it is run into the groove will more than likely prevent the joint from closing. If using furniture clamps, have them adjusted to approximately the right opening, to save time.

Lay the boards good side up into the clamps (or clamp boards), which should be protected with waxed paper. Start the joint together with hand pressure or with light taps of the mallet. Protect the work with a scrap of wood. Then slowly apply pressure alternately to the clamps to draw the joint together evenly along its entire length. Put the third clamp across the other side of the work and tighten it to the same pressure. Then go back and tighten all the clamps until beads of glue appear all along the joint. Quickly scrape off the excess glue and wipe the surface clean with a damp sponge. This is important

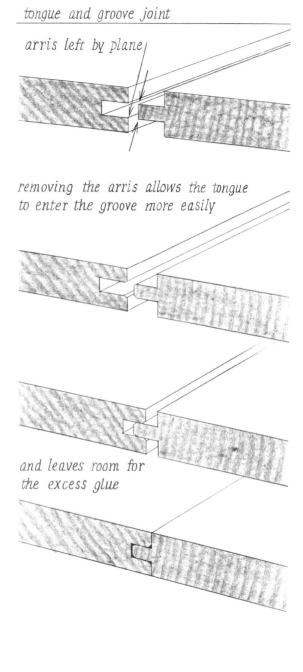

tongue and groove joint

arris left by plane

removing the arris allows the tongue to enter the groove more easily

and leaves room for the excess glue

because most glues repel stains and finishes, making light spots on the finished work. Stand the work aside to dry overnight.

TRIMMING TO WIDTH

Remove the clamps and use a jack or jointer plane to smooth one edge of the glued-up panel, using the same technique as when jointing new lumber (see *Woodworking Practices*, p. 28). Set the cutter iron for a fine cut and make one or two full-length passes. Take off no more wood than is necessary to level the edge and make it straight and square.

At each end measure across from this good edge and mark the width with pencil. Lay a straightedge on the marks and connect them

gluing up a pair of boards with clamp boards and wedges

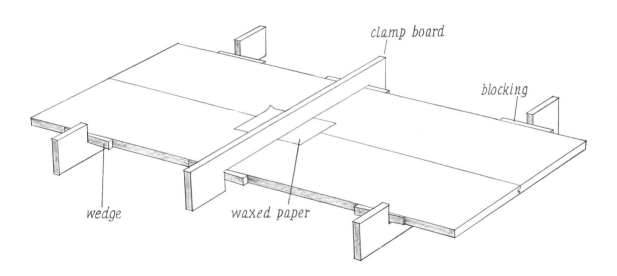

by drawing a line the full length of the work. Then hold the work in the vise and joint the edge exactly to the line, checking the width with the rule after each stroke of the plane, at both ends and in the middle. Also check with the try square frequently from one end of the work to the other. If the amount of wood to be removed is 3/8 inch or more, trim off the bulk of it with the ripsaw and then joint the edge down to the line.

SQUARING THE ENDS

To trim the work to finished length, hold the carpenter's square against one edge of the work and draw a pencil line across one end. Use a fine-toothed crosscut saw (12 pt. or 14 pt.) to trim the surplus wood to the line. Then smooth the end-grain saw cut. Clamp a pair of straight battens flush with the end of the work and stand it on end against the bench with one edge held in the vise for support. Use the block plane to plane the battens as well as the work itself, working from both sides toward the middle. Hold the plane level and check the work frequently with the try square. Then measure the finished length from this good end, square a line across the other end, trim off the surplus wood, and plane the saw cut smooth and square in the same way.

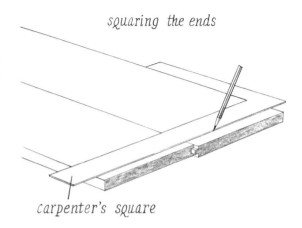

squaring the ends

carpenter's square

squaring the end of a glued-up panel

battens

C-clamp

square

lathebox: dimensions and construction details

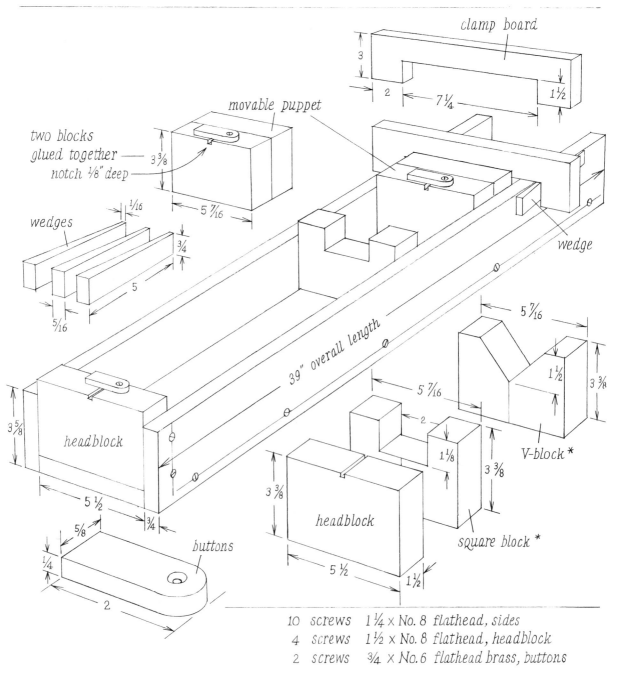

clamp board

3

2   7¼   1½

movable puppet

two blocks
glued together
notch ⅛" deep

3⅜

5⁷⁄₁₆

wedge

wedges

¹⁄₁₆

¾

5

⁵⁄₁₆

39" overall length

5⁷⁄₁₆

1½   3⅜

V-block *

headblock

3⅝

5⁷⁄₁₆

2

1⅛

3⅜

5½   ¾

square block *

buttons

3⅜

⅝

¼

headblock

2

5½   1½

10 screws   1¼ × No. 8 flathead, sides
 4 screws   1½ × No. 8 flathead, headblock
 2 screws   ¾ × No. 6 flathead brass, buttons

* V-block and square block for Pine Dressing Table

94

Turned Legs

Making turned legs without a lathe is not as complicated as the number of illustrations might suggest. As is often the case, the simpler the procedure, the more detailed the explanation required. This method is really quite simple and produces very good results with the use of ordinary hand tools.

As used here, the terms *turned* and *turning* refer not only to working in the round but also to shaping legs and posts that are square-tapered and octagonal-tapered.

Because it is essential to have both hands free to manipulate the drawknife, spokeshave, plane, and file with satisfactory control, and because these tools require considerable force, the work must be held securely yet without the risk of damaging it. A homemade lathebox is the most practical answer. By using a square block or a V-block under the work, it can be locked in a stationary position, or left free to rotate with the blocks removed. And the lathebox can be held in the vise or taken out and set aside temporarily without disturbing the work, when the bench and vise are needed for other jobs.

The lathebox shown in the illustration can be built from inexpensive lumber and will take furniture squares up to 3 inches square and

head and tail blocks for long work

wedge

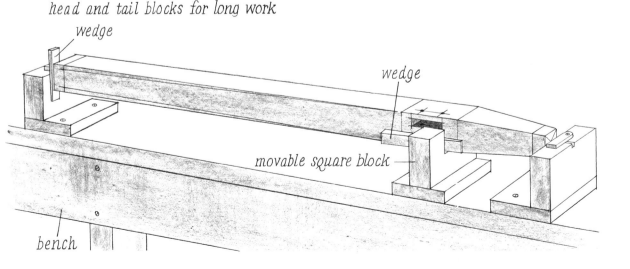

wedge

movable square block

bench

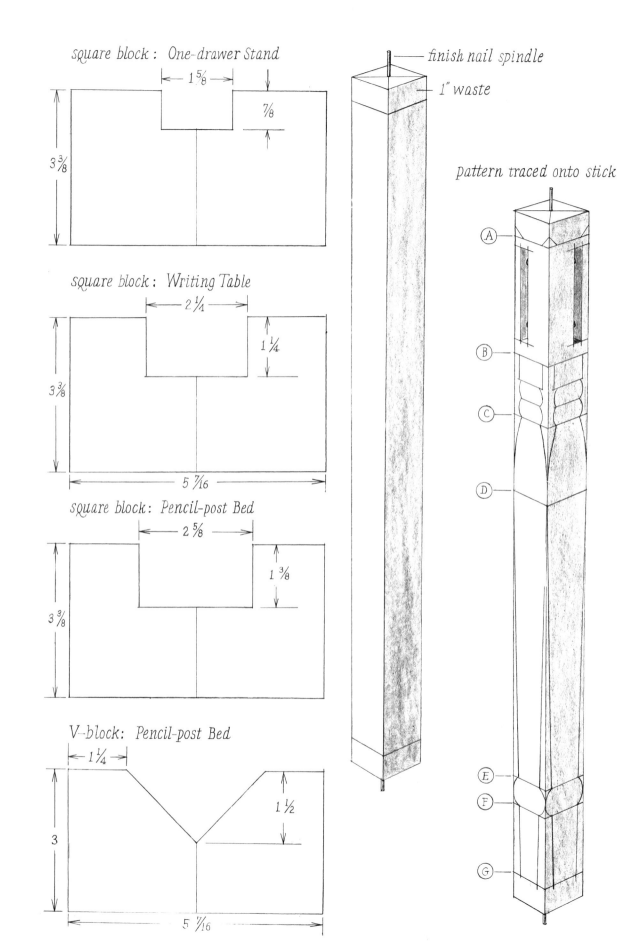

square block: One-drawer Stand

$1\frac{5}{8}$

$\frac{7}{8}$

$3\frac{3}{8}$

square block: Writing Table

$2\frac{1}{4}$

$1\frac{1}{4}$

$3\frac{3}{8}$

$5\frac{7}{16}$

square block: Pencil-post Bed

$2\frac{5}{8}$

$1\frac{3}{8}$

$3\frac{3}{8}$

V-block: Pencil-post Bed

$1\frac{1}{4}$

$1\frac{1}{2}$

3

$5\frac{7}{16}$

finish nail spindle

1" waste

pattern traced onto stick

A
B
C
D

E
F

G

34 1/2 inches long. For extra long sticks such as the posts for the *Pencil-post Bed,* individual head and tail blocks can be attached to the top of the workbench and used with similar square and V-blocks. Note that those shown are made to fit the 1 7/8-inch furniture squares for the *Pine Dressing Table.* Other sizes require special blocks as indicated in the diagrams.

ROUND TURNING

The procedures and illustrations on the next pages describe the making of legs for the *Pine Dressing Table,* but they are typical for round-turning any similar furniture parts.

Before starting to shape a leg in the lathebox, prepare the furniture square as follows:

1.   Draw diagonal lines on both ends to locate the centers. Then drive an 8d finish nail about 3/4 inch into each center to form spindles. Cut off the nails to leave another 3/4 inch projecting, using heavy cutting pliers or a hacksaw.

2.   Mark off the 1-inch waste sections across both ends and carry these marks over onto all four sides of the stick. These waste sections are mainly to prevent otherwise damaging the finished ends of the leg, but they also provide reference points from which to measure and check the work in progress. They are not cut off until the leg is completely finished.

3.   Tape the leg pattern to the work to prevent its slipping, aligning the straight side of the pattern with one edge of the stick. Use a sharp, soft pencil to trace carefully around the pattern from top to bottom. Remove the pattern, flop it over, and tape it down aligned with the other edge of the stick. Trace around pattern as before.

4.   Then, referring to the pattern diagram in the project chapter, lay off all the reference lines, using the try square and pencil. In the case of the *Pine Dressing Table,* these lines are

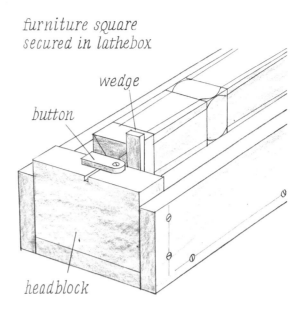

furniture square secured in lathebox

wedge

button

headblock

designated A, B, C, D, E, F, and G. Trace the pattern and the reference lines onto all four sides of the furniture square in the same way, as shown in the illustration.

Put the stick into the lathebox and turn the buttons over the spindles so the work stays put. Put the lathebox in the vise. Wedge the clamp board across the box to hold the puppet tight, as illustrated on page 94. Then, using a tenon saw or a fine-toothed backsaw (12 pt. or 14 pt.), make light cuts on lines B, C, E, F, and G. Saw only about 1/16 inch deep. If these parting cuts are sawn too deep, the tool marks will remain and spoil the appearance of the finished work; they are deepened a little at a time as work progresses. Saw across the corners first, then level off the saw and complete the cuts. Repeat similar scoring cuts on all four sides of the work. Hold the furniture square firmly for this work by using the V-block or by a wedge between the end of the stick and the headblock.

scoring with tenon saw

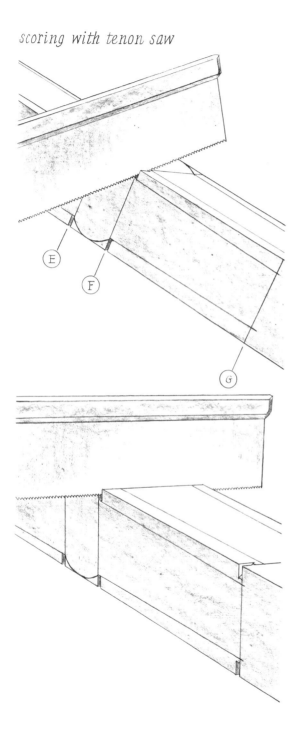

SQUARE SHAPING

Turning a leg by this method follows a set sequence: first shape it square in section to the outlines of the traced pattern; then make it octagonal in form; and finally round it off.

Start with the section of the leg between C and D. Put the square block in place under the furniture square and wedge it up tight. With a 1/2-inch chisel held bevel-up, pare off wood following the curved lines, using hand pressure

paring to the curve with a chisel

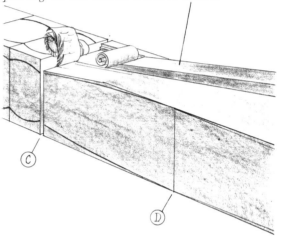

alone (no mallet). Take narrow slices. This gives better control and less chance of slipping than attempting great, wide cuts. Chisel right up to the saw cut. Using the hands alone forces you to pare thinner and thus avoid cutting too deep. Pare close to the lines, *but leave them showing.* It is especially important not to lose the reference lines at D, as they mark the greatest diameter of the leg. Do not clean out the shavings at C—that comes later.

When this first side has been pared to shape, it is necessary to retrace the curved lines that were removed with the wood. From the original pattern trace off and make a patch pattern to fit up against the shoulder you have just made. Then rotate the work in the lathebox and shape

retracing the curves with a patch pattern

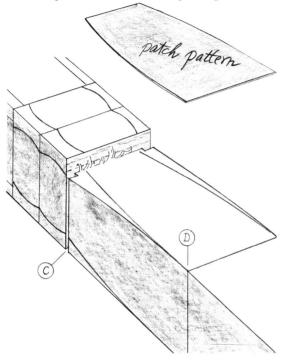

the opposing side in the same way. Then go on and shape the remaining two sides.

Deepen the saw cuts on all four sides at E and F (either side of the bulb). Then use a 1/2-inch chisel to cut pockets on all four sides of the leg above E and below F. Also cut pockets on all four sides at G. The purpose of these pockets is to establish square sections above and below the bulb to which to work.

Next taper all four sides of the leg from D to E, keeping it square in section. For this oper-

saw cuts deepened on all four sides

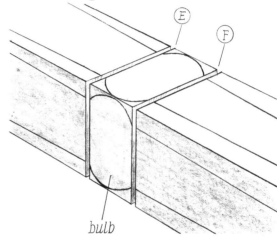

bulb

square-shaped from C to D

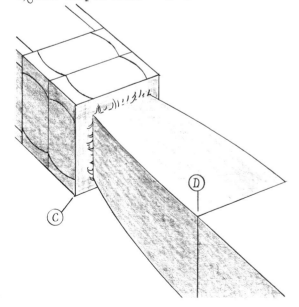

pockets cut

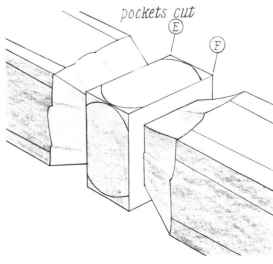

ation, leave the square block in place under the leg, wedge it good and tight, and tighten the wedges as needed while work progresses. Use the drawknife to rough out this part of the work. Hold it with the bevel of the blade down and at an angle to the length of the work in order to get a slicing action which makes cutting easier and gives better control. Shave thin slices rather than heavy splinters, frequently checking the layout lines on both sides of the stick.

After removing most of the wood with the drawknife, use the spokeshave set for a fine cut to smooth up the surfaces. A small bullnose plane will get into the tight spots just above E, or you can pare carefully with a 1-inch chisel held bevel-up. Remove wood close to the lines, but leave them showing. Don't worry about tool marks, they are cleaned off when it comes to rounding. The main thing is to keep all four sides of this taper as nearly square as possible, or the next stage of making the octagonal shape will be difficult. This can be checked by measuring

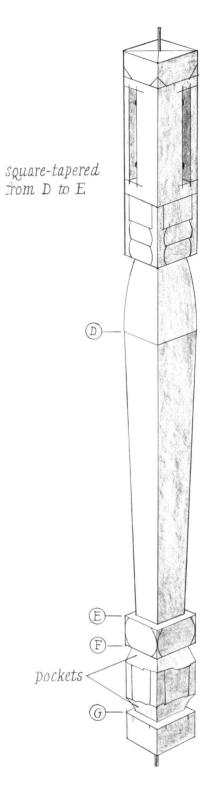

square-tapered from D to E

D

E

F

pockets

G

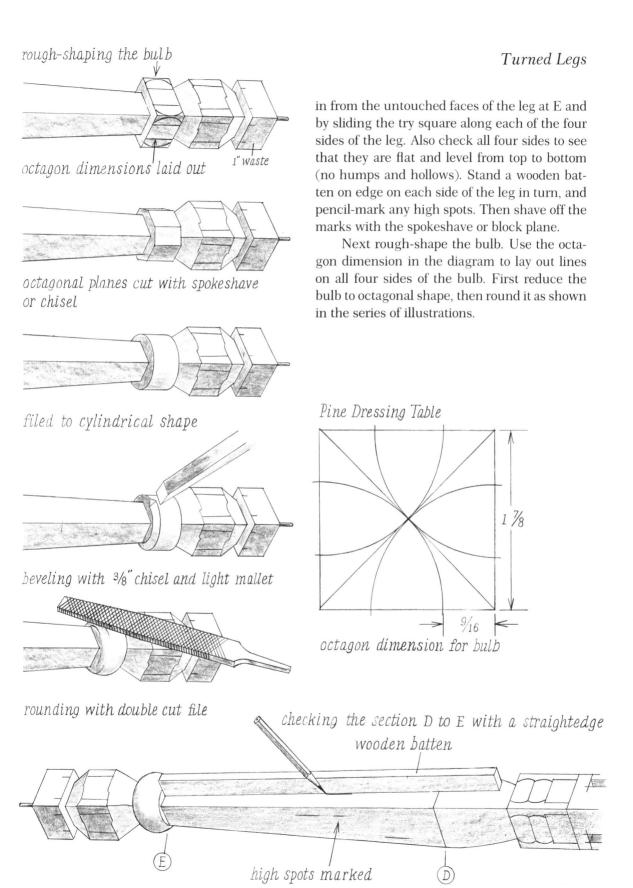

rough-shaping the bulb

octagon dimensions laid out

1" waste

octagonal planes cut with spokeshave or chisel

filed to cylindrical shape

beveling with ⅜" chisel and light mallet

rounding with double cut file

in from the untouched faces of the leg at E and by sliding the try square along each of the four sides of the leg. Also check all four sides to see that they are flat and level from top to bottom (no humps and hollows). Stand a wooden batten on edge on each side of the leg in turn, and pencil-mark any high spots. Then shave off the marks with the spokeshave or block plane.

Next rough-shape the bulb. Use the octagon dimension in the diagram to lay out lines on all four sides of the bulb. First reduce the bulb to octagonal shape, then round it as shown in the series of illustrations.

Pine Dressing Table

1 ⅞

⁹⁄₁₆

octagon dimension for bulb

checking the section D to E with a straightedge wooden batten

E

high spots marked

D

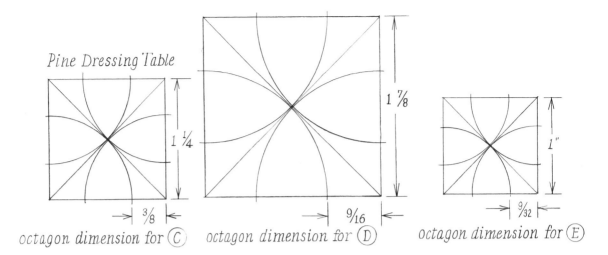

Pine Dressing Table

octagon dimension for Ⓒ   octagon dimension for Ⓓ   octagon dimension for Ⓔ

OCTAGONAL SHAPING

This stage of the work dramatically changes the appearance of things. As the edges are beveled off and the form is altered from square to octagonal, the final shape of the leg begins to emerge. For additional illustrations of octagonal shaping, see *Pencil-post Bed*, p. 265–269.

Start with the section between C and E. Use the dimensions in the octagon diagrams for C, D, and E and tick off pencil marks at all three points on all four sides of the leg. Then use a straightedge and pencil to draw connecting lines from D to E as shown in the illustration. The marks at D are connected to those at C by drawing freehand pencil lines. All of these finished markings are shown in the illustration. Before cutting these bevels down to the guidelines, make short beveled chisel cuts at C to outline the octagonal shape.

beveled chisel cuts to outline octagon

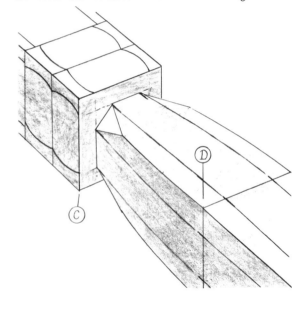

drawing the octagon lines

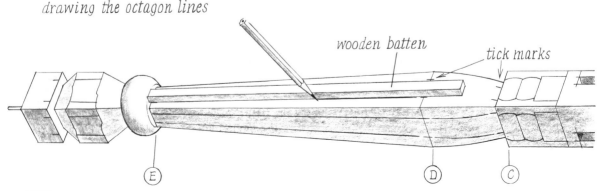

wooden batten

tick marks

Beveling the Edges

Achieving satisfactory roundness from one end of the leg to the other depends primarily on how accurately the bevels correspond to the guidelines. And this in turn depends on taking off wood only a little at a time. If you have a really light touch, the drawknife can be used, but the

spokeshave is the safer tool, as it never takes a very big bite and tends to leave a smoother, more finished surface.

Always work down from point D to avoid cutting against the grain, and up from point D toward the top for the same reason. Again, shave as close to the lines as possible without obliterating them.

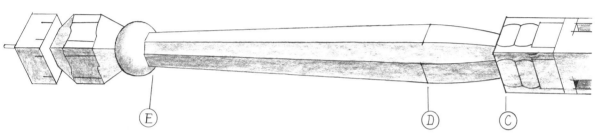

octagonal shaping completed from C to E

shaping the foot

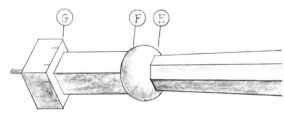

square–shaped between F and G

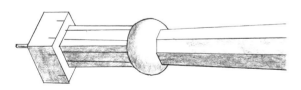

octagon lines laid out

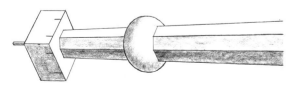

octagonal shaping completed

At this point, use a 10-inch double-cut flat bastard file to fair up and smooth all eight surfaces. Be careful not to file too close to the shoulders at C and the bulb at E, otherwise they may be irreparably nicked and damaged.

Shaping the Foot

Next, work the foot end of the leg to size, using the chisel to take out wood between the pockets at F and G, making this part of the leg square in section. Then lay out octagon lines as before, using the same measurement as for E. Pare the bevels with the chisel and then smooth them with the 10-inch file.

Beveling the Eight Edges

The square stick had four edges and the octagonal form has eight. The next stage of turning is to chamfer off these eight to make sixteen. This job is done strictly by eye using the 10-inch file. Again, work the file down from D to the foot of the leg, and up from D to the shoulder at C. Like any other cutting tool, a file cannot be run against the grain without leaving a ragged surface. The main thing as always is not to cut too fast or too deep. File one or two edges experimentally and then try to work the others to match. Any minor irregularities can be corrected just before the final rounding.

When shaping the curved section C to D, it is a good idea to use a cardboard template made from the original pattern. As you work, hold the template on one edge of the lathebox while you rotate the leg slowly. This way, imperfections can easily be spotted, marked with pencil lines, and filed off a bit more.

using a template to shape the curved section C to D

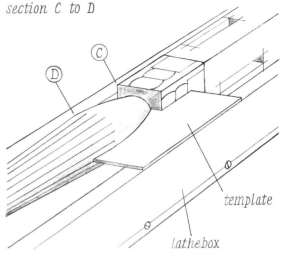

template

lathebox

Shaping the Top Section

The part of the leg from B to C is round in section and is shaped in the same way. First, refer to the original pattern and lay out lines to mark the dimensions of the section B to C, and carry these marks over onto the end grain of the shoulder at C. Use the chisel and mallet to pare this part down to size, keeping it square in sec-

lines laid out for section B to C

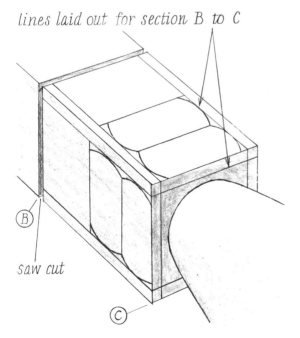

saw cut

paring with the chisel

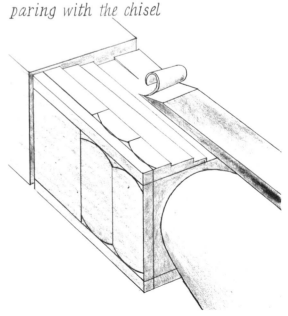

Pine Dressing Table

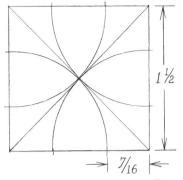

1 ½

7/16

octagon dimension for Ⓑ

tion. Then lay out octagon lines to the dimensions in the diagram, and carefully pare the bevels down to these lines.

Chamfer off the eight edges as before, using the 10-inch file. Then continue filing to make this section cylindrical in form. Pick up the dimensions for the two rings from the pattern and lay them out as shown in the illustration. The simplest way to do this is to hold the pencil steady on the mark while you slowly rotate the leg in the lathebox.

octagon lines laid out

filed to cylindrical shape

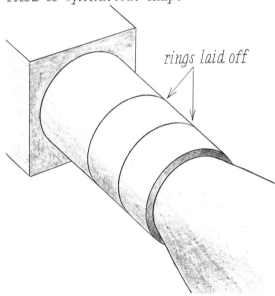

rings laid off

octagonal bevels pared

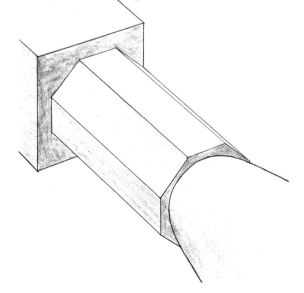

Then make shallow saw cuts clear around, sawing exactly on the lines. Saw only about 1/16 inch deep. Take up the 10-inch file and set one corner into a saw cut. File round and round in the saw cut to make a V-trough. Rotate the leg in the lathebox with one hand while you file with the other, counting and using the same number of file strokes at each rotation. Do the other one in the same way. Then round up the rings to the approximate shape with the file, as you did with the bulb.

filing round and round in the saw cuts

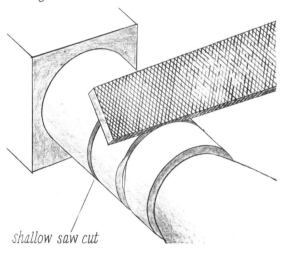

shallow saw cut

FINAL SHAPING

The round work produced by this hand-turning method will not have the mechanical perfection of a power lathe job. Despite the most exacting attention to accuracy in taking the work from square to octagonal to round, there will probably be a swelling here or an out-of-round section there. Yet if each stage of the work has been measured, laid out, and executed accurately and slowly, the final shaping and sanding will produce a turning that is remarkably uniform, and one that has the stamp of your own personality.

With all roughing-out completed, spin the leg round smartly several times in the lathebox to watch it in motion. Any glaring bulges and flat places will show up immediately. Mark these spots with a soft pencil, then use the file to remove the marked areas along with a scant amount of wood. Spin the leg again and repeat the process. This filing should be done with patience and restraint, as the work is close to the point where no spare wood remains.

Continue this process of turning, testing, marking, and filing over the whole main section of the leg from B to E. To assist in this refinement, make a simple template in which are cut half-circles corresponding to the diam-

Pine Dressing Table

half-circle diameter template

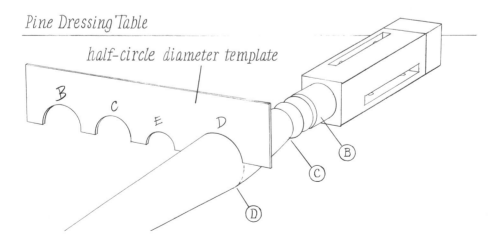

eters at three or four fixed station points along the leg. Mark the stations on the edge of the lathebox, and hold the template on the mark when testing. Work over the other sections of the leg with the same methods.

Sanding

When things look shipshape and test to your satisfaction, switch from the file to sandpaper (see *Sanding,* p. 132). Wrap the paper around a thin, flat stick of wood and with one hand sand lightly down and across the leg at a slight angle as you slowly rotate it with the other.

final touches with a half-round file

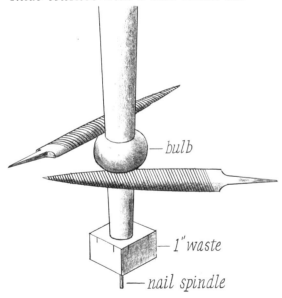

— *bulb*

— *1" waste*

— *nail spindle*

Final Touches

Now go back over the leg and use a fine, half-round file to clean out and sharpen the confined areas that the coarser tools couldn't reach: the shoulder at B, the groove between the rings, the junction at C, and the sections above and below the bulb—E and F. By using the flat as well as the thin edge of the file, these areas can be smoothed and made fair with the adjacent wood.

For a more highly polished surface, clamp the leg bottom end-up in the vise between pieces of scrap wood to protect it, and use a 1-inch strip of sandpaper backed with masking tape (see *Sanding,* p. 132). Hold it in both hands and use a shoeshine stroke, turning the work in the vise in order to smooth all the surfaces uniformly.

The last step is to cut off the 1-inch waste sections at top and bottom. To avoid marring the finished work, lay it on an old towel with the bulb end of the leg in the V-block over several folds of thick cloth. Hold the leg firmly with one hand, and use the backsaw held tight against the shoulder of the waste section at G. The top end of the leg can be laid in the miter box to trim off the other waste at A.

SQUARE TAPERING: TWO SIDES

The legs for the *Writing Table* are tapered on the two inside faces only, leaving the outside corner of the leg straight. Prepare the furniture squares as follows:

1. Draw diagonal lines on both ends to locate the centers. Then drive an 8d finish nail about 3/4 inch into each center to form spindles. Cut off the nails to leave another 3/4 inch projecting, using heavy cutting pliers or a hacksaw.

2. Mark off the 1-inch waste sections across both ends and carry these marks over onto all four sides of the stick. These waste sections are mainly to prevent otherwise damaging the finished ends of the leg, but they also provide reference points from which to measure and check the work in progress. They are not cut off until the leg is completely finished.

3. Tape the leg pattern to side 4 of the work to prevent its slipping, aligning the straight side of the pattern with the outside straight corner of the stick, as shown in the illustration. Use a sharp, soft pencil to accurately trace along the pattern from the start-of-taper mark clear to the bottom.

4. Remove the pattern, tape it to the opposing side 2 of the stick aligned as before, and trace the taper line. Draw a line across the bottom end of the stick (on the end grain) to connect these lines, and X-mark the waste wood. Use the try square and pencil to draw the start-of-taper lines across all four sides of the stick.

5. Put the furniture square bottom-end up in the vise and use the backsaw to make a 3/4-inch-deep cut about 1/16 inch *outside* the taper line. This helps prevent cutting the taper too deep.

Then put the stick in the lathebox with the square block under it to immobilize the work. Wedge the clamp board across the box just behind the movable puppet (see the illustration on page 94). Tap a wedge between the square block and the work, and another between the top of the leg and the puppet.

Use the drawknife or a 1-inch chisel and mallet to pare wood down to the level of the saw cut. Start at the foot of the leg and work toward the top, but don't cut too close to the start-of-taper lines. They should be left showing until the very last. Continue shaving with the drawknife, or use the spokeshave or plane (9-inch smoothing or jack rabbet) to bring the surface down not quite to the taper lines on both sides

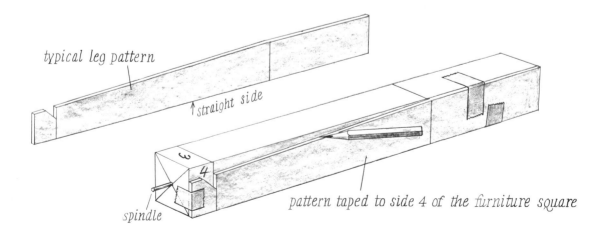

typical leg pattern

↑*straight side*

spindle

pattern taped to side 4 of the furniture square

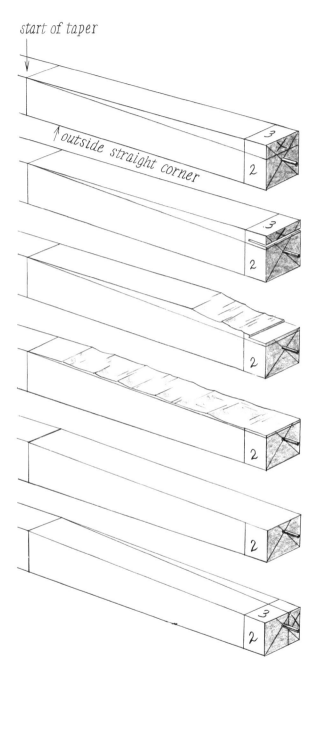

start of taper

↑outside straight corner

of the stick. Keep the cut surface as level as possible.

When the taper has been rough-shaped, use a jack or jointer plane set for a fine cut to make a few full-length strokes to dress the surface exactly to the taper lines, again working from the top toward the foot of the leg.

Redraw the 1-inch waste mark across the surface just planed. Then tape the pattern to side 3, aligned with the outside straight corner of the stick, and trace the taper as before. Remove the pattern, rotate the stick in the lathebox, flop the pattern over and trace it on the opposing side 1. Draw a line across the end of the stick (on the end grain) to connect these lines, and X-mark the waste wood.

Make a 3/4-inch-deep saw cut outside the taper line as before, then replace the stick in the lathebox with side 4 on top. Put the square block under it and tap the wedges up tight. Cut this taper in the same way. Finally, redraw the 1-inch waste marks on the tapered surfaces.

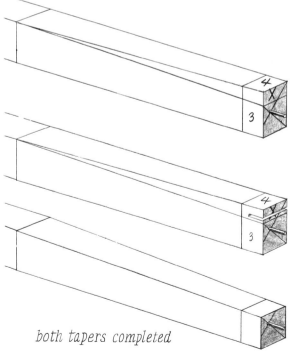

both tapers completed

SQUARE TAPERING: FOUR SIDES

The legs for the *One-drawer Stand*, the *Breadboard-top Table*, and the *Pencil-post Bed* are tapered on all four sides. Prepare each furniture square as follows:

1. Draw diagonal lines on both ends to locate the centers. Then drive an 8d finish nail about 3/4 inch into each center to form spindles. Cut off the nails to leave another 3/4 inch projecting, using heavy cutting pliers or a hacksaw.

2. Mark off the 1-inch waste sections across both ends and carry these marks over onto all four sides of the stick. These waste sections are mainly to prevent otherwise damaging the finished ends of the leg, but they also provide reference points from which to measure and check the work in progress. They are not cut off until the leg is completely finished.

3. Use the try square and pencil to draw the start-of-taper lines across all four sides of the stick.

4. Tape the leg pattern to side 2 of the work to prevent its slipping, aligning the straight side of the pattern with one edge of the stick. Use a sharp, soft pencil to accurately trace along the taper of the pattern from the start-of-taper line clear to the bottom.

5. Remove the pattern, flop it over to the opposite edge of the stick and tape it in place. Trace the taper line as before.

6. Turn the stick over and trace two corresponding taper lines on side 2, as shown in the illustration. Draw lines across the bottom end of the stick (on the end grain) to connect these taper lines, and X-mark the waste wood.

Put the furniture square bottom-end up in the vise and use the backsaw to make 3/4-inch-deep cuts about 1/16 inch outside the taper lines. Then put the stick in the lathebox—side 3 on top—with the square block in place under it to

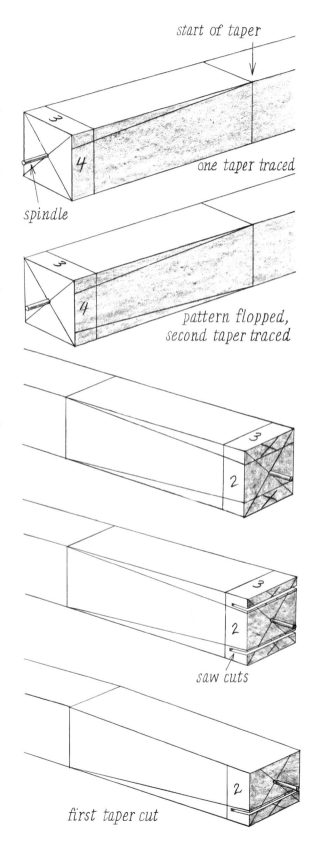

start of taper

spindle

one taper traced

pattern flopped, second taper traced

saw cuts

first taper cut

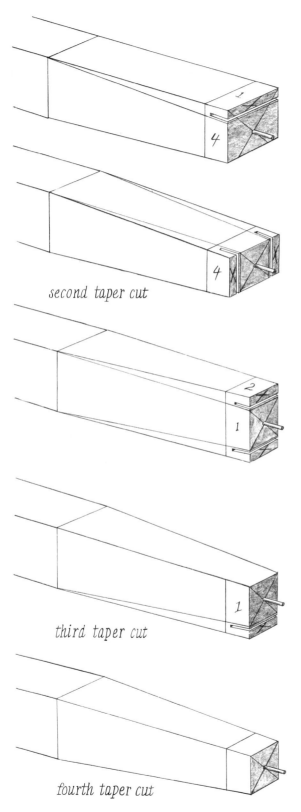

second taper cut

third taper cut

fourth taper cut

immobilize the work. Wedge the clamp board across the box just behind the movable puppet (see the illustration on page 94). Tap a wedge between the square block and the work, and another between the top of the leg and the puppet.

Use the drawknife or a 1-inch chisel and mallet to pare wood down to the level of the saw cut, as described above in "Square Tapering: two sides." Work from the top of the taper toward the foot of the leg, but don't cut too close to the start-of-taper lines. They should be left showing until the very last. Continue shaving with the drawknife, or use the spokeshave or plane (9-inch smoothing or jack rabbet) to bring the surface down not quite to the taper lines on both sides of the work. Keep the cut surface as level as possible.

When the taper has been rough-shaped, use a jack or jointer plane set for a fine cut to make a few full-length strokes to dress the surface exactly to the taper lines, again working from the top toward the foot of the leg.

Redraw the 1-inch waste mark across the surface just planed. Then rotate the stick in the lathebox so that the opposing side 1 is on top. Wedge the work in place and taper this side in the same way.

Then use the pattern again to trace taper lines on opposing sides 1 and 3. Redraw the 1-inch waste lines on both these sides. Rotate the stick so that side 2 is on top, wedge it up tight, and cut the taper.

Finally, rotate the stick one more time with side 4 on top and cut the last taper. Redraw the 1-inch waste lines.

Drawer Construction

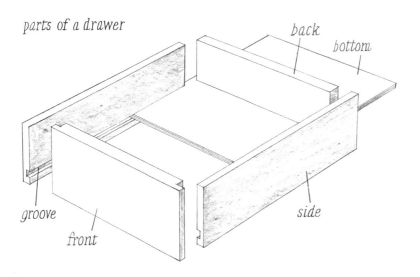

parts of a drawer

back

bottom

groove

front

side

While it has a structural resemblance to a box, a drawer is much more than a simple container, and must be built to meet special requirements. The joints must be strong, especially those at the front which are the points of greatest strain as the drawer is opened and shut, often with a heavy hand. Since these joints are exposed when the drawer is pulled out, they should also be laid out, cut, and fitted as neatly as possible. And because a drawer is a moving part, accurate measuring and fitting are especially necessary to ensure that it will slide in and out with ease even when heavily loaded, and without dragging or sticking.

The two construction methods described here make use of the dovetail, the groove, and the cross-grain rabbet. The details of making and fitting these joints are described and illustrated in *Making Joints*, page 52, page 60, and page 85, and may be referred to as needed.

marking dowel pinhole centers

center punch

drawer side

DOVETAIL CONSTRUCTION

This was the traditional method and is still the strongest and most durable way to put together a drawer. While cutting the dovetails may be somewhat more time-consuming than other joints, the final results generally justify the additional labor.

A drawer should be built only after the frame of the furniture has been completed, as it must be measured and fitted to the actual dimensions of the drawer opening itself, not those given in the list of materials, which are for reference only. And a drawer should be built from front to back, because how nicely it runs in and out depends largely on how carefully the drawer front fits the opening.

DRAWER FRONT

Cut the drawer front to rough size. Then use a sharp block plane set for a fine cut to shave the top and bottom edges and the end grain of both

partly closed dovetail joint

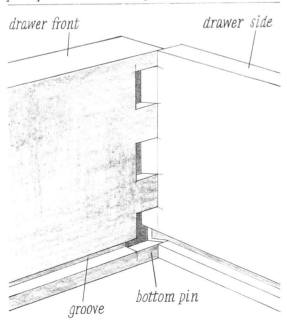

drawer front   *drawer side*

groove   *bottom pin*

ends until it fits into the opening in the furniture with a clearance of no more than 1/16 inch at the top and each side. Keep the plane level and use slow, steady strokes to make the edges square and true.

DRAWER SIDES AND DOVETAILS

Next, cut the drawer sides to rough size and carefully trim them with the block plane to the same height as the fitted drawer front. Be sure to make their height the same front and back, or the drawer may stick when finished.

Lay out the dovetails on their front ends, using the dimensions given in the particular project. At the same time locate and punch-mark the pinhole centers for the back joints, but do not drill these holes until later. Then cut the dovetails (see *Making Joints*, p. 52).

DRAWER FRONT AND PINS

With the dovetails cut, scribe their outlines onto the ends (end grain) of the drawer front, tracing one set and then the other. Be sure to mark both parts of each joint with pairs of letters, to avoid confusion in assembling them (see *Woodworking Practices*, p. 33). Then cut the pins. This procedure is described and illustrated in *Making Joints*, page 56–58.

GROOVES

Next, shoot grooves in the drawer front and in both drawer sides into which the bottom board will be fitted. Note that the grooves should be located so that they do not cut away part of the bottom pins, or the joint will be weakened. Using the dimensions specified in the particular project, adjust the grooving plane and make a trial groove. Then shoot an identical groove in the drawer front and in each of the drawer sides. There is no groove in the drawer back. The bottom board is nailed to its under edge.

DRAWER BACK

Cut the drawer back to size from measurements taken directly from the drawer front. For height, measure from the top edge of the drawer front to the top of its groove; and for width, measure shoulder to shoulder between the joints as shown in the illustration. Make the saw cuts with the backsaw and miter box to keep them square and clean. Plane the top and bottom edges smooth and square with the block plane.

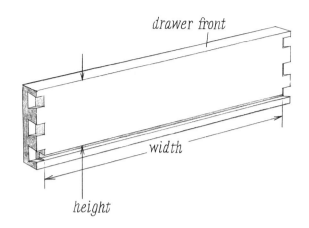

drawer front

width

height

jigboard

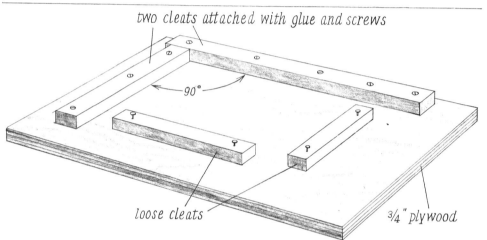

two cleats attached with glue and screws

90°

loose cleats

¾" plywood

ASSEMBLY

This job goes much more easily with the aid of a homemade jigboard and a clamp board (see *Woodworking Practices,* p. 35). The jigboard holds the parts of the drawer square while the clamp board holds them securely while the pin-holes are being drilled and the pins driven. And once assembled, the jigboard and drawer can all be set aside for the glue to dry, leaving the workbench free for other work.

Start assembly with the drawer front. Put it end-up in the vise between pieces of scrap wood. Spread glue sparingly on the sides only of the dovetails and of the pins as well. Pick up the drawer side and lay the dovetails over the pins, and start the joint together. Use a mallet

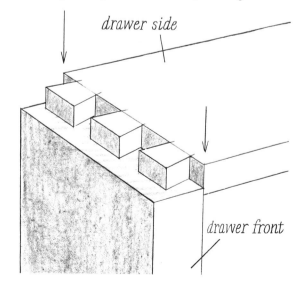

starting the glued dovetail joint together

drawer side

drawer front

assembling second drawer side

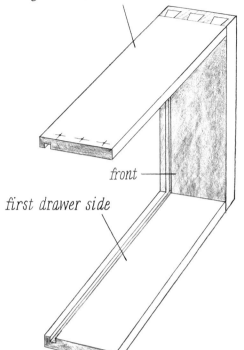

front

first drawer side

and a scrap of wood laid over the work to gently tap the joint shut. Immediately clean off any excess glue with a damp sponge.

Take the work out of the vise and lay it with the drawer side flat on the jigboard. Glue and attach the other drawer side in the same way, and wipe off any excess glue.

As quickly as possible and without racking the freshly glued joints, lay the drawer bottom-up into the jigboard, sliding it into the corner against the cleats. Tack one of the loose cleats tight against the inside of the drawer front, and another against the inside of the drawer side

assembling a drawer in the jigboard

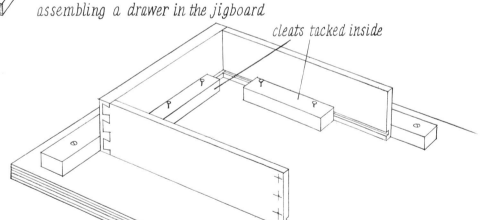

cleats tacked inside

away from you. Set the back of the drawer in place. Then lay the clamp board across the assembly as shown in the illustration, tap it down on top of the drawer sides, and wedge it up tight. Then tack a loose cleat against the outside of the near drawer side. Lay a board across the drawer with a heavy weight on top (a gallon can of paint, nine-pound anvil, or three or four clean bricks wrapped in paper). Set the whole works aside to dry overnight.

DRAWER BOTTOM

Cut the drawer bottom to size after measuring the drawer itself. For width, measure between the side grooves; and for length, from the inside of the front groove to the outside of the drawer back. The bottom should be fitted to slide into the grooves without forcing and with no side-to-side play, as it is the bottom board that holds the drawer in square alignment. Plane the edges with the block plane, a little at a time, trying it in place each time. And use the try square frequently to keep all four corners as nearly square as possible. After fitting, sand the inside surface to final smoothness (see *Sanding*, p. 132).

DRILLING PINHOLES

For this job, leave the work in place on the jigboard but remove the weights and, temporarily, the clamp board. The drawer back is glued in, not so much for strength as to prevent its slipping out of alignment while the pinholes are being drilled. Remove the cleat nearest you and drive the nails back flush, ready to be used again. Take out the drawer back and spread glue on both its ends (end grain). Also spread glue on the back edges of the drawer sides. Let the glue stand until tacky, then put the back of the drawer in place again, making sure that it is flush with the back end of the drawer sides. Lay the clamp board across the drawer and wedge it up tight. Then nail the loose cleat back in place, pushing it firmly against the drawer side while you drive the nails. Slide the drawer bottom in place in the grooves and drive 2 nails partway into the drawer back. Before drilling the pinholes, tap the whole drawer down flat onto the jigboard and check the wedges once again.

With the hand drill, drill the pinholes through the drawer side facing you, and about 1 1/4 inches into the end of the drawer back.

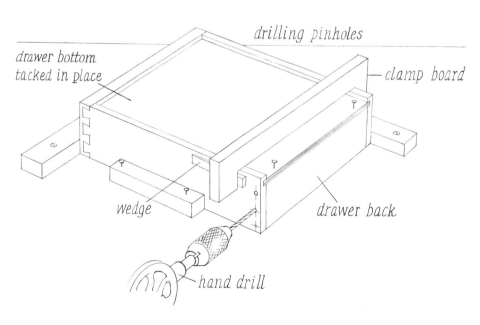

drilling pinholes

drawer bottom tacked in place

clamp board

wedge

drawer back

hand drill

Use a stop over the drill bit to gauge the holes all the same depth (see *Woodworking Practices*, p. 38). Replace the board and weights or have someone press down on the drawer while you drill. Clean the sawdust from the hole each time by pulling the drill back out while still turning it.

DOWEL PINS

Sandpaper a length of dowel to make it an easy-push fit into the pinhole. Then cut the pins about 1/8 inch longer than the total depth of the hole. Slightly taper their entering ends with a file or sandpaper (see *Making Joints*, p. 79).

To drive a pin, wipe glue round it for about half its length. Start the glued end into the hole, and while someone holds down the drawer, drive the pin. As each pin is driven, clean off any excess glue with a damp sponge. Do not trim the pins flush until both joints have been pinned and the glue has thoroughly dried.

When one side has been pinned, turn the jigboard around and work from the other side to make the other joint in the same way. Set the finished work aside to dry overnight. If the cleat is in the way of drilling one of the holes, leave it until the rest of the work is dry, then remove the work, put it in the vise and drill the last holes.

Trimming the Pins

When the work is dry, take it out of the jigboard and cut off most of the projecting pins with a backsaw (see *Making Joints*, p. 79). Then use a double-cut file to clean off the rest flush with the drawer sides.

At the same time, dress off the dovetails flush with the sides of the drawers as shown in the illustration. File in one direction only—toward the back of the drawer, to avoid chipping the sharp front corners of the front. To make the drawer run more easily, slightly bevel

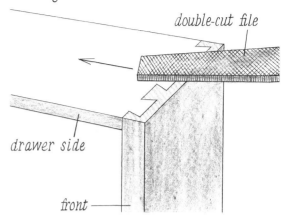

dressing the dovetails flush

double-cut file

drawer side

front

back ends of drawer sides slightly beveled

the back ends of the sides with a stroke or two of the block plane, or with the double-cut file.

Finish nailing in the drawer bottom by driving home the 2 nails already started and adding other nails as required in the specifications.

FITTING THE DRAWER

Try the drawer in the furniture to see if it runs smoothly and without sticking. If it sticks, locate the friction points and use the block plane set for a very fine cut to shave off a little wood at each point. Then sand these areas smooth.

RABBET CONSTRUCTION

In this method, the drawer parts are cut, fitted, grooved, and the drawer sides punch-marked for pinholes in the same order and as described above in "Dovetail Construction"; except that in place of dovetails, cross-grain rabbets are cut in both ends of the drawer front to the dimensions given in the particular project, and the sides fitted into them flush and secured with glued dowel pins.

After fitting the drawer front to the opening in the furniture, lay out and cut the rabbets (see *Making Joints*, p. 83) to the specified dimensions.

ASSEMBLY

Stand the four parts of the drawer frame bottom-up into the jigboard as shown in the illustration. Nail a movable cleat tight against the inside of the drawer back and another against the inside of the drawer side away from you. Adjust the other side and the drawer front in place and hold the whole works together with a length of hard, nonstretch twine tied round the drawer and tightened with a tourniquet pin. Nail movable cleats against the outside of the drawer front and the near side. Lay the clamp board across the assembly and wedge it up tight. Have it as close as possible to the joint without

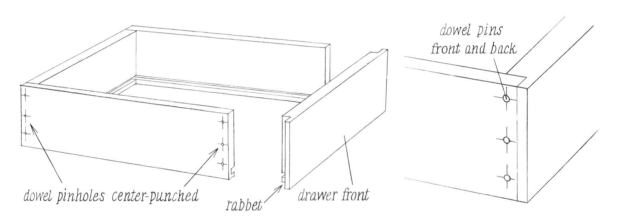

dowel pinholes center-punched   rabbet   drawer front   dowel pins front and back

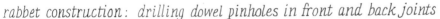

rabbet construction: drilling dowel pinholes in front and back joints

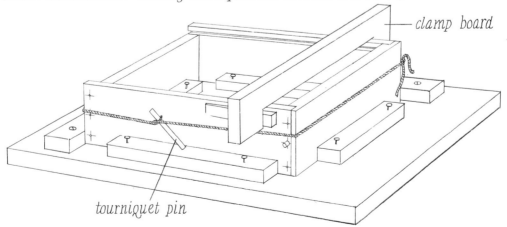

clamp board

tourniquet pin

obstructing the operation of the drill. Tighten the tourniquet again.

Cut the dowel pins and slightly taper their entering ends. Then drill the pinholes, starting with the front joint. Glue and drive all the pins in one side. Wipe off any excess glue with a damp sponge. Then turn the jigboard around and work from the other side to complete the other joint. Clean off the excess glue as before. Keep the tourniquet and the clamp board tight. When both front joints are done, lay a board across the work with a heavy weight on top (a gallon can of paint, nine-pound anvil, or three or four clean bricks wrapped in paper). Then leave the work to dry overnight.

DRAWER PULLOUT STOPS

In addition to the usual stops fastened to the back end of the drawer runners to control how far in a drawer goes, it is a good practice also to install a pullout stop as well, or the drawer may be damaged in coming all the way out and falling to the floor.

Slide the drawer about one-third its own length into the furniture. Draw a pencil line on the drawer bottom from underneath, against the inside edge of the drawer rail. Take the drawer out.

Cut a piece of wood 1/2 inch thick, 2 inches wide, and the same length as from the pencil

drawer pullout stop

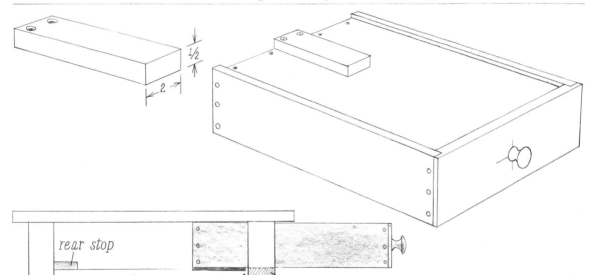

rear stop

drawer runner

drawer rail

stop strikes against drawer rail

When the glue has dried, shift the clamp board to the back of the drawer and pin the back joints in the same way. The drawer bottom can then be fitted and nailed in, and the final details finished as described above in "Dovetail Construction."

line to the back of the drawer. Drill and countersink 2 screw holes 3/8 inch from one end as shown in the illustration. Start 1 x No. 6 flathead screws into the holes. Slide the drawer in place again, and working from underneath, screw the stop to the drawer, flush at the back.

Drawer Construction

The stop can be cut off shorter to allow the drawer to come out farther, but if too much is cut off, the weight of drawer and contents may put a strain on the furniture.

DRAWER PULLS

The type of brass pull shown in the illustration is installed by boring two holes to accommodate the threaded posts. First measure and mark the center of the drawer with a light pencil line. Dismantle the pull and, using the backplate as a template, lay it on the drawer front centered on the center line. Shift the plate up or down to the position you prefer. If centered exactly top to bottom, the pull may appear either too high or too low, depending on its particular design. When this position has been determined, mark through the holes in the plate with a pencil. Remove the plate and check the horizontal alignment by drawing a horizontal pencil line running through the centers of both post marks. Then mark their centers with a center punch. Drill the holes, making them a fraction larger than the diameter of the posts.

Next, measure and cut the posts to a length that fits the thickness of the drawer front. Lay the assembled drawer pull flat against the face of the drawer with the threaded post (minus the nut) resting on its top edge. Thread on a nut and turn it up until it touches the inside of the drawer front. Then back it off 1/16 inch and mark the spot by nicking the post with the edge of a file. Take the posts out and cut them to the same length. Clamp the threaded end in the machinist's vise and use a hacksaw to cut outside the file nick. If a vise is not available, use a pair of heavy lineman's pliers. Clean up the sawn ends with a file so that the nut will start easily.

To attach the drawer pull, assemble the post with the bail and hold these parts together while you feed the posts through the backplate and into the holes in the drawer front. Thread on

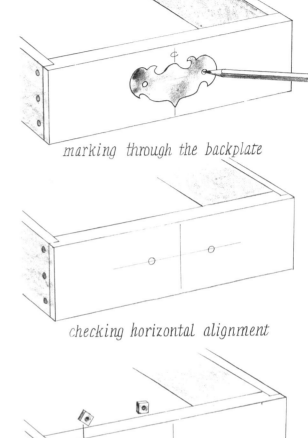

marking through the backplate

checking horizontal alignment

installing a hardwood drawer pull

nut   post   bail   backplate

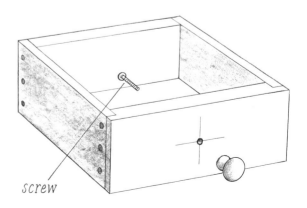

screw

the nuts and bring them up not quite tight. Try the bail to see that it lifts and drops easily. If not, rotate the posts until the bail swings free. Then tighten the nuts with a wrench and carefully file the projecting threaded ends of the posts smooth and flush.

FURNITURE HARDWARE

These typical listings of hardware suppliers were picked at random from woodworking, hobby, and home workshop magazines, and from newspapers and telephone directories.

Acorn Manufacturing Company
Mansfield, MA 02048

Ball and Ball
463 West Lincoln Highway
Exton, PA 19341

Box 1776
Cohasset, MA 02025

Craftsman Wood Service Company
2727 South Mary Street
Chicago, IL 60608

Elvstrom USA Inc.
PO Drawer A
725 Post Road
Guilford, CT 06437

Fer Forge, Ltd
PO Box 511
Hanover, NH 03755

Holland Manufacturing Company
1300 Bank Street
Baltimore, MD 21231

Horton Brasses
Nooks Hill Road
PO Box 95
Cromwell, CT 06416

Imported European Hardware
4295 South Arville
Las Vegas, NE 89103

Jamestown Distributors
22 Narragansett Avenue
Jamestown, RI 02835

Kemp Hardware Supply Company
PO Box 529
Paramount, CA 90723

Minnesota Woodworkers Supply Company
925 Winnetka Avenue North
Minneapolis, MN 55427

Paxton Hardware
7818 Bradshaw Road
Upper Falls, MD 21156

Period Hardware
123 Charles Street
Boston, MA 02114

Sta-Put Fastener Manufacturing Company
3900 Vero Road
PO Box 7342
Baltimore, MD 21227

Tremont Nail Company
PO Box 111
Wareham, MA 02571

Woodcraft Supply Corporation
41 Atlantic Avenue
PO Box 4000
Woburn, MA 01888

typical fast-pin butt hinge

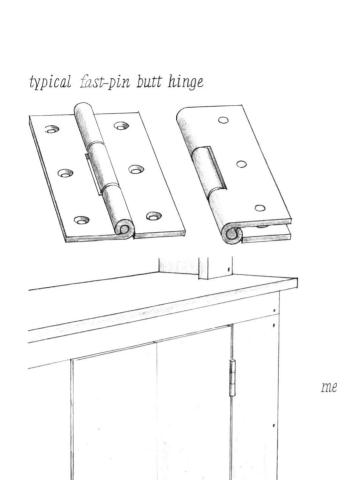

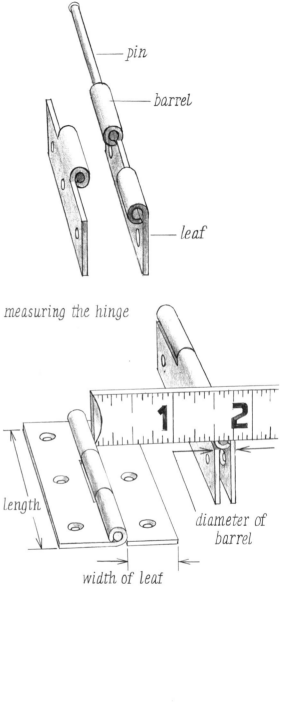

pin

barrel

leaf

measuring the hinge

1

2

length

diameter of
barrel

width of leaf

detail

*hinge barrel
set clear of the
door face*

Hanging Doors

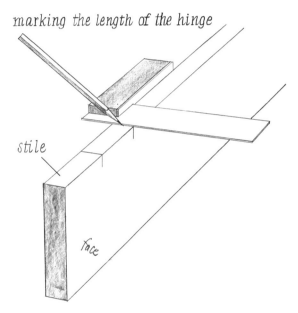

marking the length of the hinge

stile

face

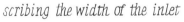

scribing the width of the inlet

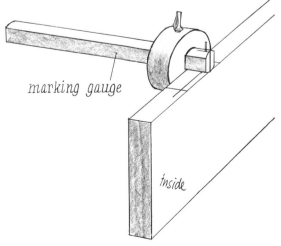

marking gauge

inside

The hinges specified for the hutch and cupboards are of the fast-pin butt type having two leaves permanently joined by a pin through the barrel. One leaf is recessed in an inlet cut into the edge of the door, and the other in an identical inlet cut into the edge of the stile or frame of the furniture.

For the door to operate properly, these matching inlets should be cut to the same dimensions—length, width, and depth—and positioned so that the barrel of the hinge is set clear of the face of the door, allowing it to open back flat against the front of the furniture.

MEASURING AND LAYING OUT

Measure the length and width of the leaf, and the diameter of the barrel, as shown in the illustration. Use the try square and a sharp pencil to mark off the length of the hinge, and carry these marks over onto the edge of the stile. Then use the marking gauge to scribe the width of the inlet (width of hinge leaf) on the edge of the stile. The last dimension—the depth—is the most exacting to measure and lay out, as it is usually only a fraction more than the thickness of the hinge leaf. It is also critical to the proper operation of the door: if the inlets are too deep, there will be too little clearance between the edge of the door and the stile, preventing the door from shutting. On the other hand, when the inlets are too shallow, the clearance will be excessive, leaving an unsightly gap. The following equation can be used to find the correct depth of inlet:

$$depth\ of\ hinge\ inlet = \frac{diameter\ of\ barrel\ \text{MINUS}\ amount\ of\ clearance}{2}$$

EXAMPLE:

diameter of barrel	$\frac{1}{4}''$
clearance	$-\frac{1}{16}$

$$\frac{3}{16} \div 2 = \frac{3}{32}$$

Set the marking gauge to the depth of inlet and scribe a line on the face of the stile. If the width of the hinge leaf is the same as the thickness of the stile, scribe a similar line on its inside face.

scribing the depth of the inlet

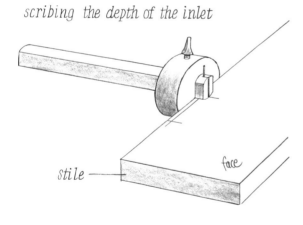

stile — face

TRIAL INLETS

Before starting the actual work, cut a pair of trial inlets on two scraps of wood, attach the hinge, then make adjustments in your calculations as needed. Use a sharp 1/2-inch chisel and a mallet to cut the inlets. First outline the inlet as shown in the illustration. Set the chisel a fraction inside the mark, holding it perpendic-

ular with the chisel bevel toward the inlet. Give the chisel a light rap with the mallet to score about 3/32-inch deep. Work clear around the inlet, scoring as accurately as possible to the lines. Then pare out both ends of the inlet—but not to full depth. Use the chisel bevel-down to pare out the middle, working from the center toward the ends.

Continue paring a little at a time, keeping the bottom of the inlet as flat and level as possible. As you get closer to the scribed bottom line, hold the chisel bevel-up and shave paper-thin slices, working in from the side. Try the hinge in the inlet. If it is too tight lengthwise, don't pound it in. Taking it out again will splinter off wood at the ends. Set the chisel across one end of the inlet, the bevel toward the inlet. Push the chisel down by hand to trim off just a thin slice from the end of the inlet. Then lay the hinge in place, fold up the other leaf, and inspect your work. The barrel of the hinge should lie parallel to the stile, neither cocked up at one end nor too low at the other.

outlining the inlet

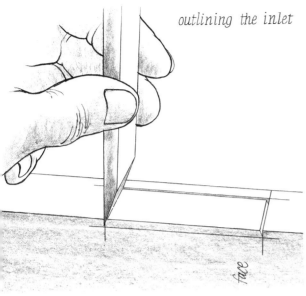

hinge should lie parallel to the stile

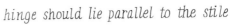
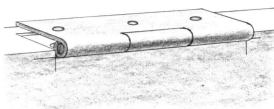

paring out the ends

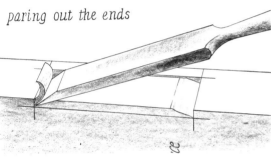

paring out the middle of the inlet

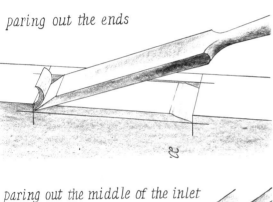

punching a hole for the middle screw

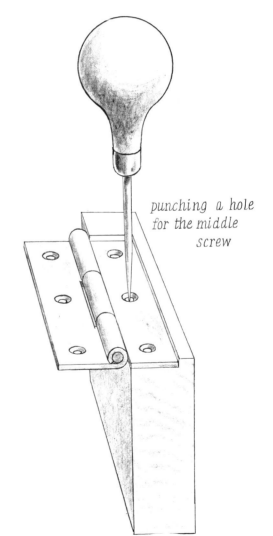

shaving down to the scribed bottom line

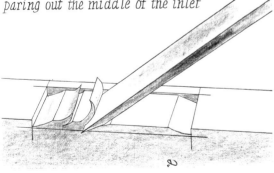
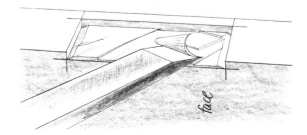

Cut a similar trial inlet in the other piece of scrap wood. Attach the hinge to both pieces by driving a screw in the center hole of each leaf. Push the leaf tight into the inlet, and with the awl punch a starting hole in the center of the hinge hole. Drive the screw. Attach the other leaf in the same way. Fold the two parts shut to check the alignment of the hinge barrel and the amount of clearance. Note that the center of the barrel should align with the center of the clearance space.

FITTING THE DOOR

Hold the door up and try it in the opening of the furniture. If it was made a trifle oversize as it should have been, the first job is to trim the edges of the door until it fits into the opening with a clearance of 1/16 inch at both sides and at the top. Use a jack or jointer plane on the side edges and a block plane on the end-grain top edge (see *Woodworking Practices*, p. 28, p. 29). Set the plane for a fine cut. Plane one or

trial inlets in scrap wood

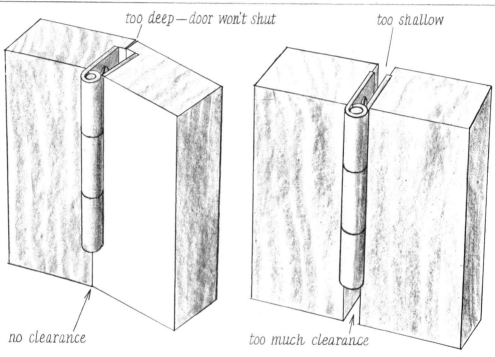

too deep—door won't shut

too shallow

no clearance

too much clearance

CUTTING THE ACTUAL INLETS

The most convenient practice is to cut the inlets in the stile *before* attaching it to the furniture, and then locate and cut the inlets in the door *after* the stile has been fastened in place.

Lay out and cut both hinge inlets in the finished stile as described above. Then nail the stile in place on the furniture, preparatory to fitting the door.

two strokes, holding the plane level to keep the edge square. Before planing any more, make three shims from 1/16-inch-thick cardboard. Try the door in place again with a shim wedged at the top, and the bottom of the door blocked up as shown in the illustration. Try shims at both sides as well. The object is to make the door a snug fit with all three shims in place.

DOOR INLETS

When the door has been fitted, leave the shims in place and transfer the location of the hinge inlets from the stile to the door, using the carpenter's square as shown in the illustration. Then lay out the inlets as before. Put the door in the vise back-edge up and cut the inlets. To be on the safe side, make these door inlets just a shade shallow—they can be pared a bit deeper if necessary.

*fitting the door and
transferring location of hinge inlets*

HANGING THE DOOR

Attach both hinges to the door temporarily by driving the middle screw in each hinge. Fold the hinges shut and try the door in place, sliding the hinge leaves into the stile inlets. Replace the shim in the crack at the open edge of the door. If the clearance here is less than 1/16 inch—and the shim will not go in—remove the door, remove the hinges, and shave the door inlets just a fraction deeper: a fraction meaning no more than the thickness of a piece of paper. If there is too much clearance, on the other hand, make paper shims and spot-glue them into the inlets under the hinges, as shown in the illustration. Then put the hinges back on the door with the 2 temporary screws, and try the door in place again.

When everything has been adjusted, remove the door and drive all the screws in the

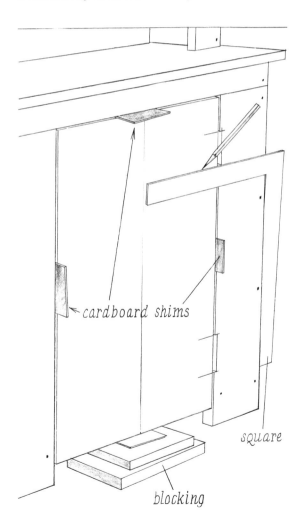

cardboard shims

square

blocking

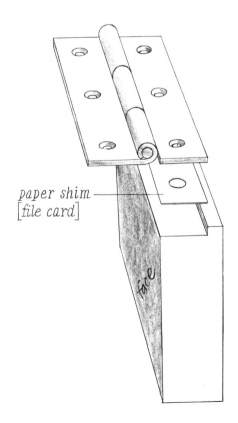

*paper shim
[file card]*

face

127

door-half of the hinges. Before attaching the other half of the hinges to the furniture, attach the door cleats, which have been left until now simply to make it easier to hold the door in the vise.

Attach the other half of the hinges to the stile of the furniture. Open the hinges and hold the door back flat against the front of the furniture in fully opened position, its inside facing out. Have someone hold the door while you carefully slide the free hinge leaves into the stile inlets. Press them tight into the inlets. Hold the door steady while you use the awl to punch screw starting holes in the center of the hinge leaves. Then drive these 2 screws. If you are working with hardwood, drill pilot holes in the punched marks. Try the door a few times to make sure it opens and closes smoothly. If it drags against the stile, shave a little off the edge of the door with the block plane, holding it tipped at an angle to cut a slight inward bevel. Then drive the remaining screws.

Hinges and screws are often sold as a package, but it is wise to try a screw in the hinge to make sure that the head of the screw seats flush with the surface of the leaf or slightly below. Otherwise, an oversize screw may crowd the clearance and cause the door to pop open.

SURFACE HINGES

Butterfly, H, and H & L hinges are less work to install than butts as they are simply screwed to the face of the door and cabinet. But they are also very conspicuous and should therefore be chosen with the size and style of the furniture in mind.

To install hinges of this type, first fit and wedge the door in place with shims, as described above. Mark the vertical position of the hinge with a lightly drawn horizontal pencil line. Then hold the hinge in place on the line, with the hinge barrel centered on the clearance space, and mark the outline of the middle screw hole

in each half of the hinge. Use the awl to punch 1/8-inch-deep center holes. Lay the hinge in place and drive these 2 screws. Repeat the process for the other hinge. Remove the shims and open and shut the door a few times to check its operation. Then punch holes and drive the remaining screws.

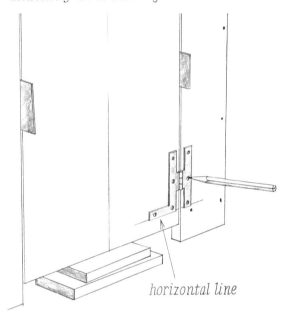

attaching an H & L hinge

horizontal line

DOOR BUTTON

The simplest hardware for holding a cupboard door shut is a wooden button attached with a flathead brass screw. A button can be made from scrap wood in less time than it takes to tell about it.

Use a hardwood such as maple, cherry, walnut, or mahogany, all of which wear much better than pine. Cut the button to size and mark its center with intersecting lines. Then drill and countersink the screw hole, using a drill slightly larger than the diameter of the screw shank. The button should turn freely on the screw. Bevel and sandpaper the under corners and

detail: door button

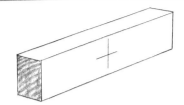

under edges slighty rounded

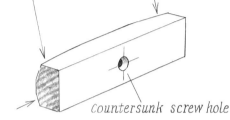

countersunk screw hole

locating position of door button

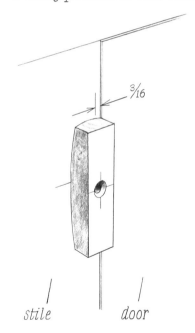

stile   *door*

turned hardwood knob and screw

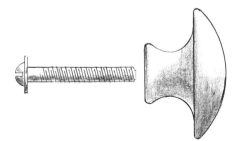

edges of the button so that when turned it will engage the edge of the door without gouging the wood.

To attach the button, hold it against the stile about 3/16 inch back from the edge as shown. Use the awl to punch through the button and make a starting screw hole in the stile. Push the screw through the button, twist it into the starting hole, and drive it tight. Then back the screw out just enough to allow the button to turn easily but not so much so that it drops away by itself and disengages from holding the door.

DOORKNOB

Turned hardwood knobs come in a variety of diameter sizes and are attached with a pan-headed screw which is usually sold with the knob. As these knobs are often rather rough, they should be thoroughly sanded to final smoothness before being attached (see *Sanding*, p. 132).

Lay out the location of the knob. Use the try square to draw a light horizontal pencil line, and the rule to measure in from the open edge of the door. Draw a vertical pencil line against the end of the rule to mark the center of the screw hole. Hold a center punch on the intersection of the lines and tap it lightly with the hammer to make an indentation in which to start the drill point. Clamp a piece of waste wood to the back side of the door and drill a hole slightly larger than the diameter of the screw, clear through the door and into the waste. This prevents splintering the exit side of the hole.

Push the screw through the hole from the back. Start the knob onto the screw and turn it up tight while holding a screwdriver in the slot of the screw. If the knob still turns after tightening the screw, the screw is too long. Remove it, cut a little off the end with a hacksaw, clean up the screw threads with a triangular file, and then replace it. The knob should be made absolutely tight.

Finishing Wood

Finishing is the last stage in the completion of a piece of furniture, and it is just as important as the materials, time, and workmanship that have gone into its construction. Without question one good reason for applying a finish to raw wood is to enhance the appearance of its grain and color; another is to protect the wood against the ravages of dirt, stains, and spills, as well as producing a surface that is practical to clean and maintain. But the main purpose of a finish is to retard the penetration of moisture and resist the effects of temperature changes which together cause the wood alternately to expand, contract, or change shape. Wood is not fully protected unless the finish is applied to all its exposed surfaces. For example, if the undersides of tabletops and shelves are not treated, expansion and contraction of one side will almost certainly result in warping.

Finishing cannot be done hurriedly in a day or two. It requires patient experimentation and testing of materials on scraps of the same wood you are using, as well as paying close attention to procedures—especially sanding and allowing enough drying time. Yet, considering how the appearance and the durability of the furniture are affected, this work is time well invested.

There is on the market an almost bewildering profusion of wood finishes of all types. They are roughly grouped as transparent (varnish, shellac, lacquer, and penetrating oils that retain the natural grain and color of the wood) and opaque (paint that covers and completely hides the wood and its grain and color). The finishes discussed here have been put through several tests on various kinds of wood, and have been selected because they require no special equipment, skill, or experience, and are comparatively easy to apply.

In selecting a finish, the following factors must be taken into account: (1) the specie and grain pattern of the particular wood used, (2) the abuse to which it may be subjected, (3) the color and general appearance you want, and (4) the amount of time and effort you are willing to spend. But keep one important thing in mind: to achieve a good finish, the surface condition of the wood and the type of finish must be planned in advance with respect to one another before you put saw to wood.

SURFACE PREPARATION

This consists mainly of sanding the entire furniture with progressively finer grits of abrasive paper until you get the degree of smoothness you want. No matter what finish you apply, the condition of the surface *must be clean*—dents raised, nail holes filled, dried glue spots removed, pencil lines, scratches, and rough spots sanded off. The smallest scratch will show up clearly when the finish is applied and rough spots will absorb stain faster, resulting in a blotchy appearance.

Begin by wiping the surface with a clean lint-free cotton cloth. Then carefully examine each side of your project from every angle. Mark any blemishes with white chalk. Run your fingers over the surface to locate the rough spots— they are difficult to see. Keep in mind that some imperfections may add character to the wood, but remove the ones that might be unsightly.

Next, remove the doors, doorknobs, latches, hinges, drawers, and drawer pulls. Remove the scrolled backboard of the *Pine Dressing Table* so that the tabletop can be sanded and the table set bottom-side up to finish the underside and the legs. Plug all screw holes with facial tissue to prevent any stain or finish from running into the inside. If the piece is to be painted, then recess all visible nailheads with a nail set and fill the holes with a wood patching compound as described below in "Filling Holes."

RAISING DENTS

Use the tip of your finger to apply warm water to the dent, filling it to slightly above the surface. As the wood absorbs the water, add more until the cells have expanded to their original size and the dent has raised a bit higher than the surface around it. It will shrink as it dries. Allow it to dry thoroughly before sanding. For deep dents, place a wet cloth on the depression and press a hot iron over the cloth to create

steam. The moisture and heat will expand the wood cells. Again, it is important that the dent is raised slightly higher than the surface around it, and that it is completely dry before sanding.

FILLING HOLES

Wood fillers are used to fill small holes and other minor surface imperfections, and should not be confused with paste wood fillers which are used to fill pores in open-grain wood. Wood fillers are referred to as wood patch (latex), wood dough, plastic wood paste, and glazing compound. They are available ready-mixed in neutral and some wood colors. All fillers will take paint and clear finishes, but not all of them will accept stain. While some manufacturers claim that their fillers will absorb stain uniformly, they also caution that the wood surrounding the patched area will accept the stain differently. No matter what the manufacturer claims, always test the filler on a scrap of the same wood before using it on your furniture project. This is the only way to judge how it will match the wood tone and how well it absorbs stain.

Make some trial nail holes in the scrap wood. Then cover the area around the hole with masking tape to protect the wood from absorbing any of the filler which may cause a halo to appear around the patch when the stain or finish is applied. Apply the filler with a small palette knife or a nail. Press it in and mound it slightly above the surface. The filler will sink as it dries. If it sinks below the surface, add more. If the hole is a deep one, add the filler in layers, allowing each one to dry hard before adding another. This helps to prevent its cracking and pulling away from the sides of the hole as it dries. When it is thoroughly dry, remove the masking tape and use a sanding block to sand it level with the wood surface, sanding with the grain. Wipe the surface clean and make sure no bits of filler remain, as they will prevent the stain or finish from penetrating into the wood. Examine the patch to see how well the tone of the filler blends with the wood. If you are planning to stain, apply some stain over the test patch to see how it is absorbed.

Some woodworkers make their own filler by mixing fine sawdust or sanding dust of the wood they are using with creamy yellow wood glue which has been diluted 50 percent with water. Mixed to a thick paste, it's applied to the wood in the same way as commercial fillers. Make sure it is completely dry before sanding smooth and that no bits of paste remain on the surface. Wood generally darkens as it ages, but most commercial plastic fillers do not, and may even lighten.

REMOVING GLUE SPOTS

Dried glue spots left on the surface prevent both stain and finish from penetrating into the wood. Removing them is one of the hardest things to do, but you can try sliding a flat file (minus the handle) back and forth over the spot. Press down on the file with fingers and thumbs, and keep it parallel with the grain. Then sand the area.

SANDING

Sanding is probably the most important part of finishing. Not only does it remove surface scratches and pencil lines, level raised wood cells and filled nail holes, but it is also the process used to develop the overall surface smoothness necessary for a fine finish. While it can be a tedious job, it is also exciting to see and feel the wood surface becoming smooth under your touch. Developing surface smoothness is accomplished by using progressively finer grits of sandpaper and following the cardinal rule: *always sand with the grain*. Sanding across the grain cuts the wood fibers and produces surface scratches that are often impossible to remove.

SANDPAPER

There are four types of coated abrasive papers used in woodworking: flint, garnet, aluminum oxide, and silicon carbide. Flint is the least expensive and the least desirable. It clogs and tears easily and does not wear well. The reddish-colored garnet paper has better cutting qualities and many woodworkers prefer it for preparing raw wood for finishing. But it is not as strong as aluminum oxide or silicon carbide, the two papers most often used for furniture work. Aluminum oxide, also called *production paper*, is hard and durable and works best on hardwoods. Silicon carbide has a very fast cutting action and can be used wet or dry. It is a nonclogging paper ideal for sanding softwoods and for acquiring an extrasmooth surface, as well as for sanding between finish coats, and for polishing the final finish coat.

Grit Size

The grade or grit size specifies the coarseness or fineness of the abrasive and is usually printed on the back of the sandpaper in one of three ways: the aught system (1/0 to 10/0), by numbers (20 to 600), or according to texture (coarse, medium, fine). The lower the number, the coarser the grit.

Backing

Also printed on the back is the weight (thickness) of the paper backing. This is indicated by the letters A, C, D, and E. A-weight is the thinnest paper stock, making it the most flexible, and is coated with fine mineral grain. It is also known as *finishing paper*. C and D are medium weight with medium grains and are known as *cabinet paper*. E-weight is a heavy, durable, paper not generally used in furniture finishing.

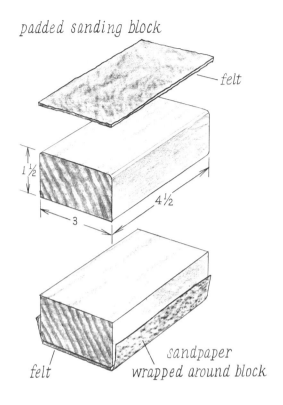

padded sanding block

felt

$1\frac{1}{2}$

3

$4\frac{1}{2}$

felt

sandpaper wrapped around block

always sand with the grain

Coating

The term *open-coat* means that the abrasive grains cover between 50 and 75 percent of the paper, leaving more space around each grain so that it does not clog as quickly when used on softwood. *Closed-coat* indicates that the grit covers the entire backing paper and will clog faster. But it cuts faster and works best on hardwoods.

HOW TO SAND

A standard 9 x 11″ sheet of sandpaper can be cut into working pieces by folding and then tearing along the fold with a straightedge. When cut in half to make two 5 1/2 x 9″ pieces, each one can be folded in thirds and used when sanding with the palm of the hand. Cut into quarters (4 1/2 x 5 1/2″), the pieces are a perfect size to fit around a sanding block. Or, several of these quarter-sheets can be folded in half and slipped one inside the other like pages of a book. These extra layers serve as a cushion when sanding tight areas where a block cannot be used.

Use a sanding block to sand flat surfaces. Since most woods have both hard and soft areas, sanding with a block produces a smoother and more truly level surface. Without a block, the fingers push the sandpaper deeper into the soft areas while it simply rides over the hard ones. A sanding block helps avoid rounding over edges and corners, and is essential when sanding end grain (see *Woodworking Practices*, p. 40). Make a block 1 1/2 x 3 x 4 1/2″ from a piece of scrap wood. Plane it smooth and round the long edges a bit to prevent their tearing the sandpaper. Pad it by gluing a piece of felt to the bottom. This will cushion the paper and prevent scratches when wood particles build up between the sandpaper and the surface of the work. Wrap the sandpaper around the bottom and up over

SANDPAPER CHART

Purpose	Grit	Grade	Description
Final sanding prior to applying finish	120	3/0	Fine
	150	4/0	
	180	5/0	
	220	6/0	Extrafine
	240	7/0	
	280	8/0	
	320	9/0	Superfine
	400	10/0	
Final sanding prior to applying paint	120	3/0	Fine
	150	4/0	
	180	5/0	
	220	6/0	Extrafine
Finish sanding between coats	600		Superfine

the sides, gripping it with your thumb and fingers. Never tack it to the block. Having several blocks of different sizes makes it convenient to choose the best one for the job. For moldings and other curved sections, wrap sandpaper around a length of wooden dowel or other blocks cut to fit concave or convex surfaces.

Use the sandpaper chart to select the correct abrasive grit size. Don't start with a coarse grit expecting to get the work done faster. It only makes deep scratches that are time-consuming to remove and may even damage the wood beyond repair. Take more time and begin with a fine grit—120 for softwood and 150 for hardwood. Then move to increasingly finer grits until you get the smoothness you want. How far you go depends on the ultimate surface you want and on the type of finish you plan to use. Both soft- and hardwoods become even silkier when finish-sanded up to 400. This is more noticeable with penetrating finishes, which soak into the wood and leave the wood surface in its natural state, than with a built-up surface finish such as varnish, polyurethane, or paint. Sanding between finish coats should always be done with 600-grit abrasive paper. However,

before starting to sand your work, try the different grit sizes on scrap pieces of the same wood to see and feel the effects they produce. To avoid breathing the sanding dust, wear a nontoxic particle mask.

Sanding Techniques

1. Have the work in a horizontal position, especially when extensive flat areas are to be sanded. Lay large pieces such as cupboards on their sides and then, as each side is completed, turn the work over. Be sure to place protective padding under the furniture to avoid damaging the wood, but don't use newspapers as the ink transfers to the wood and is difficult to clean off.

2. *Always sand with the grain,* using straight back-and-forth strokes and an even hand pressure. Sanding with a circular motion or across the grain cuts the wood fibers and produces scratches that are almost impossible to remove.

3. Sand with uniformity. Don't sand one area with 180-grit abrasive and another with 220, as the rougher area will absorb more stain as

well as more finish. The same thing happens when you sand lightly in one place and with heavy pressure in another. Remember that sanding affects the degree to which wood absorbs stains and finishes.

4. Brush the surface frequently to remove sanding dust, and blow it out of tight corners. Check the sandpaper and block every so often to avoid the build-up of dust. Bang it on the edge of the workbench to loosen the dust, or clean it with a stiff brush.

5. Turn the paper from time to time and when it gets clogged or worn spots begin to show, discard it for a new piece.

6. Inspect the wood surface frequently, using your fingers to detect rough spots that are hard to see.

7. When sanding close to edges, be careful not to let the block tip over the edges or they will be rounded.

8. Sand plywood following the direction of the grain. First look at the edge to see the thickness of the outer veneer, and be careful not to sand a hole clear through.

9. For sanding turned legs, cut strips of 400- or 600-grit sandpaper about 1 1/2 inches wide, and back it with masking tape. Hold the strip by the ends and with some tension pull it back and forth shoeshine style to clean off and smooth any tool marks. Then use folded sandpaper in the palm of your hand to lightly sand with the grain.

10. After final sanding and before raising the grain, dull the sharp edges and corners of the work. Use 600-grit paper over a padded block, stroking lightly along the edges with the grain. Slightly rounded edges allow something for the finish to take hold of and will not chip as easily as when applied to a razor-sharp edge.

11. When sanding between finish coats, wet-sand with 600-grit wet-or-dry paper over a padded sanding block. Wet the surface with plain water and sand lightly in long, overlapping strokes in the direction of the grain. Keep the area wet as you work. The water acts as a lubricant and keeps the paper from loading up with sanding dust that scratches the surface. From time to time dip the paper in water to wash away the wet sanding dust. As you wet-sand, periodically wipe the area dry with a clean cloth or paper towel and inspect the surface carefully.

RAISING THE GRAIN

Although after sanding the surface may feel as smooth as silk, there are some damaged fibers remaining pressed down into the wood by the sanding process. When the first coat of stain or finish is applied, these fibers will stand up like tiny whiskers, causing a rough and sometimes blotchy finish. To remedy this, sponge the entire surface with warm water, following the grain. Use just enough water to moisten the surface and be careful not to miss any areas. The moisture causes these fibers to swell and raise above the surface. Allow the wood to dry completely. Then give the surface a light sanding with 600-grit paper wrapped around a sanding block. Go lightly—the object is to remove just the whiskers without cutting into the surface, which would then only produce more whiskers.

Raising the grain is recommended for an extremely smooth surface. If you plan to use a water stain, then the grain *must be raised* before the stain is applied.

TACK RAG

With the final sanding completed, the surface must be given a thorough cleaning. First, wipe it with a clean cloth and go over it with a vacuum cleaner. Then, to be sure that every speck of dust is removed, wipe the surface down with a tack rag. A tack rag is a sticky cloth that will pick up the minutest traces of dust and is used not only for the final wipe before the stain or finish is applied, but also when sanding between finish coats. Most paint and hardware stores carry them, or you can make your own. Simply dampen a 24-inch square of cheesecloth or clean cotton cloth with turpentine. Then sprinkle 1 teaspoonful or more of varnish on the cloth and wring it to distribute the varnish. The tack rag should be barely damp and sticky and not leave a mark on the surface of the wood. Fold the edges to the center to keep loose threads from unraveling, then bunch it together loosely and wipe. Store it in a screw-top jar, and occasionally add a drop of turpentine to keep the rag moist. When it begins to fill with sanding dust, discard it and make a new one.

WOOD SEALERS

Sealers are applied to wood to act as a bonding layer between the wood and the finish coat; to prevent uneven absorption of stain or finish in wood species that have both hard and soft grain; and to prevent the porous end grain from soaking up too much stain. And sealers are brushed over certain stains to prevent their bleeding through and muddying the finish coat. Read the stain label carefully as some contain their own sealer, in which case an additional sealer coat is not needed. Do not apply a sealer over wood that is to be water-stained or finished with penetrating resin-oil.

While there are many prepared sealers on the market, it is a simple matter to make your own. A coat of thinned varnish is an excellent sealer and bond for a varnish finish, just as thinned polyurethane works well for a polyurethane finish. Follow the manufacturer's directions for thinning with mineral spirits. A wash coat of shellac can also be used to seal the wood, and where necessary the stain. But if the final finish is to be polyurethane, don't use shellac as a sealer, since it is not compatible with urethane and will not bond well.

Shellac is an excellent sealer and primer for surfaces that are to be painted. It fills the pores and hardens the wood fibers, preventing the paint from soaking deep into the wood. Shellac is also used to seal wood knots and sap streaks that otherwise usually leak up through and discolor the painted finish.

Shellac Wash Coat

Shellac is a natural resin processed in the form of dried flakes which are then dissolved in denatured alcohol. White shellac is the type generally used on both light and dark woods and is the bleached form of natural shellac which is an orange color. It is manufactured in 2-, 3-, 4-, and 5-lb. cuts, the term *cut* specifying the proportion of shellac to alcohol. For example, a 3-lb. cut consists of three pounds of shellac flakes dissolved in one gallon of denatured alcohol. Most stores stock either the 3-lb. or 4-lb. cuts. Because shellac has a poor shelf life, buy only what you need for the job, and check the expiration date on the can.

Use a 1/2-lb. cut shellac for a wash coat to seal wood before staining and to seal the stain, if necessary, before applying the finish coat. To get a 1/2-lb. cut from a 3-lb. cut shellac, mix one part shellac with four parts denatured alcohol; from a 4-lb. cut, make the proportions one to five. To seal and prime wood before painting, use a straight 3-lb. cut shellac.

Though they are not often exposed to view, the underside and the inside of drawers will absorb moisture and may warp unless they are sealed. Apply one coat of a 3-lb. cut shellac to keep the surfaces clean and help prevent the wood from warping. Or, use a thinned coat of varnish or polyurethane.

Applying Shellac

Stir—don't shake—the shellac carefully and thoroughly. Shaking causes air bubbles to form in the liquid which are then transferred to the work. Don't work directly from a full can. Use a container large enough to hold what you will need and still have enough space above the shellac so that you can tap the tip of the bristles lightly against the inside wall of the container to remove excess shellac from the brush. Immediately replace the lid on the shellac can. When thinning shellac with denatured alcohol, stir the mixture well to blend thoroughly.

Good lighting is important. Place the furniture so that the light is directly in front of you as you apply the shellac. In the glare from the light on the work surface you can easily see each brush stroke and avoid overlapping.

Use a new, natural bristle brush—one as wide as possible for large areas and a narrower one for small areas and end grain. Buy the best available—a top quality bristle brush will do a better job. Slap the brush in the palm of your hand and scrub your fingers over the tips of the bristles to work out any dust and loose bristles.

Apply the shellac with a full brush and brush in the direction of the grain in even, full-length strokes. Cover as much area as you can with each stroke without forcing the shellac from the bristles. Remember, shellac is quick-drying and doesn't spread the way varnish and paint do. Reload the brush and continue brushing in parallel rows in one direction, being very careful not to overlap the strokes or you will have an uneven seal which will show up when the stain is applied. Allow four to five hours for the shellac to dry thoroughly, longer in wet or humid weather. Then sand lightly with 600-grit paper wrapped around a padded block. Be extremely careful when sanding—the idea is to remove just the tiny whiskers raised on the surface, not the shellac. Wipe the surface with a tack rag to remove all sanding dust.

Shellacking Techniques

1. Have the surface to be shellacked in a horizontal position to facilitate brushing long, even strokes without overlapping, and to avoid any runs and sags which might occur with vertical application.

2. Give the surface one last thorough wipe with the tack rag before starting.

3. Start with the least visible part of the work such as the back of a hutch or the underside of a tabletop, and work toward the front or the more visible part. Begin on the far side and work toward you to avoid reaching over and dripping shellac, dust, and lint on the wet area. Take advantage of the natural breaks in the surfaces of the furniture as places at which to begin and end the brush strokes. When shellacking the inside of the cupboards or the *Armoire*, work from the back out toward the front.

4. Dip the brush into the shellac about one-third its bristle length and gently brush back and forth on some scrap wood or a clean heavy paper bag to work the shellac through the bristles. Then dip the brush into the shellac again and tap the bristles against the inside wall of the container to remove any excess shellac. Don't remove too much—you should have a full brush. *Never drag the brush across the rim of the container* as this produces tiny bubbles which run back into the can and will be transferred to the work.

5. Lay on the shellac, holding the brush at a 45-degree angle so that it flows from the bristles onto the wood. Don't bend them. Brush in the direction of the grain in long, even strokes, covering as much area as you can with each stroke without forcing shellac from the bristles. Reload the brush and start the second stroke next to the first, and make it the same length. Be careful not to overlap the brush strokes or you will have an uneven seal. Continue brushing in one direction until the area is covered.

6. Don't let the brush drag or fall over the edge as it will leave a fat deposit of shellac on the horizontal and vertical surfaces.

7. When applying shellac to end grain, be careful not to let any of it run onto the adjacent flat surfaces.

8. Apply shellac to molding in lengthwise strokes.

9. On inside corners, brush out from the corner, covering the horizontal surface first, then return the brush to the corner and stroke it up to coat the vertical surface.

10. On turned legs, brush around small turnings, then brush lengthwise strokes on flat surfaces and on long turned areas.

PASTE WOOD FILLER

In the process of wood finishing, using a paste wood filler is more a matter of taste than a necessity. While sanding smooths the surface of the wood, it does not fill the pores of open-grained woods such as oak. And if a high-style, mirror finish is wanted, then a wood filler is used to fill the pores and make them level with the surface. However, if you like the natural texture of an open-grained surface and want to keep it that way, or if you are planning to apply a penetrating finish to your furniture, then skip this step completely.

Paste wood filler is a thick paste of powdered silex, linseed oil, and japan drier. It is available in natural as well as various wood tones, but the natural color is what most stores carry, one reliable brand being Benjamin Moore's Benwood. It can be applied under a clear finish, or before or after staining. And this wood filler can be tinted with universal colors or with some of the same stain that is to be used on the furniture. Paste wood filler must first be thoroughly mixed and then thinned with mineral spirits to the consistency of heavy cream. When wet, its color is similar to that of peanut butter, but it dries to a lighter shade.

Applying Paste Wood Filler

Spread a generous amount of paste wood filler across the grain to work it into the pores, then brush with the grain. Use an old, short, bristle brush that is stiff enough to spread the filler but not to push it up out of the pores. Allow it to set for five to twenty minutes, or until it starts to lose its wet look and begins to dull. Fold a clean piece of burlap or an old rough towel to fit your hand and rub the filler across the grain in a circular motion, forcing it into the pores while at the same time removing any excess from the surface. Then wipe the surface with a clean cloth in the direction of the grain. Keep wiping until all the filler has been removed from the surface, but *wipe gently* to avoid removing it from the pores. Timing is critical. If you start rubbing too soon, most of the filler will be cleaned out of the pores. And if you wait too long or have covered too large an area, and the filler becomes sticky or crusted on the surface, wiping will also lift some of the filler out of the pores. Since this is a tricky wiping technique, practice applying filler to scrap pieces of the same wood you are using before applying it to your furniture.

Allow the filler to dry twenty-four hours. Then sand the area lightly with 400- or 600-grit paper over a padded sanding block. Clean off the sanding dust and wipe the surface with a cloth dampened in mineral spirits, wiping in the direction of the grain. Any traces of filler left on the surface will dull the appearance of the wood when the final finish is applied.

STAINING

The staining of wood is also a matter of personal taste and preference. While some feel that stain is essential to a good finish, others believe that it should be applied only to wood that lacks interesting color and grain, or when the appearance of newness is so important a factor that it must be made to look old. Woods that have naturally beautiful color and grain should not be stained at all. They can be given a transparent finish simply to bring out and enhance these characteristics. With time and gentle handling, all wood develops its own richness of color, and there is not a stain to be had that quite equals the distinct beauty of wood aged to a natural patina.

Applying a clear finish will intensify the color and emphasize the grain as the wood seasons and continues its natural process of coloration. But it will also darken the color somewhat—the degree depending on the particular specie and its natural hue. For example, walnut, mahogany, rosewood, butternut, cherry, and teak will become darker than maple, birch, and pine, which are woods with a lighter hue.

To get an idea of how a piece of wood will look with a transparent finish, dampen a cloth with mineral spirits and wipe it over the surface. The color of the wet surface is a pretty close approximation of what it will look like, but the resins in the actual finish will make it a bit more spectacular. If you want to modify the color of the wood, or give it an aged look, then staining is required.

All stains are transparent, or translucent, which means that they change the color of the wood by actually dyeing it. It must also be noted that stain is not a finish. Stained wood is still raw wood, subject to the ravages of moisture, heat, and dirt. It must therefore be treated as such and have a finish applied over it for protection. There are finishes that contain stain or to which Universal Tinting Colors may be added (see "Coloring," p. 148), and when they are applied to raw wood, staining, sealing, and finishing are all done in one operation. Don't use varnish or lacquer stain finishes—they do not penetrate and almost completely hide the grain.

Of the many types of wood stains available, most fall into one of three categories: pigmented oil wiping stain, penetrating oil stain, and water stain. Each one possesses certain advantages and disadvantages. Oil stains are convenient and easy to apply, water stains are the most brilliant and transparent in color and will not fade.

PIGMENTED OIL WIPING STAIN

A pigmented stain consists of very fine particles of color pigment *suspended* in a solvent. When applied to wood, these fine particles are deposited in the surface pores and merely color the top layer of wood. Although the grain may still show through, it is likely to be somewhat clouded. For this reason pigmented stains are not the best choice for woods that have a distinctive and attractive grain or figure. They are often used to partially obscure an unattractive or too prominent a grain. Pigmented stains come in a variety of colors and are easy to control because they are neither penetrating nor quick-drying. Properly applied and wiped off they are good for soft, close-grained woods such as pine, since the pores are smaller and less susceptible to clogging.

Before applying a pigmented oil wiping stain, partially seal all end grain with a wash coat of shellac (see "Wood Sealers," p. 136), being careful not to slop over the edges onto the flat surfaces of the work. Stir the stain thoroughly and then frequently during application to keep the pigment in suspension and prevent its settling to the bottom of the can. Otherwise, the color will not be uniform. Apply the stain with a brush or a lint-free cloth, working in the direction of the grain. Let it set for five to fifteen minutes, depending on the manufacturer's directions. Then, wipe the stain with a clean cloth, working in the direction of the grain.

The sooner the stain is wiped, the lighter the color will be. If a darker shade is preferred, apply a second coat after the first has dried. If the color is too dark, wipe it with a cloth dampened in mineral spirits. When staining is completed, set the work aside to dry for twenty-four hours before applying a stain sealer, if one is required, or the final finish.

PENETRATING OIL STAIN

In this type of stain the coloring substance is completely *dissolved* in the solvent, which means that the stain penetrates more deeply into the pores and fibers, emphasizing the wood's natural grain or figure. Clear and transparent, these stains are more resistant to fading than pigmented oil wiping stains. For these reasons, they are especially good for both soft- and hardwoods, especially those with an attractive grain or figure and a uniform texture. Softwoods which are more porous and have an alternating soft and hard grain tend to soak up more stain in the soft layers than in the hard ones, giving the surface a streaked appearance. This can be controlled somewhat by first sealing the wood with a wash coat of shellac which allows the stain to penetrate more evenly. Of course, the end grain of both hard- and softwoods should also be sealed to prevent its staining darker than the other surfaces (see "Wood Sealers," p. 136). Penetrating oil stains come ready-mixed in standard wood tones. But rather than relying entirely on the manufacturer's color chart, always make tests on scraps of the wood you are using before making a final decision.

Apply the oil stain with a clean, flat, bristle brush or folded lint-free cloth, working in the direction of the grain. Avoid overlapping the strokes as much as possible. Allow the stain to penetrate for five to twenty minutes, depending on the manufacturer's directions. Then wipe the stain with a clean, cotton cloth in the direction of the grain to remove any excess and to even up the color. The longer the stain remains on the surface, the darker the color will be. If a deeper color is wanted, apply a second coat after the first has dried. If just a hint of color is desired to give new wood a warmer look, wipe the stain immediately after applying it. Allow twenty-four hours for the stain to dry before applying a stain sealer, if one is required, or the final finish.

WATER STAINS

Prepared by mixing powdered aniline dyes and water, these stains are often used by professional wood finishers and purists. They penetrate deeply, show the grain clearly, and give the wood a very natural look. Wood in its natural state in the tree is composed of millions of tiny cells which are filled with water (sap). When the tree is cut into lumber and dried, the water in these cells is displaced by air. Dry, seasoned wood absorbs water more naturally and more evenly than it does oil, the water penetrating and filling the cells in about the same way as did the sap.

These water-soluble, powdered dyes come in a wide range of colors and when dissolved in water are pure and clear—almost brilliant. They are quick-drying, leave no muddy film on the wood surface, do not fade, and are inexpensive.

The stain is prepared by dissolving one ounce of powdered dye in a quart of hot (not boiling) distilled water. The color can be strengthened by adding more dye, made lighter with more water, or modified with the addition of other colors. Carefully measure the powdered dye before mixing it with water and make a note of the quantity. Then if more stain is needed later, you will be able to duplicate the color. Allow the solution to cool to room temperature before using it.

There are three disadvantages to using water stains: (1) few paint and hardware stores carry the powdered dyes, although they can be ordered from some woodworkers' supply catalogs, one of which is Albert Constantine and Sons, Inc., 2050 Eastchester Road, Bronx, NY 10461; (2) the wood grain must first be raised before the stain is applied (see "Raising the Grain," p. 135); and (3) it is not the easiest stain to apply with a brush because it penetrates the surface quickly and deeply, making it difficult to blend the stain from one brush stroke to the next to get a uniform color and to avoid overlapping and streaking. Although a spray gun is the ideal tool for applying water stain, good results can be obtained with a brush. Use a nylon brush—as wide a one as possible so that the surface can be covered with a minimum number of strokes. Apply the stain with a full brush, brushing in the direction of the grain in even, full-length strokes. Cover as much area as you can with each stroke without bending the brush to force the stain from the bristles. Reload the brush and start the second stroke next to the first, making it the same length and being careful not to overlap the brush strokes or you will get an uneven color. Work quickly, and continue brushing in one direction until the whole area is covered. Then wipe the surface in light, even, full-length strokes in the direction of the grain, using a clean cotton cloth. To prevent the end grain from absorbing too much stain, first wet it with clear water, then stain and wipe immediately. Or, first seal the end grain with a wash coat of shellac (see "Wood Sealers," p. 136). Allow twenty-four hours for the stain to dry before applying the finish coat.

SELECTING A COLOR

Buy only a good quality stain from a reputable paint, hardware, or building supply dealer. When selecting a color, don't rely alone on the manufacturer's color chart, or on stained wood samples. *Always do your own testing.* Apply the stain to a scrap of the same wood you are using—and to plywood if it is part of the construction—but first sand the wood to the smoothness you want. Apply the stain in daylight; artificial lighting does not show the true color of stains. Wait until the stain has thoroughly dried before you decide on the color. Then take the trial one step further and apply the final finish over the stain. The resins in varnishes and penetrating oils tend to intensify the color and may even darken it a bit.

Each manufacturer has his own version of the various wood color tones and the names they are given. You can intermix the shades of one brand, but it is not advisable to mix brands. When you have found and tested the shade you like, buy enough stain to complete the whole job. If more than one can is required, stir and mix the contents of both cans together to avoid any possible color differences.

Remember, there are several factors that affect the final color of a stain: the type of wood, how well its surface is prepared, in what concentration the stain is applied, and the length of time elapsed before the stain is wiped. Bear in mind also that no stain will uniformly produce the same color on each and every kind of wood.

STAINING TECHNIQUES

1. Make sure the surface has been properly sanded. A rough spot absorbs more stain than the smooth areas around it, causing light and dark spots.

2. Go over the entire surface with a tack rag to remove any specks of dust lodged in the pores of the wood.

3. Have plenty of clean, lint-free cloths on hand for wiping up excess stain.

4. Apply stain with the work surface in a horizontal position to get an even distribution of stain. When staining vertical areas, work from the bottom toward the top to prevent runs.

5. Start with the least visible part such as the back of a cupboard or the underside of a table and work toward the front or the more visible areas.

6. Use a brush to apply stains—it is much neater. Use a wide brush for large surfaces, and a narrow one for end grain and other small areas.

7. Use a full brush and try to take the same amount each time you dip it into the stain. But don't overload it so much that stain drips or

puddles on the surface. Avoid spattering uncovered areas.

8. Apply the stain with light, long, quick strokes, always brushing with the grain.

9. Do not let the brush drag over the edges of the work where the stain will collect and darken.

10. Take advantage of the natural breaks in the surfaces of the furniture as places at which to begin and end the brush strokes.

11. As each section is stained, be sure to allow the same amount of penetration time before wiping. This helps to achieve uniformity of color.

12. Use a fairly dry brush on end grain because it soaks up more stain—and more quickly—than other areas.

13. Color can be controlled better by applying two light coats rather than one dark one. Apply the second coat only after the first has completely dried.

14. Always work in the direction of the grain when wiping up excess stain. Use a uniform pressure to wipe and remove the stain evenly.

15. Be careful not to remove too much stain when wiping corners and edges, or they will be much lighter than the rest of the work.

16. To prevent spontaneous combustion, spread soiled wiping cloths to air out and dry before disposing of them.

TRANSPARENT FINISHES

There are two basic types of transparent finishes: surface and penetrating. Surface finishes are built-up layers of a protective film such as varnish, shellac, and lacquer, producing a hard, transparent coating on the surface. Of the three, varnish is recommended as the most suitable for the furniture projects here because it is more durable and offers more protection to the wood surface than shellac, and is easier to apply than lacquer, which is fast-drying and

requires some expertise and special equipment.

Penetrating finishes are nondrying oils and resin-oils which soak deep into the wood pores and emphasize the natural color and grain. They are the easiest to use and not only give the wood an attractive natural uncoated look but a protective finish as well. The penetrating resin-oils are similar to varnish, but they dry in the pores and between the wood fibers, rather than on the surface.

VARNISHES

Modern varnishes are formulated with synthetic resins and are an improvement over the old, natural-resin varnish. They are easier to apply, faster drying, tougher, and more durable. They are specified by their resins: alkyd, polyurethane, phenolic, and vinyl. The alkyds and polyurethanes are the best for furniture finishing.

Alkyd-based varnishes give the wood a deep, rich appearance and are resistant to water and alcohol. Additional coats are applied to get the depth or built-up look you want. For a soft, hand-rubbed look, use a satin finish varnish, but test it first on a scrap piece of the same wood you are using, as one manufacturer's satin finish may be glossier than another's. While all varnishes are clear, they generally have an amber color which changes the color of raw wood as well as stained wood. As for yellowing, alkyd varnishes vary from brand to brand. For the best results, buy the best quality varnish from a reputable dealer.

Polyurethane varnishes, particularly the satin and antique types, also produce an excellent top coat and are recommended where a clear, hard finish is needed. They are tougher than the alkyd varnishes and more resistant to water, heat, alcohol, and chemicals. They are also clearer in color, tend to yellow less, and dry to the touch in three to four hours, thus eliminating some of the dust problems of the slower drying varnishes. The one disadvantage of polyurethane is that it does not bond well over shellac.

Phenolic-resin varnishes are called *spar varnish* or *marine varnish* and are designed primarily for outside work. They are slow-drying and never really harden, thereby allowing the wood to swell and shrink without damaging the finish. They are also the most yellowing.

The vinyl-resin varnishes are clear, fast drying, and best used on floors, wall paneling, interior trim, and bar tops.

Two major hazards in varnishing are air bubbles forming in the varnish and being brushed onto the wood, and dust particles settling on the varnished surface while it dries. For the best results, start work with a fresh, new can of varnish. Never shake it. Shaking causes air bubbles to form in the liquid which are next to impossible to brush out, and once the varnish is dry, they are even more difficult to sand out. Don't work directly from a full can. Pour into a separate container, such as a clean coffee can, only the amount you expect to use each time. Immediately replace the lid on the can. The container should be large enough to hold what you will need and still have enough space above the varnish level so that you can tap the tip of the bristles lightly against the inside wall of the container to remove excess varnish from the brush. As you pour into the container, hold it at an angle so that the varnish runs down the sloping side of the can. This helps avoid air bubbles. Should they appear, however, cover the container tightly to exclude air and let the varnish rest for several hours or until the bubbles can rise to the surface and disappear.

If at all possible varnish in a room that can be closed off from the rest of the house in order to help control the movement of dust-laden air stirred up by human traffic and heating equipment. Ideally, the room temperature should be between 65 and 80 degrees. Too hot a room makes the varnish flow more freely, causing runs and sags, while a cold room stiffens and prevents it from speading smoothly and evenly. Avoid varnishing in damp or humid weather. A clear, dry day with high barometric pressure is ideal.

Good lighting is also important. Place the furniture so that the light is directly in front of you as you varnish. In the glare from the light on the work surface you can quickly see any areas missed with the brush as well as particles of dust that settle on the wet varnish. Use a new, natural-bristle brush about 3 inches wide for large areas, and a narrower one for end grain and small areas. Buy the best available—a top quality bristle brush will do a far better job. Slap the brush in the palm of your hand and scrub your fingers over the tips of the bristles to work out any dust and loose bristles.

Applying Varnish

The first coat of varnish should be thinned according to the directions on the can. It seals the wood and creates a base to which subsequent coats can bond. Again, tilt the container so that the thinner will not plunge directly into the varnish and create air bubbles. Stir gently with a clean paddle and mix the liquids thoroughly. Apply the first coat of varnish as evenly as possible, first brushing with the grain, then across the grain, and finally tipping off the varnish with a fairly dry brush, as described below in "Varnishing Techniques." Allow it to dry at least twelve hours, then sand lightly with 600-grit paper over a padded sanding block. Remove all sanding dust and wipe the surface with a tack rag. Apply the second and any subsequent coats full strength straight from the can. Allow each coat plenty of drying time before wet-sanding. The exception to this is polyurethane varnish, the second coat of which must be applied within a specified time before the first coat hardens too much and prevents the second coat from adhering in a tight bond. Otherwise, a lot of sanding will be necessary to give the hardened coat enough tooth to hold the next coat. Read the manufacturer's label carefully and follow the directions.

Always allow the alkyd varnishes more drying time than the manufacturer recommends. Each coat should be left to dry really hard—twenty-four to thirty-six hours, depending on ventilation and room temperature—before lightly sanding and applying the next coat. The longer the drying time, the better the sanding job, and the better the adhesion of the next coat.

When the second coat has hardened, wet-sand it with 600-grit wet-or-dry paper and a padded sanding block. Wet the surface well with plain water and sand lightly in long, overlapping strokes in the direction of the grain. Keep the area wet as you work. The water acts as a lubricant and keeps the paper from loading up with varnish particles that scratch the surface. From time to time dip the paper in water to wash off the slurry of water and sanding dust. Don't sand too much, just enough to remove any specks of dust and to smooth out the brush marks. As you wet-sand, periodically wipe the area dry with a clean cloth or paper towels and inspect the surface carefully. When it looks nice and smooth, move on to the next area. If you should cut through to the wood in any one spot, wipe the surface clean and let dry. Then apply another coat of varnish to the entire surface, let it dry hard, and resand.

Varnishing Techniques

1.   Have the surface to be varnished in a horizontal position to facilitate flowing the varnish evenly and to avoid runs and sags which are likely to occur with vertical applications.

2.   Give the surface one last thorough wipe with the tack rag before starting.

3.   Start with the least visible part such as the back of a hutch or the underside of a tabletop, and work toward the front or the more vis-

ible part. Begin on the far side and work toward you to avoid reaching over and dripping varnish, dust, and lint on the wet area already covered. Don't work too large an area at one time. Take advantage of the natural breaks in the surfaces of the furniture as places at which to begin and end the brush strokes. When varnishing the inside of the cupboards or the *Armoire*, work from the back out toward the front.

4.   Dip the brush into the varnish about one-third its bristle length, and brush gently back and forth on scrap wood to work the varnish through the bristles. Then dip the brush into the varnish again and tap the bristles against the inside wall of the container to remove any excess varnish. Don't remove too much—you should have a full brush. *Never drag the brush*

removing excess from the brush

separate container ——

laying on varnish

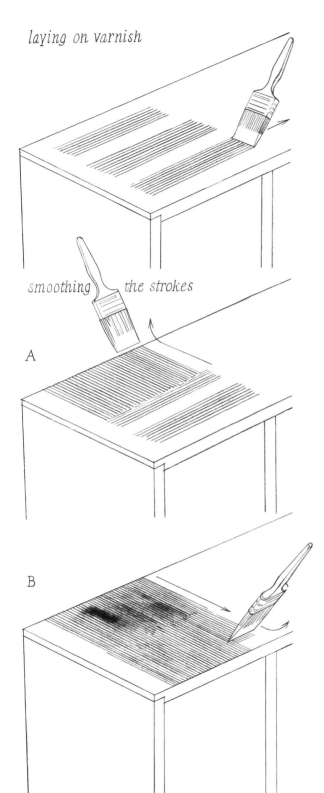

smoothing the strokes

A

B

across *the rim of the container* as this produces tiny bubbles which run back into the can, are picked up by the brush, and transferred to the work surface.

5. Lay on the varnish, holding the brush at a 45-degree angle so that the varnish *flows* from the bristles onto the wood. Don't bend the bristles. Start the first stroke about 2 inches in from one corner and 2 inches in from the far edge, and brush with the grain to where you have decided to break. Stroke the brush with the grain firmly but smoothly to avoid forming bubbles. Start the second stroke a brush-width away from the first, and make it the same length. Keep the brush full enough so that the varnish is flowed on rather than dragged on. Repeat this process, laying on varnish until you have covered the area.

6. Smooth out the varnish strokes by placing the brush in the center of the coated area and brush *across the grain* to the far edge, lifting the brush just at the edge. Don't let the brush drag or fall over the edge as it will leave a fat deposit of varnish on the horizontal surface and an extra deposit on the vertical. Return the brush to the center and repeat this procedure to distribute the varnish to the opposite edge. Next, to smooth out the varnish to the

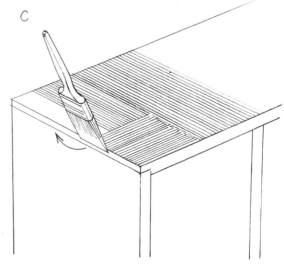

C

two remaining edges, start the brush one-third of the way into the coated area and brush with the grain, again lifting the brush just at the edge. Inspect the surface for any bare spots. It's easier to cover them now than when you begin to level the varnish. Remove any bristles that come loose from the brush by lifting them gently at one end with the tip or corner of the brush. Pick them off the brush with your fingers, then brush the area again. Use the point of a bamboo skewer or a round toothpick to lift off any dust particles. Then smooth the area with the tip of the brush.

7.   To level off the varnish it is now tipped with a dry brush. Have a clean, wide-mouthed jar at your side and dry the brush from time to time by pressing it against the inside of the rim. Any bubbles that form will fall into the jar instead of the varnish container. Hold the brush almost vertical to the surface. Start the brush stroke at the edge and brush with the grain, *using just the tips of the bristles*, again lifting the brush as you reach the other edge. Continue tipping in rows until the entire varnished surface has been leveled. Dry the brush from time to time as needed.

8.   Continue flowing on varnish, smoothing, and tipping until the entire work surface is covered. Stroke from the unfinished into the finished area. If, when making the final tipping strokes with new varnish into that previously applied, the overlapping joint doesn't blend and level out in a minute or two, it means that the varnish is beginning to set before the new varnish is tipped in. Work a smaller area so the meeting edge won't set before you get back to it again.

9.   Apply varnish to molding in lengthwise strokes.

10.   On inside corners, brush out from the corner, covering the horizontal surface first, then return the brush to the corner and stroke up to coat the vertical surface.

11.   On turned legs, brush around small

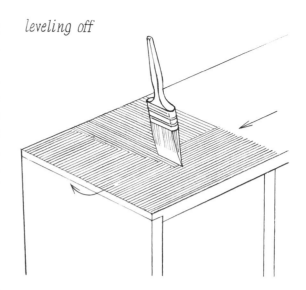

leveling off

turnings, then brush lengthwise on the flat surfaces and on long turned areas. For the final tipping, work from the middle part of the leg toward the top and the bottom.

Applying Polyurethane

1.   Follow the directions 1 through 4 given above for "Varnishing Techniques."

2.   Hold the brush at a 45-degree angle so that the polyurethane flows from the bristles onto the wood. Brush with the grain and in one direction only, using a minimal number of brush strokes. Avoid working back into it. Since polyurethane is more self-leveling than alkyd varnish, it does not need to be smoothed out and leveled by tipping.

3.   Don't bend the bristles. Stroke firmly but smoothly to avoid forming bubbles.

4. Reload the brush frequently, but be careful to avoid surface flooding. If puddles or sags appear, wipe up the excess with a dry brush. Have a clean, wide-mouth jar at your side to dry your brush by pressing it against the inside rim. Any bubbles that form will fall into the jar instead of the container.

5.   Follow instructions 9 through 11, remembering to brush in one direction only.

PENETRATING FINISHES

There are basically two penetrating finishes: the natural oils such as linseed and pure tung oil, both of which require a lot of rubbing and take a long time to dry; and the resin-oils which are oils that have been converted to resins, dissolved in a solvent, and mixed with driers. When this solution combines with oxygen, it becomes a polymerized solid.

For many wood finishers these clear, penetrating resin-oils come the closest to producing a perfect finish. They are the easiest to apply, dry quickly so there is never a mildew or fungus problem, require very little rubbing, and are easy to maintain. They soak deep into the wood pores, bring out the natural color of the wood, and emphasize the beauty of its grain. And except for a slight darkening of the wood's natural color, the surface looks uncoated and very natural because the resins have dried in the pores and between the wood fibers rather than on the surface. For this reason, the smoothness and quality of the wood are of paramount importance because the finish will be only as good as the surface to which it is applied. Penetrating resin-oils are durable and resistant to water, alcohol, heat, and household chemicals. But should a surface repair be necessary, simply wet-sand the area lightly with superfine grit paper and some additional resin-oil, then buff it dry.

There are many commercial resin-oils on the market—almost every paint manufacturer has one. Study the labels and ingredients and read the directions carefully to decide which one will best fit your needs. Make tests on scrap pieces of the same wood you will use—and plywood if it is part of the construction—before applying it to your furniture. Remember, penetrating resins will change the color of the wood a bit more than varnish.

APPLYING PENETRATING FINISHES

Two penetrating resin-oil finishes which have proven satisfactory are the natural Watco Danish Oil Finish, which gives the wood a warm low luster finish, and Formby's Low Gloss Tung Oil Finish, which produces a satin sheen without the built-up see-through look of varnish.

To apply Watco, shake the container thoroughly and pour a generous amount on the surface, spreading it with your hand. Be careful not to let any run off the edges. Having the work surface in a horizontal position will make application much easier. Wet-sand the surface with 600-grit wet-or-dry sandpaper over a padded sanding block. Use light hand pressure and sand with the grain. As the oil penetrates the wood, the fine sanding dust mixed with the oil is worked into the pores to level the surface. Add more oil to any dull spots that appear, and continue sanding for about fifteen minutes or until the surface starts to get a little tacky. Then wipe it clean with a soft cotton cloth and leave the work to dry overnight. The first coat of Watco can also be applied while preparatory sanding with 320 wet-or-dry sandpaper. Either way, before applying the second coat, lightly sand the surface with 600-grit paper, and wipe carefully with a tack rag to remove all sanding dust. Apply the second coat, but this time rub the oil in with your hand. The heat generated by hand friction helps the oil to penetrate.

Keep wetting and rubbing the surface until it will absorb no more oil. Then wipe it completely dry with a clean cloth, using long, parallel strokes. The oil must either be rubbed into the surface or wiped off dry. After about thirty minutes check the surface and wipe off any shiny spots of oil that may have resurfaced. Any traces of oil left on the surface harden into an unpleasant shiny surface film. To remove traces of dried oil, add Watco to soften them and then wipe them away with a cloth. Set the work aside to dry overnight. You can apply any number of coats to get the look that you want. Each successive coat adds depth to the finish. Porous woods will naturally require more than hardwood. Allow the final coat to dry twenty-four hours. Then cover the surface with a thin film of Watco and lightly wet-sand with 600-grit wet-or-dry sandpaper for about ten minutes. Wipe it dry and buff it vigorously to a soft warm luster, using a soft clean cloth.

Formby's Tung Oil Finish is a blend of tung oil and varnishes and is a very durable finish. To apply it, pour some finish into the palm of your hand and rub it into the wood. Continue rubbing with the grain until the oil is completely worked into the fibers of the wood. Then let it dry overnight. Before applying a second coat, lightly sand the surface with 600-grit paper, then wipe off the sanding dust with a tack rag. Now rub the second coat into the wood, and let it dry overnight. This should produce a low-luster sheen. For a glossier look rub in additional coats until you get the degree of shine that you want, allowing each coat to dry overnight before applying the next one.

COLORING

Watco Danish Oil is also available in several shades of walnut and oak, and in cherry and fruitwood, all of which can be intermixed to obtain other wood tones. When applied as directed to raw wood, the staining, sealing, and finishing are all done in one operation.

Natural Watco Danish Oil or Formby's Tung Oil Finish can be mixed with Universal Tinting Colors. These colors are made from pigments usually triple-ground to ensure maximum strength. The color dissolves in the oil and as the oil soaks into the wood, so does the color. Universal Tinting Colors are available in standard colors and most hardware, paint, and artist's supply stores carry them. They should not be confused with artist's oil colors whose pigment particles are a bit larger.

Almost any wood tone can be developed with just four colors: raw sienna, burnt sienna, raw umber, and burnt umber. Experiment with different combinations of these earth colors mixed with oil and test each shade on scrap wood. Then mix in some yellow ochre and see how the color is altered.

When you have decided on a color combination, make up a base mixture for testing. For example, measure 4 teaspoons of oil (Watco or Formby's) into a white cup (for better color visibility). Add 1/4 teaspoon burnt umber, 1/8 teaspoon burnt sienna, and 1/8 teaspoon of yellow ochre. Stir until all the pigment is thoroughly mixed. Next, measure 2 tablespoons of oil into a clean container and add 1 teaspoon of the base mixture you have just made, and stir to blend it well. Test this solution on a 1 x 6 x 14" scrap of the same wood you are using, having first sanded it to final smoothness. Because these pigments tend to separate quickly and settle to the bottom, it is necessary to stir the mixture frequently.

First, rub a very thin coat of oil over the surface, then pour 1 teaspoon of the solution onto the wood and rub it in with your hand, working in the direction of the grain. (If the color is too light, add more of the base mixture to the solution and make a note of the amount. If it is too dark, add more oil and note the amount.) Continue rubbing the mixture into the surface, and when it begins to feel a bit tacky, wipe with a clean cloth, in the direction of the grain. Allow twenty-four hours for the stain to dry. Then apply a coat of clear oil and rub it in by hand. Again, wipe off any excess oil on the surface, and leave the work to dry. This second coat will seal in the color. Continue adding additional coats of clear oil until you get the luster or shine that you want. Allow the final coat to dry twenty-four hours. Then, if you are using Watco, cover the surface with a thin film of oil and let it stand for about ten minutes. Wipe dry and buff vigorously to a soft, warm luster, using a soft cloth.

Keep an accurate record of the mixtures you make, so that when you have gotten the color you want—and have tested it—you will be able to multiply the ingredients and make the same color in a quantity large enough to do the whole piece of furniture.

PLAIN PAINTING

Paint is a clear vehicle with pigment added to give it color and to make it opaque. It is an ideal finish for furniture constructed with mixed woods, or wood with unattractive grain or unsightly knots. Paint has been used for centuries to beautify furniture and painted furniture has been and continues to be an imaginative and creative way to add color to a room. Today, paints are available in an almost unlimited range of colors—from creamy pastels to earthy terra-cottas. There are no set rules to govern the use of colors—the choice is yours to make, and your color choice can make the furniture blend in or stand out in a room.

Paints are divided in two basic groups: alkyd (oil-based) and latex (water-based) in flat, low luster, semigloss, and gloss finishes. The alkyds are more durable and resist stain better. Use a low-luster alkyd enamel for a soft rubbed look, or a semigloss enamel if you want a bit more shine on the surface. But do some testing on scrap pieces of the same wood because the degree of luster and gloss will vary from one brand to another. *Never* use an inferior paint. Buy the best quality and from a reputable dealer.

Although paint will hide the color and grain of wood, any surface defects will show up once the paint has dried. Therefore, all the procedures described in "Surface Preparation," page 131, should be followed to achieve a good painted finish. However, you don't have to sand the surface as smooth as you would for a transparent finish: sanding up to 220-grit abrasive is fine enough.

PRIMER COAT

Before applying paint, the raw wood must be primed, or given a first coat, to keep the paint from soaking unevenly into the wood, and to create a strong base to which it can adhere.

An alkyd enamel underbody is a good primer, but since it is a flat white it should be tinted to the approximate color of the paint you are using, otherwise an extra coat of paint may be necessary in order to completely cover the primer.

Bear in mind, however, that primers do not seal knots against their leaking through into the paint and staining it. To take care of this, the wood should first be sealed with a coat of white pigmented shellac-base primer (often referred to as stain-killer) or, which is much simpler, one coat of 3-lb. cut white shellac, which seals the knots and primes the surface all in one operation (see "Wood Sealers," p. 136).

APPLYING PAINT

If at all possible, paint in a room that can be closed off from the rest of the house in order to help control the movement of dust-laden air stirred up by human traffic and heating equipment. Ideally the room temperature should be between 65 and 80 degrees. Good lighting is also important. Place the furniture so that the light is directly in front of you as you paint. In the glare from the light on the work surface you can quickly see any areas that have either puddled or sagged and spot any loose bristles on the wet surface.

Use a new, natural bristle brush 2 to 3 inches wide for large areas, and a narrower one for small sections. Buy the best—a top quality brush does a far better job. Slap the brush in the palm of your hand and scrub your fingers over the tips of the bristles to work out any dust and loose bristles.

Mix the paint thoroughly with a wooden paddle. Don't work directly from a full can. Use a container large enough to hold what you will need and still have enough space above the paint so that you can tap the tip of the bristles lightly against the inside wall of the container to remove excess paint from the brush. Immediately replace the lid on the paint can.

Apply a full coat of paint as evenly as possible, first brushing with the grain, then stroking across it, and finally tipping off the paint with a fairly dry brush. Allow the paint to dry twenty-four hours or more before sanding. The paint must be hard-dry before sanding and applying the next coat. Don't rely on the manufacturer's drying time—paint takes longer to dry on a sealed, or nonporous surface, as well as when it has been heavily applied. Test the surface by pressing a fingernail into it. If an indentation shows, then the paint has not completely hardened. Allow more drying time.

When the first coat has hardened, wet-sand it with 600-grit wet-or-dry paper over a padded sanding block. Wet the surface well with plain water and sand lightly in long, overlapping strokes in the direction of the grain. Keep the area wet as you work. The water acts as a lubricant and keeps the paper from loading up with paint particles that scratch the surface. From time to time dip the paper in water to wash away the wet sanding dust. Don't sand too much—just enough to remove any specks of dust and to smooth out the brush marks. As you wet-sand, periodically wipe the area dry with a clean cloth or paper towel and inspect the surface carefully. When it looks nice and smooth, move on to the next area. If you should cut through to bare wood in any one spot, wipe the surface clean and let it dry. Then apply another coat of paint over the entire surface, let it dry hard, and resand.

Apply two or three coats, wet-sanding with 600-grit wet-or-dry paper between each coat. After sanding the final coat, wipe it dry, and then buff it vigorously to a soft warm luster, using a soft clean cloth.

PAINTING TECHNIQUES

1. Have the surface to be painted in a horizontal position to facilitate flowing the paint on evenly and to avoid runs and sags which are likely to occur with vertical applications.

2. Give the surface one last thorough wipe with the tack rag before starting.

3. Start with the least visible part such as the back of a hutch or the underside of a tabletop, and work toward the front or the more visible part. Begin on the far side and work toward you to avoid reaching over and dripping paint, dust, and lint on the wet area already painted. Take advantage of the natural breaks in the surface of the furniture as places at which to begin and end the brush strokes. When painting the insides of cupboards or the *Armoire*, work from the back out toward the front.

4. Dip the brush into the paint about one-third its bristle length and brush gently back and forth on a piece of scrap wood or a clean paper bag to work the paint through the bristles. Then dip the brush into the paint again, and tap the bristles against the inside wall of the container to remove any excess paint. Don't remove too much—you should have a full brush. *Never drag the brush across the rim of the container* as this tends to bunch the bristles which prevents an even flow of paint on the surface.

5. Brush the paint on the surface in several parallel rows of even length spaced a brush-width apart, but leave about an inch of unpainted surface around the edges. Hold the brush at a 45-degree angle so that the paint flows from the bristles onto the wood. Don't bend the bristles. Work with a full brush and brush in the direction of the grain. Then brush the rows to blend them together. Next, place the brush in the center of the painted area and brush *across the grain* to spread the paint to the far edge, lifting

the brush just at the edge. Don't let the brush drag or fall over the edge as it will leave a fat deposit of paint on the horizontal surface and an extra deposit on the vertical. Return the brush to the center and repeat this procedure to distribute the paint to the opposite edge. To brush out the paint to the two remaining edges, start the brush one-third of the way into the coated area and brush with the grain, again lifting the brush just at the edge. Remove any bristles that come loose from the brush by lifting them gently at one end with the tip or corner of the brush. Pick them off the brush with your fingers, then brush the area again. Use the point of a bamboo skewer or a round toothpick to lift off any dust particles. Then smooth the area with the tip of the brush. Next, use a a fairly dry brush and hold it almost vertical to the surface. Start the brush stroke at the edge and brush with the grain, using just the tips of the bristles and again lifting the brush as you reach the other edge. Continue tipping in rows until the painted surface has been smoothed and the brush marks evened out (see also "Varnishing Techniques," p. 144).

6. Begin a new area in the same way, but brush on the rows a few inches away from the section just painted. Spread the paint to blend and then brush across the grain to spread the paint to the edges, lifting the brush just at the edges. Then brush from the newly painted section up into the old section, lifting the brush at the meeting edge. Now use a dry brush and tip the surface to level off the paint and even out the brush strokes. Continue working in sections until the painting is completed.

7. Apply paint to molding in lengthwise strokes.

8. On inside corners, brush out from the corner, covering the horizontal surface first, then return the brush to the corner and stroke up to coat the vertical surface. If puddles or sags appear, wipe them with a dry brush.

9. On turned legs, brush around small turnings, then brush lengthwise on the flat surfaces and on long turned areas. For the final tipping, work from the middle part of the leg toward the top and the bottom.

Furniture Projects

New York Hutch   155

Armoire   169

Corner Cupboard   183

Slant-back Dresser   201

Pine Dressing Table   219

One-drawer Stand   235

Breadboard-top Table   247

Pencil-post Bed   257

Writing Table   273

Blanket Chest   291

Sideboard   303

New York Hutch

HEIGHT 70   WIDTH 23   DEPTH 12

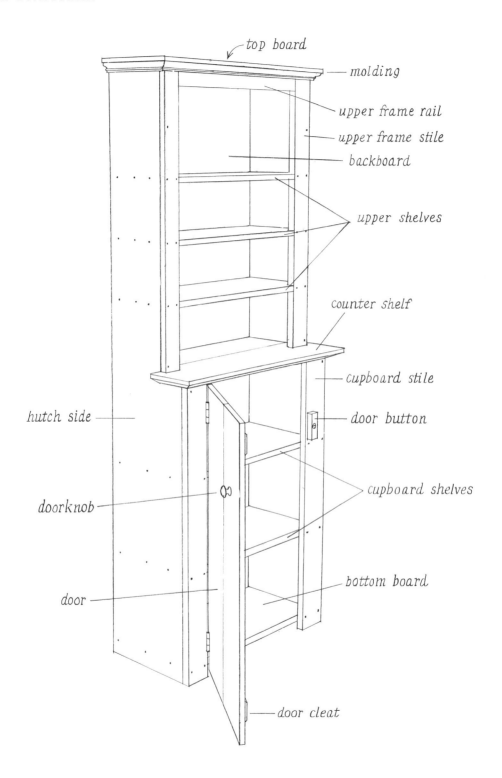

top board

molding

upper frame rail

upper frame stile

backboard

upper shelves

counter shelf

cupboard stile

door button

hutch side

doorknob

cupboard shelves

door

bottom board

door cleat

LUMBER REQUIRED

No. Pcs.	Nominal Dimensions
2	1 × 12 × 12′
1	1 × 10 × 8′
1	5/4 × 8 × 50″
1	1/4 × 2′ × 3′ fir plywood
1	1/4 × 2′ × 6′ hardwood plywood

MATERIALS

No. Pcs.	Part	Dimensions
2	hutch sides	3/4 × 10 1/4 × 70
2	counter shelf cleats	1 × 1 × 9 15/16
1	top board	3/4 × 6 3/16 × 19 1/2
1	bottom board	3/4 × 9 15/16 × 19 1/2
1	construction brace	1/4 × 2′ × 3′ fir plywood
3	upper shelves	3/4 × 7 11/16 × 19 1/2
1	counter shelf	1 × 11 11/16 × 23
2	cupboard shelves	3/4 × 9 15/16 × 19 1/2
1	backboard	1/4 × 2′ × 6′ hardwood plywood
2	upper frame stiles	3/4 × 2 × 35
1	upper frame rail	3/4 × 2 3/4 × 19
2	cupboard stiles	3/4 × 2 1/2 × 34
1	door	3/4 × 15 7/8 × 33 3/8
2	door cleats	3/4 × 2 × 14 3/8
1	doorknob	1″ round hardwood drawer pull
1	door button	5/8 × 3/4 × 2 1/2 hardwood
1	molding	3/4 or 5/8 × 1 1/4 × 6′
2	hinges	2 × 1 3/8 brass butts
quant	nails	8d finish *hutch sides to top and bottom boards*
quant	nails	6d finish *shelves, upper frame, cupboard stiles*
quant	nails	4d finish *molding*
quant	nails	1 1/4 × No. 16 wire nails *backboard*
4	screws	5/8 × No. 4 flathead *upper frame halved joints*
17	screws	1 × No. 7 flathead *door cleats*
1	screw	1 × No. 7 flathead brass *door button*
8	screws	1 1/2 × No. 8 flathead *counter shelf cleats*

New York Hutch

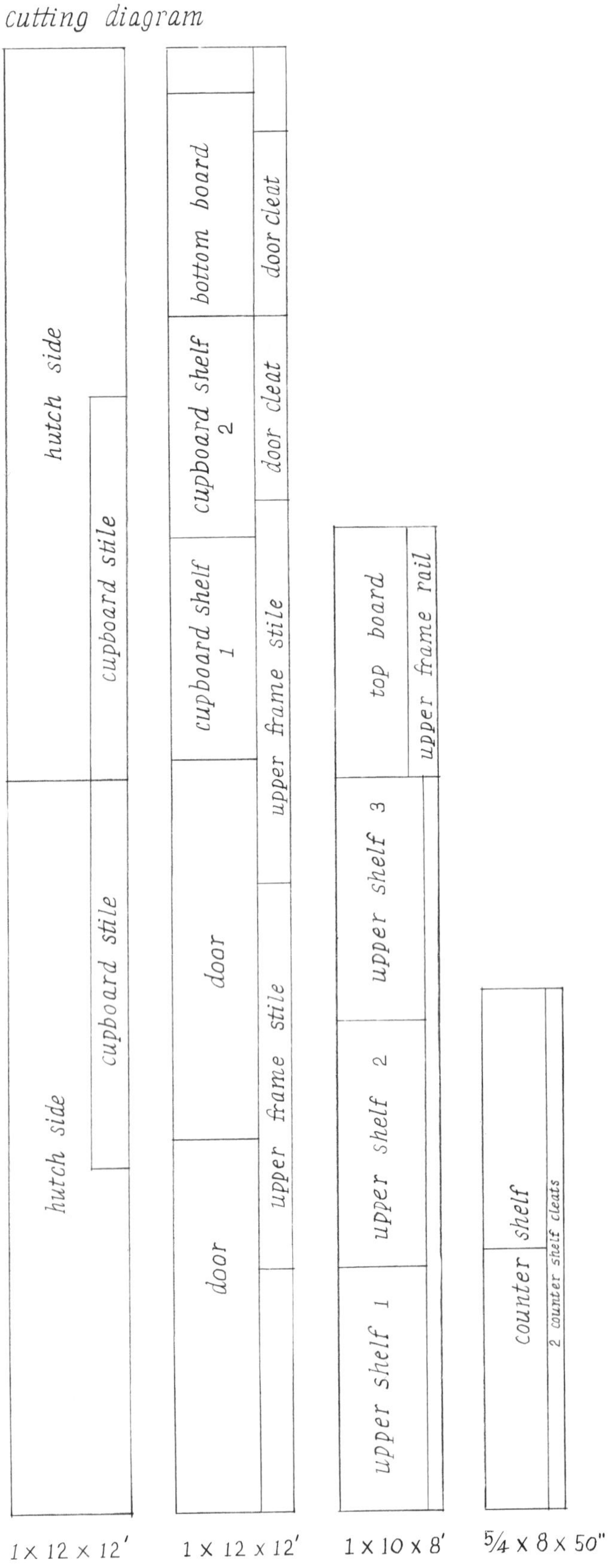
cutting diagram
hutch side
cupboard stile
hutch side
cupboard stile
bottom board
door cleat
cupboard shelf 2
door cleat
cupboard shelf 1
upper frame stile
door
upper frame stile
door
top board
upper frame rail
upper shelf 3
upper shelf 2
upper shelf 1
counter shelf
2 counter shelf cleats
1 × 12 × 12′
1 × 12 × 12′
1 × 10 × 8′
5/4 × 8 × 50″

HUTCH SIDES

Cut the two hutch sides to size and plane their edges and ends smooth and square (see *Woodworking Practices*, p. 28). Then lay out and cut the step-back notches to the dimensions shown, using a ripsaw and crosscut saw. Make the long rip cut first and the 3-inch crosscut last (the notches that the counter shelf rests on). Be careful not to saw *beyond* the inside corner (see *Making Joints*, p. 80). True up and smooth the long edge, using the block plane for most of this work. Then, with the grooving or combination

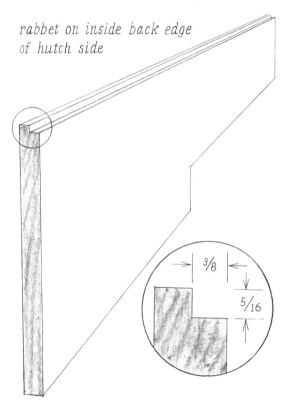

rabbet on inside back edge of hutch side

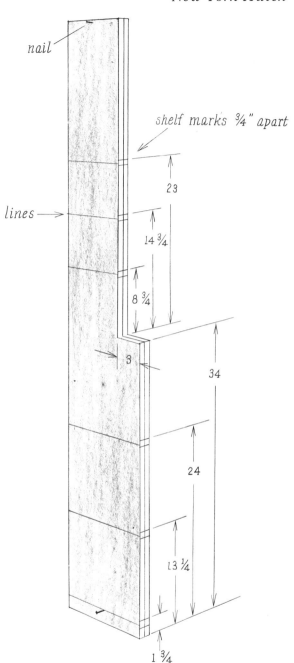

nail

shelf marks ¾" apart

lines →

plane, shoot rabbets along the inside back edges of both hutch sides (see *Making Joints*, p. 83), to the dimensions shown in the illustration. The backboard will fit down into these rabbets.

    Tack the two sides together—face sides out—with temporary nails top and bottom. Then use the try square to mark on their front edges

the positions of the upper shelves, the cupboard shelves, and the bottom board, using the measurements given in the illustration. Make two marks 3/4 inch apart for each shelf. Now use the carpenter's square centered between these shelf marks to draw nailing lines on both hutch sides. Sand the inside surfaces of both hutch

159

sides to final smoothness (see *Sanding*, p. 132).

Cut the counter shelf cleats to size, and drill and countersink the screw holes. Use the square to mark their positions, then clamp them in place—one on each hutch side and flush with the top of the step-back notch. Drive the screws.

TOP AND BOTTOM BOARDS

Cut the top board and the bottom board to size. Take special pains to plane their ends exactly square, as this establishes the width of the hutch.

ASSEMBLING THE HUTCH

Stand the hutch sides on edge as shown, and stand the top and bottom boards between them. The top board should be flush with the top of the hutch, and the bottom board aligned with the shelf marks. The edges of both boards should be flush with the front of the hutch sides and with the rabbet line at the back. Have someone help hold things together. A pair of furniture clamps tightened across the assembly is best, but it can be done with a simple clamp board as shown in the illustration (see *Woodworking Practices*, p. 35). This jig when tightened with a couple of wedges will hold things good and firm. Drill pilot holes about 1 inch in from the edge on the nailing line and drive 8d finish nails from the side into one end of the bottom board and one end of the top board. Then go to the other hutch side, drill pilot holes, and nail their other ends.

The four parts just nailed together will be wobbly and must be made square and held firm before nailing in the shelves. To do this use the 2 x 3′ plywood construction brace, tacking one

nailing top and bottom boards

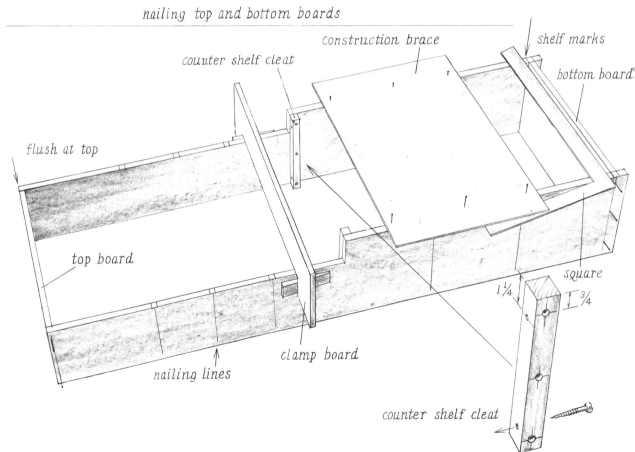

upper shelves : dimensions of notches

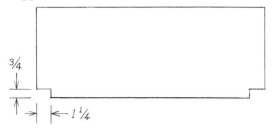

counter shelf : chamfer dimensions

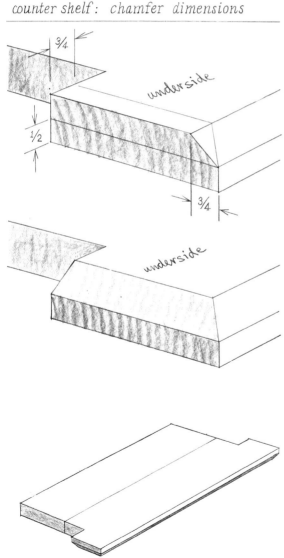

of its edges to the edge of one hutch side. Use three or four 6d finish nails, leaving the heads projecting a bit. Start nails at the other side of the plywood, then hold the carpenter's square across the hutch and in line with the bottom shelf. Get it perfectly square, then drive these nails partway into the edge of the other hutch side. These nail holes will be covered by the stiles.

Cut the three upper shelves to size and carefully cut the notches in their front corners to the dimensions given in the diagram (see *Making Joints*, p. 80). Use the block plane to shave the shelf ends smooth and square to fit between the hutch sides (see *Woodworking Practices*, p. 29). They should be snug and not fall over when they are slid into place.

counter shelf : dimensions of notches

Make the counter shelf using either an edge-butt or a tongue and groove joint to join the boards (see *Making Joints*, p. 46, p. 88). Carefully saw out the notches to the dimensions shown in the diagram (see *Making Joints*, p. 80). Then mark out and plane chamfers on its underside. Chamfer the front edge and the two short sides only. Sand the short sides (end grain) to final smoothness (see *Woodworking Practices*, p. 40). Slide the shelf in place and leave it loose for now.

New York Hutch

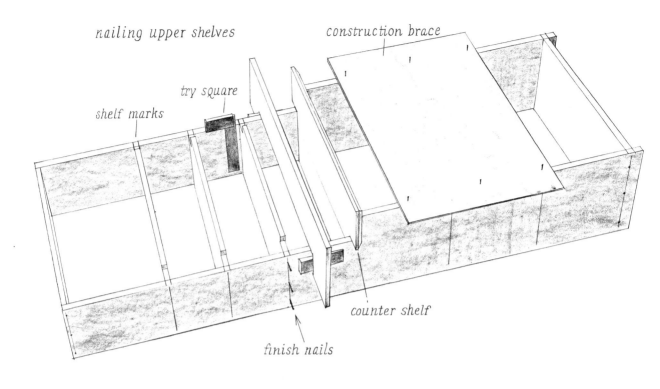

nailing upper shelves

construction brace

try square

shelf marks

finish nails

counter shelf

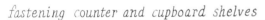

fastening counter and cupboard shelves

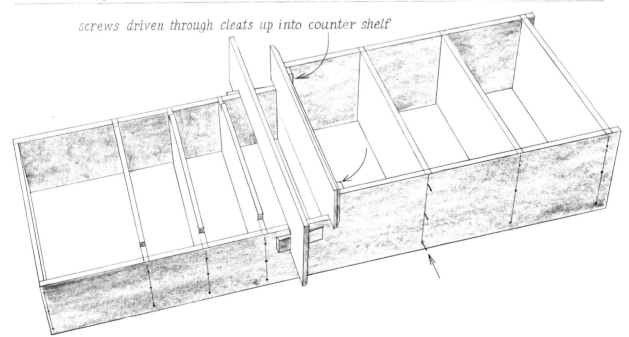

screws driven through cleats up into counter shelf

NAILING IN THE SHELVES

Adjust one of the upper shelves in position *with the notches up*. Tap the ends of the shelf into alignment with the shelf marks, and make sure that the low part of the notches is flush with the front edges of the hutch sides. Use the try square to align it front-to-back. Drill pilot holes and drive a 6d finish nail on the nailing line already drawn, about 1 inch in from the edge of the hutch side. Then go to the other side of the hutch, drill a pilot hole, and drive a nail in the other end of the shelf. Check with the square again, and drive the other nails. Nail the other shelves in the same way.

Tap the wedges of the clamp board again to bring them up tight. Remove the plywood brace, then fasten the counter shelf as follows. Tap the shelf down tight against the edges of the hutch sides and hold it there while you drive

one screw up through each cleat. Then drive the other screws.

Following this, cut the two cupboard shelves to size and nail them in place, using the same procedure as for the upper shelves. When this is done, tack the construction brace back in place, using the same nails in the same holes, and checking to make sure everything is square.

BACKBOARD

The next step is to nail in the backboard. With some help pick up the hutch and turn it over facedown. Leave the construction brace and the clamp board in place, and block the hutch up off the floor on old lumber. Put folded cloth padding over the blocking.

The width of the plywood backboard should be measured from the inside of one rabbet to the other. Measure the width of the hutch at

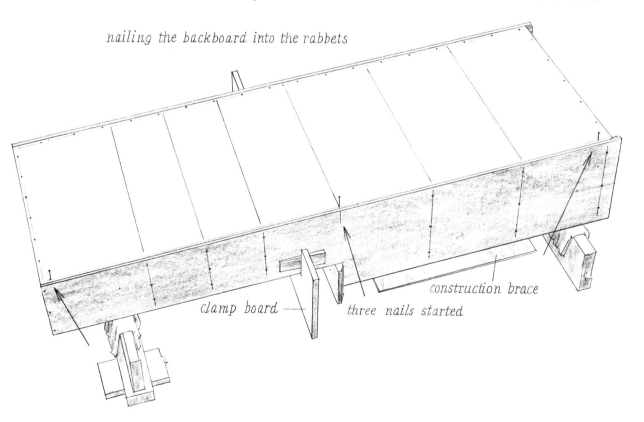

nailing the backboard into the rabbets

clamp board —   *three nails started*   *construction brace*

the top and at the bottom. The measurements should be the same, but if not, use both measurements and tailor the width to fit. The length from top to bottom is measured from the topside of the top board to the underside of the bottom board. Check your measurements again, then cut the plywood—but make it a whisker full in width. Shave the long sides with the block plane until the backboard will just drop into the rabbets. A good fit is important since the backboard acts as a brace to hold the hutch square. Before nailing it in place, sand its inside surface to final smoothness (see *Sanding*, p. 132).

Mark a pencil nailing line along one edge of the backboard 3/16 inch in from the edge. Nail clear along this one side only, spacing the wire nails about 4 inches apart and canting them a bit into the rabbet to prevent their stabbing through on the inside of the hutch.

Mark a similar nailing line along the opposite edge and along the top and bottom. Start a nail near the top, another in the middle, and a third near the bottom. But before driving them check with the carpenter's square at top and bottom. Then drive the 3 nails. Finish driving the rest of the nails.

To nail the backboard to the shelves lay the long arm of the square across the backboard and use it as a straightedge to draw nailing lines corresponding to those on the hutch sides. Then drive wire nails into the edge of each shelf spaced 4 inches apart on these nailing lines. This completes and stiffens the basic carcass of the hutch. Stand it upright and remove the clamp board and construction brace.

UPPER FRAME

The upper frame is made as a separate unit which is then nailed to the face of the hutch. Cut the stiles and rail to size, then lay out and work the halved joints (see *Making Joints*, p. 62), using the dimensions in the illustration. Drill and countersink the screw holes in the rail. To assemble the parts lay them facedown on the workbench or a piece of plywood, and have ready

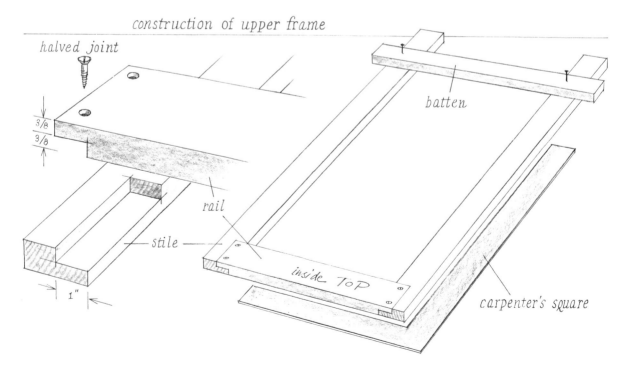

construction of upper frame

halved joint

batten

3/8
3/8

rail

stile

inside top

1"

carpenter's square

a 2-foot strip of wood to use as a batten. Wipe glue on both halves of the joints. When the glue is tacky press the joints together and drive one screw into each. Tack the batten in place after checking to get the bottom width across the stiles the same as at the top. Use the carpenter's square to check both top corners of the frame, and then drive the other screws. Wipe off any excess glue with a damp sponge. Leave the work undisturbed for the glue to dry.

Turn the upper frame faceup and draw nailing lines 3/8 inch from the outside edges of both stiles and the rail. Lay the hutch on its back. Without racking the halved corner joints, pick up the upper frame and lay it faceup on the hutch. Push the frame down so that the ends of the stiles are tight against the counter shelf. Make sure the frame is flush with the sides of the hutch at the top, then drive a temporary nail into the top board to hold the alignment. Lay the clamp board across the hutch and tap the wedge up to squeeze both stiles into the shelf notches. Use the try square to draw nailing lines across the stiles centered on the shelves. Drill a

pilot hole and drive a 6d finish nail in each stile in line with the lowest shelf. Drive the temporary nail and drill pilot holes and drive the rest of the nails as shown in the illustration.

CUPBOARD STILES

Next, cut the cupboard stiles to size and cut the inlets for the hinges in the left-hand stile (see *Hanging Doors*, p. 123). Lay out a nailing line on the outside edge of each stile, 3/8 inch in from the edge, and drill one pilot hole near the top. Start a 6d finish nail into each hole. Lay one stile in place flush with the side of the hutch. Tap it up tight under the counter shelf, then drive the nail. Use the square to carry nailing lines over from the hutch sides to the face of the stile, centered on the shelves. Again align the stile flush with the hutch side, drill a pilot hole on the nailing line centered on the bottom board, and drive a nail in this hole. Then drill pilot holes and drive the rest of the nails in the locations shown in the illustration. Nail the other stile in place in the same way.

nailing upper frame   *nailing cupboard stiles*

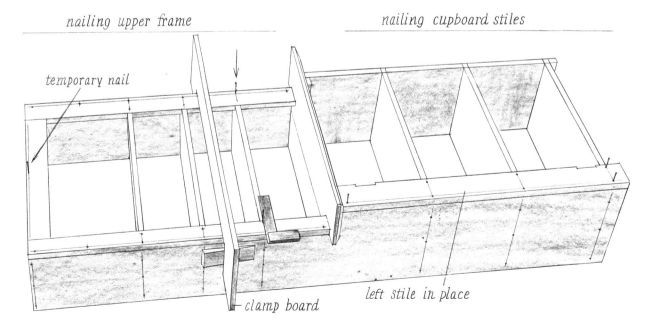

temporary nail

clamp board

left stile in place

DOOR

Make the door, joining the two boards with either an edge-butt or a tongue and groove joint (see *Making Joints*, p. 46, p. 88). Make the door 1/8 inch wider than the opening to allow extra wood for fitting. Then fit the door to the opening and locate and cut the hinge inlets (see *Hanging Doors*, p. 123). Sand the inside surface of the door to final smoothness (see *Sanding*, p. 132).

cleats : chamfer dimensions

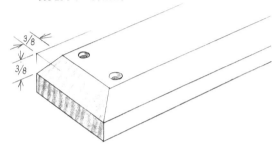

Cut the cleats to size and chamfer their edges as shown. Drill and countersink the screw holes, no closer than 1 inch to their ends or to the glued joint of the door. Then clamp them in place with C-clamps, using the carpenter's square to line them up even with the hinge inlets. Then drive the screws. Hang the door, install the doorknob, and make and attach the door button.

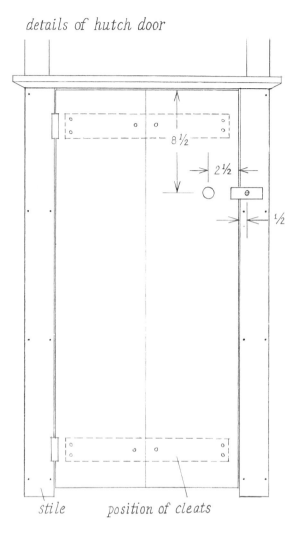

details of hutch door

stile   *position of cleats*

MOLDING

First cut the long front piece of molding, adding 4 inches to its length. Cut a 45-degree angle on one end, then measure the width of the hutch and cut the other end of the molding to 45 degrees (see *Making Joints*, p. 69). Then start 4d finish nails in the groove of the molding, one near each end, and nail it in place flush with the top of the hutch. Drive the nails only partway, in the event you have to remove the molding for fitting. Cut the side pieces of molding 3 inches longer than needed, and after mitering one end of each to 45 degrees, shave them with a 1/2-inch chisel to fit the miters of the front piece already in place. Do not sandpaper these miters, or they will show a crack when the joints are finished. Lay the side moldings in place, mark their lengths at the back of the hutch, and then use the backsaw and miter box to trim them off at a clean 90-degree right angle. Tack the side moldings in place. If the joints need no further chisel-paring, drive the nails all the way, and space other nails about 6 inches apart in the groove of the molding.

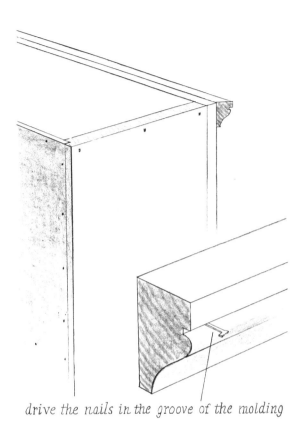

drive the nails in the groove of the molding

Armoire

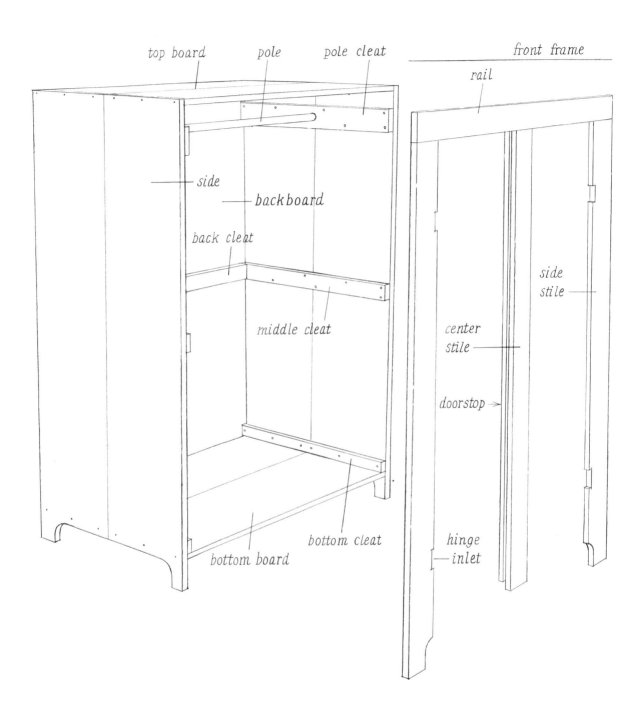

top board   pole   pole cleat   *front frame*

rail

side

backboard

back cleat

middle cleat

side stile

center stile

doorstop →

bottom cleat

hinge inlet

bottom board

LUMBER REQUIRED

No. Pcs.	Nominal Dimensions
2	1 × 12 × 10'
2	1 × 12 × 12'
1	1 × 8 × 10'
1	1 × 8 × 12'
1	1/4 × 3' × 6' hardwood plywood
1	2 1/2 × 8' cove molding
1	1 × 3' hardwood dowel

MATERIALS

No. Pcs.	Part	Dimensions
2	sides	3/4 × 22 3/4 × 55
2	pole cleats	3/4 × 3 × 22 1/2
2	middle cleats	3/4 × 2 × 22 1/2
2	bottom cleats	3/4 × 1 1/2 × 22 1/2
1	top board	3/4 × 22 1/2 × 32 1/2
1	bottom board	3/4 × 22 1/2 × 32 1/2
1	backboard	1/4 × 3' × 6' hardwood plywood
1	back cleat	3/4 × 2 × 31
1	rail	3/4 × 3 × 34
2	side stiles	3/4 × 3 × 53
1	center stile	3/4 × 2 1/2 × 50
1	doorstop	3/4 × 3 1/4 × 51
2	doors	3/4 × 12 5/8 × 48 15/16
4	door cleats	3/4 × 2 × 10 1/2
1	door button	1/2 × 3/4 × 3 1/2
2	doorknobs	1 1/4" round hardwood drawer pulls
1	molding	2 1/2 × 8' cove
4	molding brackets	3/4 × 1 × 8
1	pole	1" round × 32
4	hinges	2 × 1 3/8 brass butts
12	screws	5/8 × No. 5 flathead *back cleat, halved joints*
76	screws	1 × No. 6 flathead *cleats, door cleats, doorstop*
1	screw	1 1/4 × No. 7 flathead brass *door button*
8	screws	1 1/2 × No. 8 flathead *molding brackets*
quant	nails	8d finish
quant	nails	1 1/4 × No. 16 wire *backboard*
quant	nails	4d finish *molding brackets*
quant	nails	2d finish *molding*
2	brads	1 × No. 20 wire *molding*

cutting diagram

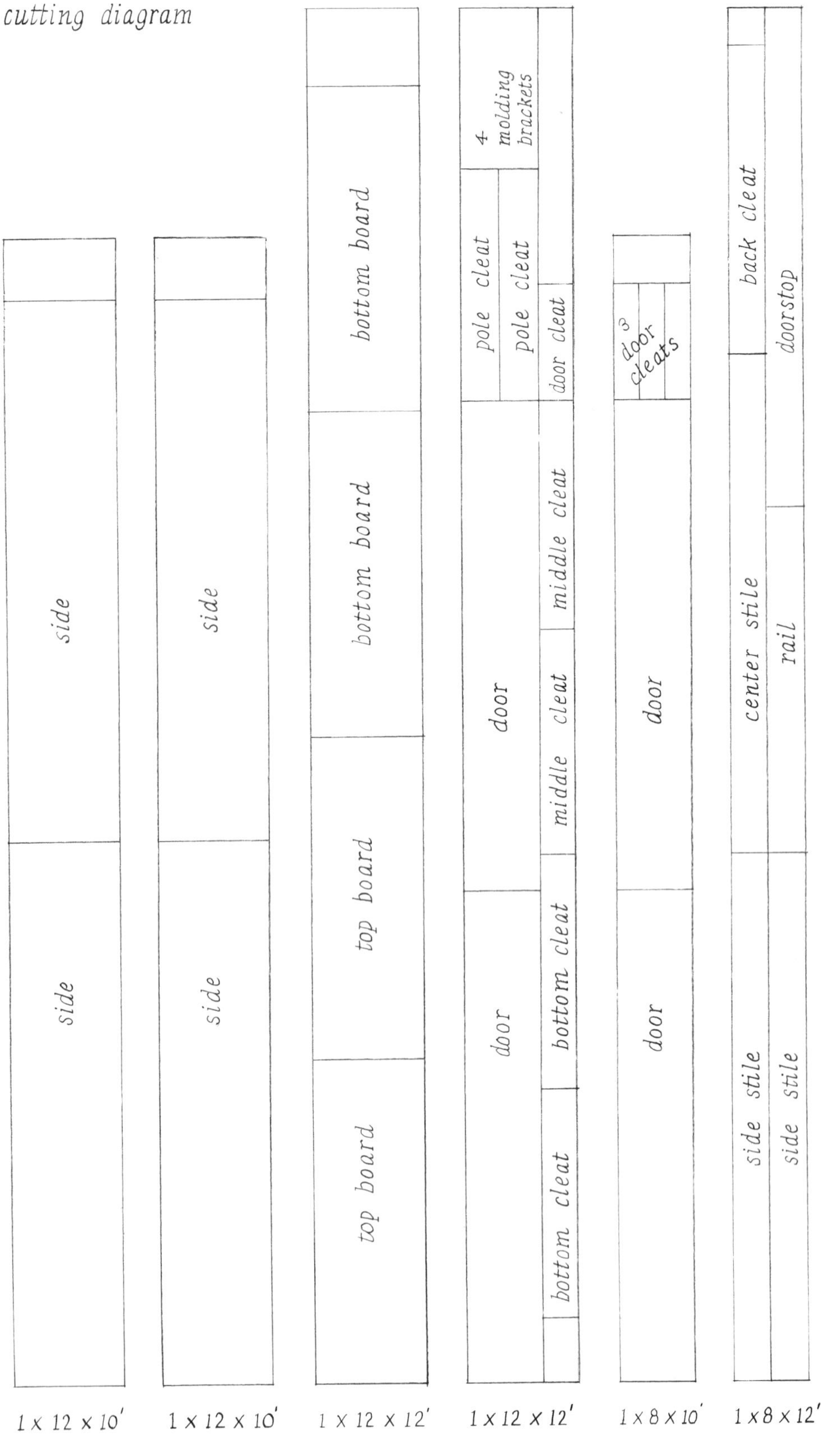

side — side — 1 x 12 x 10'

side — side — 1 x 12 x 10'

bottom board — bottom board — top board — top board — 1 x 12 x 12'

4 molding brackets — pole cleat — pole cleat — door cleat — door — middle cleat — middle cleat — door — bottom cleat — bottom cleat — 1 x 12 x 12'

3 door cleats — door — door — 1 x 8 x 10'

back cleat — doorstop — center stile — rail — side stile — side stile — 1 x 8 x 12'

shooting rabbets in side panels

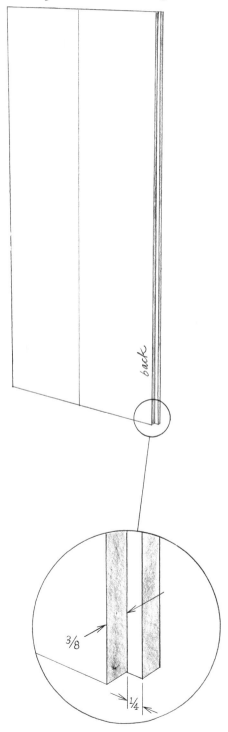

ARMOIRE SIDES

Make up the two side panels using either an edge-butt or a tongue and groove joint to join the boards (see *Making Joints*, p. 46, p. 88). Plane their edges and ends smooth and square (see *Woodworking Practices*, p. 28). Then with the grooving plane or combination plane, shoot rabbets along the inside back edges of both side panels (see *Making Joints*, p. 83), to the dimensions shown in the illustration. The backboard will fit down into these rabbets.

pattern for curved sections of sides

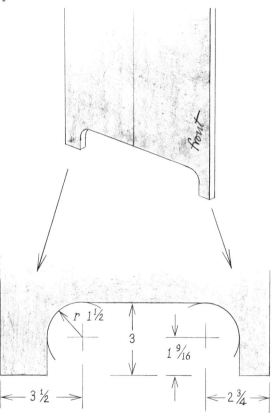

Make a pattern for the curved section of the legs from the diagram (see *Woodworking Practices*, p. 31) and trace it onto the side panels. Cut the curved sections with a coping saw. Sand the inside surface of both side panels to final smoothness (see *Sanding*, p. 132).

Cut the pole, middle, and bottom cleats to size. Bore 1 1/4-inch holes in the centers of the pole cleats, and saw one of them out to form a U-shaped notch. Drill and countersink screw holes in all six cleats, locating them no closer than 1 inch to the ends or to the glued joints of the side panels. Clamp the cleats in position and use the carpenter's square to align them. They should be flush with the front edges of the side panels and come exactly flush with the inside rabbet lines at the back. Drive the screws.

TOP AND BOTTOM BOARDS

Make up the top and bottom boards using either an edge-butt or a tongue and groove joint to join the boards (see *Making Joints*, p. 46, p. 88). Take special care to plane their ends exactly square as these boards establish the width of the armoire. Sand their inside surfaces to final smoothness (see *Sanding*, p. 132).

ASSEMBLING THE ARMOIRE

Stand the side panels on edge with their front edges up, and stand the top and bottom boards between them. The top board should be flush with the top of the armoire, and the bottom board snug against the underside of the bottom cleat. And the edges of both boards should be flush with the front and with the rabbet lines at the back. Have someone help hold things together. A pair of furniture clamps tightened across the assembly is best, but it can be done with a simple clamp board as shown in the illustration (see *Woodworking Practices*, p. 35). This jig when tightened with a couple of wedges will hold things good and firm. Use the carpenter's square to draw nailing lines on both side panels, centered on the top and bottom boards. Then use the square to check the corners. Drill 6 pilot holes and drive 8d finish nails through the side panel into one end of the bottom board. Then

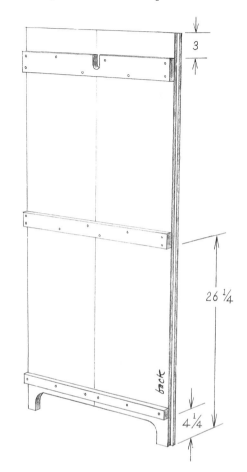

fastening cleats to side panels

drill holes and drive another 6 into one end of the top board. Then go to the other side, see that the top and bottom boards are square with the side panels, then drill pilot holes and nail their other ends. Check with the square again, then drill and countersink 4 screw holes in each end of the bottom board from underneath, and drive the screws up into the cleats. Remove the clamp board. Without racking the corners, carefully turn the armoire facedown in order to put in the backboard.

assembling the armoire

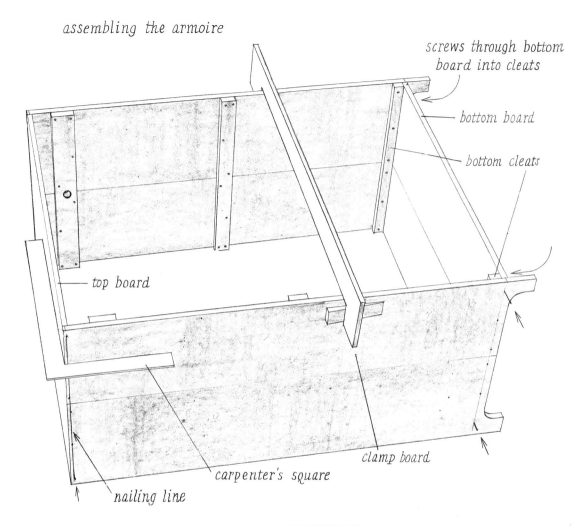

screws through bottom board into cleats

bottom board

bottom cleats

top board

clamp board

carpenter's square

nailing line

BACKBOARD

The width of the plywood backboard should be measured from the inside of one rabbet to the other. Measure the width of the armoire at the top and at the bottom. Both measurements should be the same, but if not, use both measurements and tailor the width to fit. The length from top to bottom is measured from the topside of the top board to the underside of the bottom board. Check the measurements again, then cut the plywood—but cut it a whisker full in width. Shave the long sides with the block plane until the backboard will just drop into the rabbets. A good fit is important as the backboard acts as a brace to hold the armoire square. Before nailing it in place, sand its inside surface to final smoothness (see *Sanding*, p. 132).

Lay the backboard into the rabbets and align its top edge flush with the top of the armoire. Mark a pencil nailing line along one edge of the backboard 3/16 inch in from the edge. Then set the clamp board in place and wedge it tight to hold things in position. Nail clear along this one side only, spacing the wire nails about 4 inches apart and canting them a bit into the rabbet to prevent their stabbing through on the inside. Mark a similar nailing line along the opposite side and along the top and bottom. Start a nail on the opposite edge near the top, another in the middle, and a third near the bottom. Hold the carpenter's square over one top corner of the armoire as shown in the illustration to make sure the backboard aligns flush with the armoire top. Then drive the 3 nails. Drive the rest of the

nails along the side and across the top and bottom edges. Remove the clamp board.

Lay off a pencil line across the center of the backboard to mark the line of screws for fastening the back cleat. Drill and countersink screw holes spaced about 4 inches apart as shown, and stand the armoire on its feet. Cut the back cleat to fit across the inside of the armoire from one middle cleat to the other. Then while someone holds the cleat in position, drive screws from the back side into the cleat.

FRONT FRAME

The four pieces of the front frame are put together as a separate unit which is then nailed to the face of the armoire. Cut the rail first. Its length should be the same as the overall width across the front of the armoire. Lay out and cut the three halved joints in the rail (see *Making*

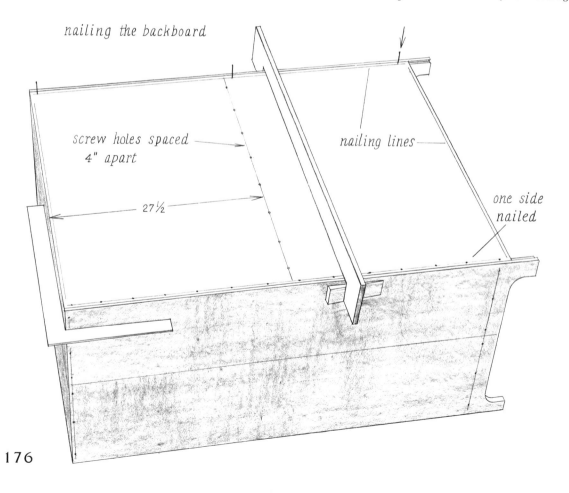

nailing the backboard

screw holes spaced 4" apart

27½

nailing lines

one side nailed

Joints, p. 62), to the dimensions given in the illustration. Then cut the side stiles to size, saw out the curved sections in their bottom ends, using a pattern made from the diagram, and cut the hinge inlets on their inner edges (see *Hanging Doors*, p. 123). Cut the center stile to size, then cut halved joints in the top ends of all three stiles, using the dimensions given in the illustration. Pare and fit the three joints with a 1/2-inch chisel as needed to make the joined surfaces come flush on the outside. Then drill and countersink the screw holes.

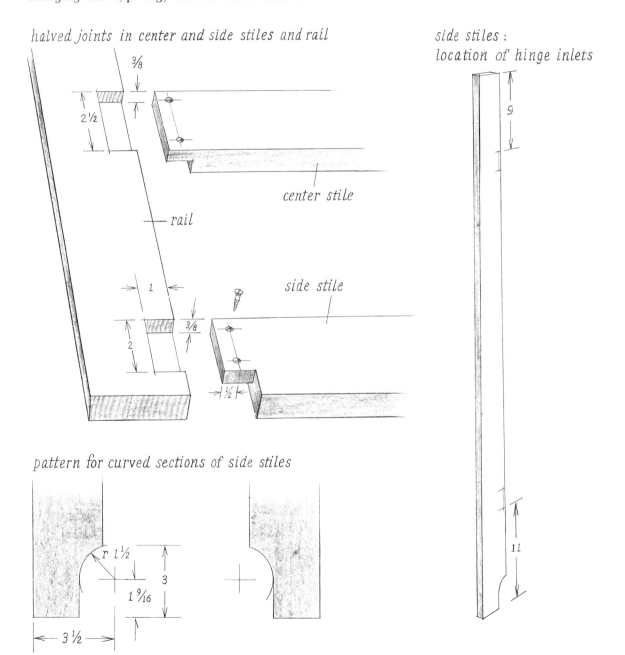

halved joints in center and side stiles and rail

center stile

rail

side stile

pattern for curved sections of side stiles

side stiles: location of hinge inlets

To assemble the frame, lay the four pieces facedown on the workbench or a piece of plywood, and have ready a 3-foot strip of wood to use as a batten. Wipe glue on both halves of all three joints. When the glue is tacky, press the joints tightly together and drive one screw into each joint. Wipe off any excess glue with a damp sponge. Tack the batten in place after checking to get the width across the stiles the same at the bottom as at the top, and to see that both door openings are the same width. Use the carpenter's square to check both top corners of the frame, then drive the other screws in the halved joints. Again wipe off any excess glue. Leave the work undistrubed for the glue to dry.

edges of both side stiles and the rail.

Lay the armoire on its back. Without racking the halved corner joints, pick up the front frame and lay it faceup on the armoire. Align its top with the top of the armoire. Drill 2 pilot holes through the rail and drive 6d finish nails partway into the top board as shown. Leave the bottom ends of the stiles loose in order to glue the sections projecting below the armoire. One at a time, lift each side stile and spread a little glue on both meeting surfaces. Then lay the stile back down and put on a C-clamp, protecting the work with scraps of wood. Check to see that the stile is flush with the side of the armoire, then tighten the clamp. Wipe off any excess glue with a damp

assembling the front frame

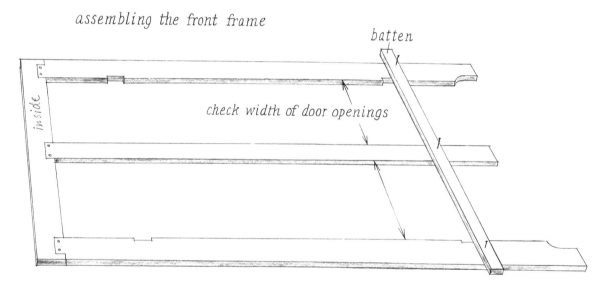

batten

inside

check width of door openings

Meantime, cut the doorstop to size and drill and countersink screw holes in the locations shown in the illustration. When the glued joints of the front frame are thoroughly dry, remove the batten and screw the doorstop to the *inside* of the center stile as shown. Note that the doorstop goes right over the halved joint of the center stile and leaves 1 1/4 inches of its lower end projecting. Turn the front frame faceup and draw nailing lines 3/8 inch in from the outside

sponge and leave the work to dry.

With the clamps still on, drill pilot holes along the edges of the side stiles and the rail, spaced about 9 inches apart. Then drive the rest of the nails. Again measure the width of the door openings. Drill pilot holes and drive 2 nails through the bottom end of the center stile into the edge of the bottom board. Then mark the location of the door button. Remove the clamps and stand the armoire on its feet.

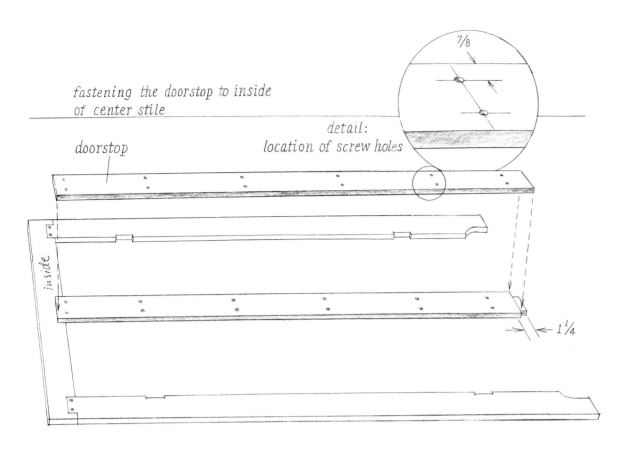

fastening the doorstop to inside
of center stile

doorstop

detail:
location of screw holes

7/8

inside

1 1/4

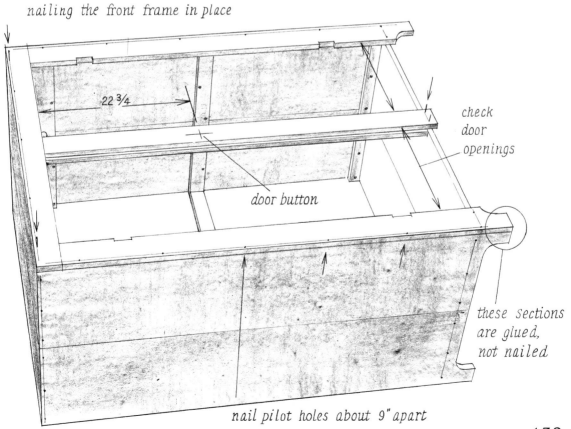

nailing the front frame in place

22 3/4

door button

check
door
openings

these sections
are glued,
not nailed

nail pilot holes about 9" apart

DOORS

Before cutting the door pieces, measure the door openings in the armoire and make each door 1/8 inch wider and longer to allow wood for fitting. Then make up the doors using either an edge-butt or a tongue and groove joint to join the boards (see *Making Joints*, p. 46, p. 88). Next, fit the doors to their individual openings and locate and cut the hinge inlets (see *Hanging Doors*, p. 123). Then sand their inside surfaces to final smoothness (see *Sanding*, p. 132).

Cut the four door cleats to size, chamfer their face edges, and drill and countersink the screw holes. Clamp them in place with C-clamps, using the carpenter's square to position them at right angles to the sides of the doors and lined up even with the hinge inlets. Drive a screw at one end of each cleat, check again with the square, then drive the remaining screws. Remove the clamps.

Hang the doors, again referring to *Hanging Doors*, page 123. Make and attach the door button in the position already marked on the center stile. Adjust the screw so that the button turns easily but still with some friction. Mark the position of the doorknobs, drill holes and fasten them in place.

MOLDING

First cut the long front piece of molding, adding 4 inches to its length. Then cut a 45-degree angle on one end, measure the width of the armoire and cut a similar 45-degree miter on the other end (see *Making Joints*, p. 69). Make the four molding brackets and drill and countersink the screw holes as shown. Attach the brackets to the top of the armoire with 1 1/2-inch screws in the locations shown—two at the front and one at each side.

Draw a light pencil line across the front of the armoire 1 1/2 inches down from the top. Then start 2d finish nails into the lower groove

door details

cleat chamfer dimensions

½ ½ ¼ ¼ ¼ ¼

1

24½

of the long front piece of molding, one near each end, and nail it in place, aligning its bottom edge with the pencil line. Tack the nails in partway, check the alignment again, them drive them flush. Drive a 4d finish nail through the top edge of the molding into the end of each front bracket. Then go back and drive 2d nails along the lower groove of the molding, spaced about 7 inches apart.

Draw similar pencil guidelines across both sides of the armoire. Cut the side pieces of molding 3 inches longer than needed, and after mitering one end of each to 45 degrees, shave them with a 1/2-inch chisel to fit with the miters of the front piece already nailed in place. Do not sandpaper the miters, or the joints will not be clean and sharp. Lay the side pieces of mold-ing in place, mark their lengths at the back of the armoire, and then use the backsaw and miter box to trim them off at a clean 90-degree right angle. Then nail them in place in the same way, and drive a 4d finish nail through the top edge of the molding into the end of each side bracket. Finally, drive a fine, 1-inch brad into each of the mitered corner joints.

POLE

Cut the pole 1/2 inch shorter than the inside width of the armoire and sand it to final smoothness (see *Sanding*, p. 132). Push one end of the pole into the hole in one pole cleat and drop the other end into the U-shaped notch of the other.

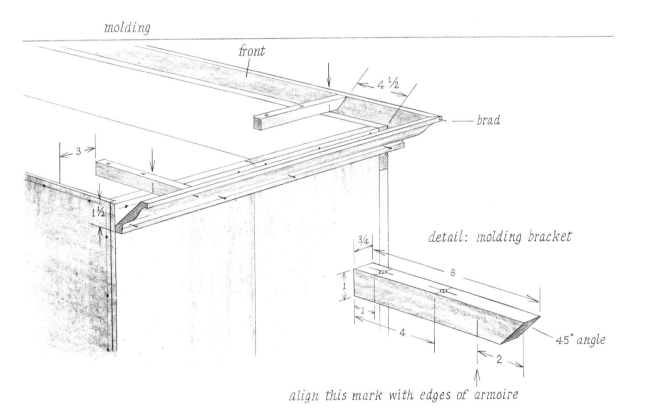

molding

front

4 ½

brad

3

1 ½

detail: molding bracket

3/4

8

1

1

4

45° *angle*

2

align this mark with edges of armoire

Corner Cupboard

HEIGHT 85   WIDTH 25   DEPTH 12¾

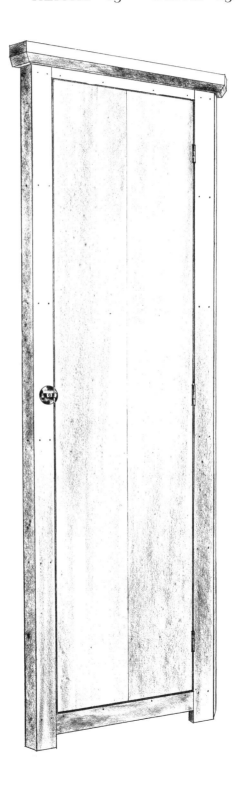

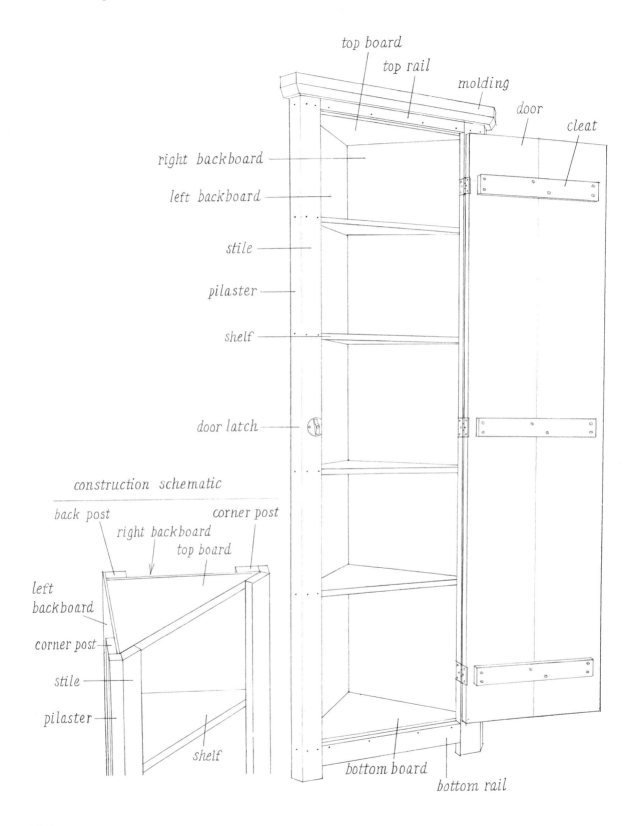

top board

top rail

molding

door

cleat

right backboard

left backboard

stile

pilaster

shelf

door latch

construction schematic

back post

corner post

right backboard

top board

left backboard

corner post

stile

pilaster

shelf

bottom board

bottom rail

LUMBER REQUIRED

No. Pcs.	Nominal Dimensions
3	1 × 12 × 8'
1	1 × 12 × 10'
1	1/4 × 3' × 7' hardwood plywood

MATERIALS

No. Pcs.	Part	Dimensions
1	right backboard	1/4 × 15 1/2 × 77 hardwood plywood
1	left backboard	1/4 × 16 1/2 × 77 hardwood plywood
1	back post	3/4 × 2 × 81 3/8
2	corner posts	3/4 × 2 × 85
1	stub leg	3/4 × 2 × 4 3/8
1	top board	3/4 × 11 × 22
1	bottom board	3/4 × 11 × 22
4	shelves	3/4 × 11 × 22
1	top rail	3/4 × 4 × 18 1/8
1	bottom rail	3/4 × 3 × 18 1/8
1	top cleat	3/4 × 2 × 20
1	bottom cleat	3/4 × 2 × 20
2	stiles	3/4 × 2 1/2 × 85
2	pilasters	3/4 × 1 1/2 × 85
1	molding	3/4 × 2 1/2 × 3'
1	door	3/4 × 18 × 78 1/8
3	door cleats	3/4 × 2 × 15 7/8
1	door latch	1 3/4″ diam brass
18	screws	5/8 × No. 5 flathead *backboards to posts*
10	screws	3/4 × No. 6 flathead *left backboard to back post*
30	screws	1 1/4 × No. 7 flathead *attach stub leg, top and bottom cleats, door cleats*
quant	nails	1 1/4 box *plywood to shelves*
quant	nails	4d finish *molding*
quant	nails	6d finish *fasten rails, stiles, pilasters*
3	hinges	2 × 1 3/8 brass butts

Corner Cupboard

cutting diagram

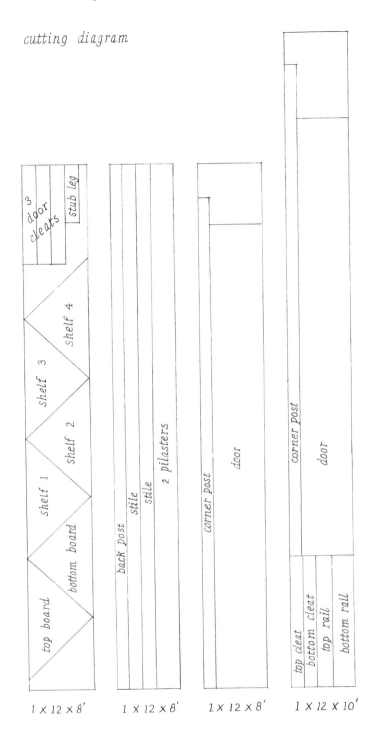

1 × 12 × 8'   1 × 12 × 8'   1 × 12 × 8'   1 × 12 × 10'

backboard panels

back post   corner post

top

top

right panel

← 15 ½ →

16 ½

left panel

front

front

screws driven from
backside into stub leg

4 ³⁄₈

4 ³⁄₈

BACKBOARDS

Cut the two plywood backboards to size and smooth their long edges with the block plane. Sand their inside surfaces to final smoothness (see *Sanding*, p. 132). Next, cut the back post and the two corner posts to size and plane their long edges. These five pieces are made up as two panels as shown in the illustration.

RIGHT AND LEFT PANELS

Start construction with the right panel. Lay the back post and a corner post down flat and place the 15 1/2-inch wide piece of plywood on top of them. Adjust the back post to come flush with the top of the plywood and with its left edge. Leave 4 3/8 inches of back post extending below the plywood. Then drill and countersink holes and drive a screw into the top end of the back post and another at the bottom end, located 1/2 inch in from the ends of the plywood.

Now attach the plywood to the corner post, again leaving 4 3/8 inches of post below the plywood. Then drill and countersink holes and drive screws top and bottom into the corner post, again located 1/2 inch in from the ends of the plywood. Make the stub leg and fasten it in place with glue and 2 screws driven from the back side of the post.

Make up the left panel. Fasten the other corner post flush with the left edge of the 16 1/2-inch wide plywood, and leave 4 3/8 inches of post extending below it. Drill and countersink holes and drive screws top and bottom as before.

Corner Cupboard

Next locate the position of the shelves. Tack the panels together face-to-face and using the try square make pencil marks across the *front edges* of both panels to the dimensions given in the illustration. These marks are used to align the top edges of the shelves when the time comes to nail them in place.

Take the panels apart and use the try square to carry these shelf marks an inch or so over onto the inside faces of both panels. Then drill and countersink screw holes 3/8 inch *under these marks* and 3/4 inch in from the edge. Drive the screws in both panels. They will be concealed when the shelves are in place.

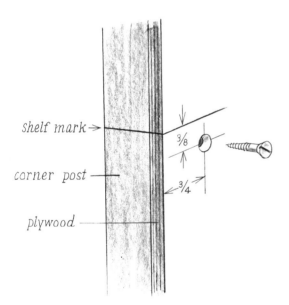

shelf mark →

3/8

corner post —

3/4

plywood —

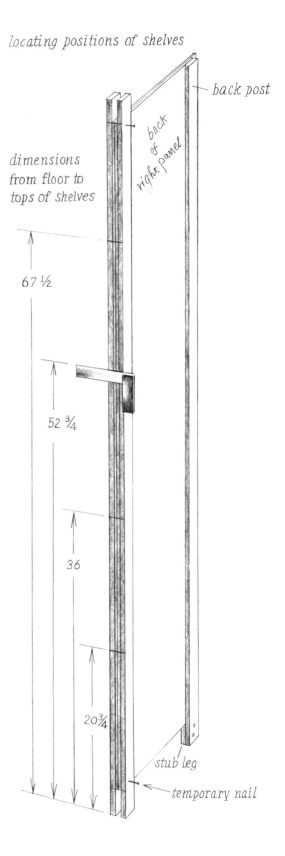

locating positions of shelves

← back post

back of right panel

dimensions from floor to tops of shelves

67 ½

52 ¾

36

20¾

stub leg

← *temporary nail*

drawing lines for nail pilot holes

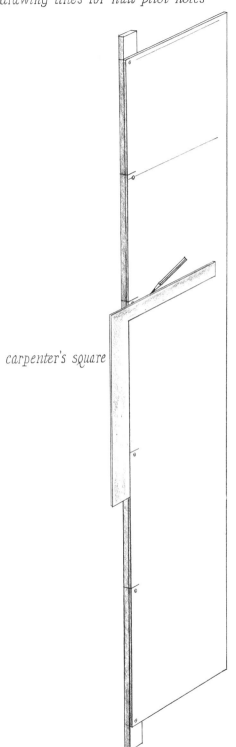

carpenter's square

Next locate and drill pilot holes through the plywood for nailing in the shelves. Start with the left panel. Lay the carpenter's square against its front edge, line it up centered on each screw, and draw pencil lines clear across the inside face of the panel. Using these as center lines, mark off and drill 1/16-inch holes through the plywood, spaced 3 inches apart as shown in the illustration. To drill corresponding holes in the right panel, again tack the panels together face-to-face making sure that they are aligned exactly at the bottom and flush at the front edge. Then, working from the back side of the left panel, drill through the holes already made and through the plywood of the right panel.

*drilling pilot holes
in left panel*

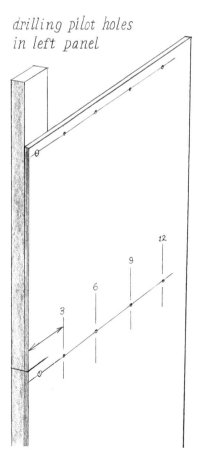

ASSEMBLING THE PANELS

Stand the right-hand panel on edge, back edge up, and lay the left-hand panel on top of it, supported by a pair of deadmen tacked to its front edge as shown in the illustration. Bring the back edges of both panels flush, then drill a 1/16-inch pilot hole and tack a nail through the plywood top and bottom into the edge of the back post to hold things in alignment. Draw a nailing line 3/8 inch in from the back edge. Drill and countersink 5 screw holes through the plywood, and drive the screws. Remove the temporary nails and drive 2 more screws in the same holes. Remove the deadmen.

assembling the panels

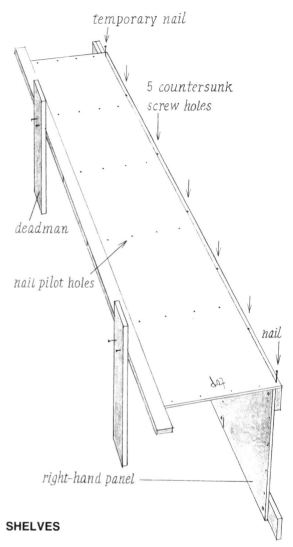

temporary nail

5 countersunk screw holes

deadman

nail pilot holes

nail

right-hand panel

top and bottom boards and four shelves

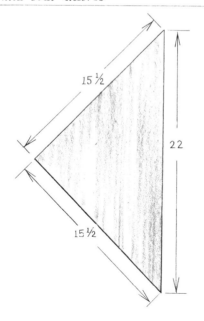

15 ½

22

15 ½

the grain should follow the longest dimension

SHELVES

Cut the top and bottom boards and the four shelves to size, and plane their three sides smooth and square with the block plane. Keep the pointed back corners square. All six of these pieces can be got out of one board 1 x 12 x 8'.

NAILING TOP AND BOTTOM BOARDS

This job is best done with a simple jig made of rough lumber as shown in the illustration. Nail one cleat to the jig and then lay the panels facedown on it. Put a board under the other end of the panels for support. Set the bottom board of the cupboard in position and nail the other cleat to the jig while pressing the panels tight against the bottom board. If necessary, drive a wedge between the cupboard and the cleat to further tighten things. Tap the bottom board flush with

nailing the top and bottom boards in place

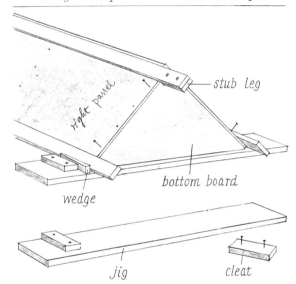

the plywood panels, then tack 3 box nails partway in through the pilot holes already drilled, as shown. Check to see that the bottom board is tight against the stub leg, then drive all the nails. Nail in the top board in the same way, flush with the plywood panels.

NAILING THE SHELVES

Lay the cupboard over on its left panel and start with the lowest shelf. Cut a short cleat and clamp it to the right panel in line with the shelf marks that mark the topside of the shelf. Adjust the cleat until it is square with the edge of the panel, then tighten the clamp. Hold the shelf solidly against the cleat while you drive box nails from the backside through the predrilled pilot holes and into the shelf.

Move the cleat along to the next shelf marks, clamp it in place and nail in the second shelf. Continue in this fashion, nailing one edge of all the shelves. Then tip the cupboard over on its right panel and use the same system to nail the other edges of the shelves. Stand the cupboard upright.

nailing the shelves

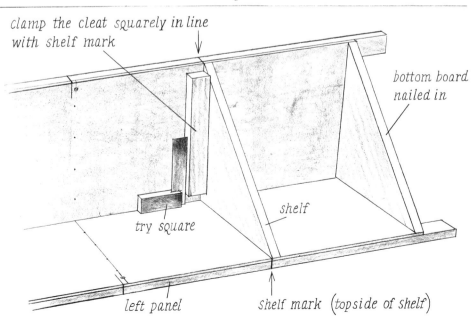

191

RAILS AND CLEATS

Cut the top and bottom rails and cleats to size,
using the backsaw and miter box to make their
ends square and clean. These pieces are made
up as two units, which when nailed to the face
of the cupboard, establish the width of the door
opening and the position of the stiles.

Drill and countersink 5 screw holes in each

nailing rail-and-cleat units in place

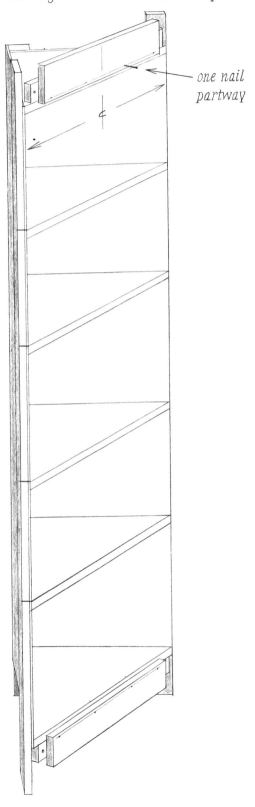

one nail
partway

rail-and-cleat units

back view

½

3/8

2½

rails   cleats

3/8

front view

3/16

top unit

nailing lines

bottom unit

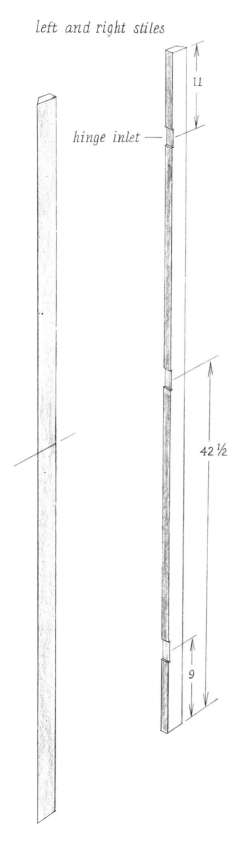

left and right stiles

hinge inlet

11

42 ½

9

cleat. Then clamp them to the rails, centered horizontally and set in 3/8 inch from the edges of the rails as shown in the diagram. Drive screws in the 3 middle holes and remove the clamps. The other 2 screws will be driven into the back of the stiles after they have been nailed in place. Then draw nailing lines on the outside of both rails 3/16 inch in from the edge, and drill pilot holes clear through for 6d finish nails (see *Woodworking Practices,* p. 37).

Fasten these units to the cupboard starting with the top unit. Stand it on top of the cupboard with the rail hanging down over the front edge of the top board. Start a finish nail into one of the holes, then center the rail horizontally. Hold the unit tight against the top board and drive the nail partway in. Check the centering again, then drive the rest of the nails. Center the bottom rail unit up under the bottom board and nail it to the cupboard in the same way.

STILES

Cut the stiles to size and joint their edges (see *Woodworking Practices,* p. 28). Using the dimensions in the illustration, locate and cut the three hinge inlets in the right-hand stile (see *Hanging Doors,* p. 123). Draw a bevel line on the inside face of each stile 5/16 inch in from the outside edge. This gives an angle of approximately 66 1/2 degrees to fit similar bevels on

bevel line on inside face of stile

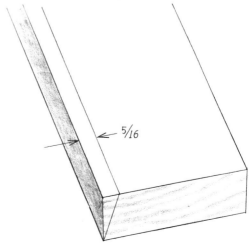

5/16

the pilasters, making a neat joint where they meet on each side of the cupboard. One at a time, tack the stiles against the front edge of the workbench, and use a long plane to cut the bevels. Plane down not quite to the bevel lines, then try the stiles in place. They may need one or two more strokes of the plane to make the inside corner of the bevel just meet the corners of the cupboard. Nail the stiles to the face of the cupboard. Stand one stile in place, resting on the floor and tight against the ends of the top and bottom rails. Have someone hold it there

nailing stiles in place

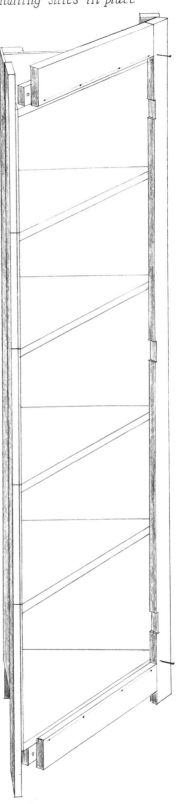

bevel angle for stiles and pilasters

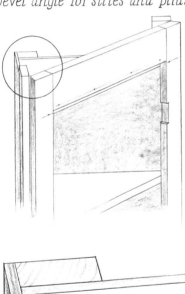

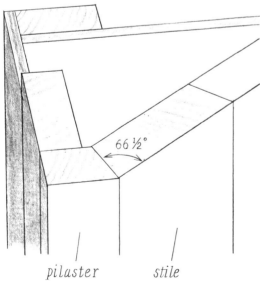

66 ½°

pilaster   stile

194

drawing nailing lines across the stiles

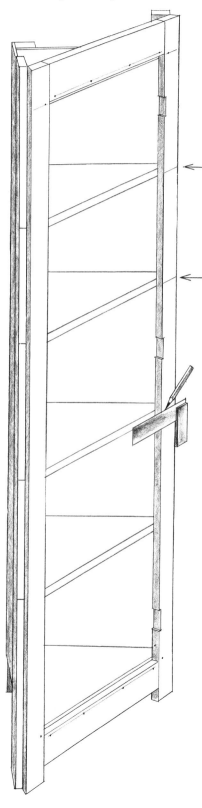

while you drill pilot holes about 1 inch deep through the stile and into the edge of the top and bottom boards as shown. Without moving the stile, drive a nail into each hole. Fasten the other stile in place in the same way.

Before driving any more nails measure across the door opening between stiles, at the top, in the middle, and at the bottom. Check to make sure that the edges of the stiles are straight by tipping the cupboard on its back and squinting along their inside edges. Center the try square on each shelf and draw nailing lines across the stiles. Drill 1-inch deep pilot holes and drive all remaining nails.

Finally, working from the back side of the cupboard, fasten the ends of the top and bottom rail-and-cleat units by driving screws through the holes already drilled.

fastening the ends of rail-and-cleat units

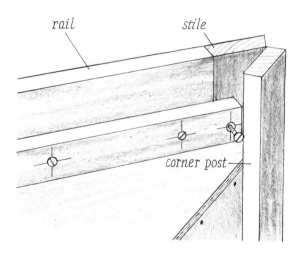

rail   stile

corner post

PILASTERS

As it is impossible to plane the bevels on the narrow pilasters when they are held in the vise, use the following system. Saw out a piece of lumber 3/4 x 3 1/2 x 87″, joint both edges, and draw a center line down its full length. Plane bevels on *both edges* by the same method as used for the stiles. As you plane each bevel, try it in place frequently and fit its angle to match the stile already nailed in place. Mark it "left" or "right" as the case may be to keep track of where it goes. Then rip the board down the center line to make the two pilasters. Leave the rough-sawn edges for now. They are planed off flush with the cupboard sides after they have been nailed in place. Mark and trim them to exact length, using the backsaw and miter box.

Hold each pilaster in place and use the try square to draw nailing lines across its face, aligned with the nails in the stiles. To nail the pilasters in place, spread glue along the beveled edges of both the pilaster and the stile. When the glue is tacky, lay the pilaster in place and squeeze it tight against the stile while you drill pilot holes and drive nails into the corner post at the top and bottom. Then drill a pilot hole and drive a nail on each nailing line, each time pushing the pilaster tight against the stile. Quickly wipe off any excess glue with a damp sponge. Leave the cupboard to dry. Plane the rough, outside edges of the pilasters flush with the sides of the cupboard.

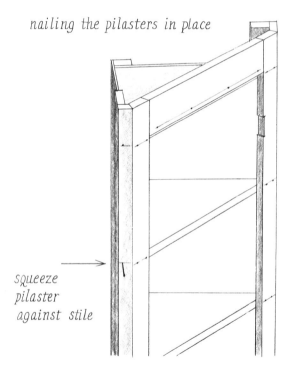

nailing the pilasters in place

squeeze
pilaster
against stile

MOLDING

First cut the long front piece of molding, adding 4 inches to its length. Miter one end to the same angle used for beveling the pilasters. To facilitate this work, make a mitering jig from a scrap of 2 x 6 lumber as shown in the illustration. Use a protractor to set the sliding T-bevel to 66 1/2 degrees, then draw a line across the top edge of the jig. Flop the T-bevel over and draw another line. Set the try square on the top edge of the jig and carry both these lines about 3 inches down over the face side. Put the jig in the vise and use a fine-toothed backsaw (12 pt. or 14 pt.) to cut a slot on each line.

To cut the miters, measure and mark off the correct length of the molding as described in *Making Joints*, page 69. Clamp the molding to the face of the jig, face out, and flush with its top edge. Use the saw in the right-hand slot to cut the first miter. Then reposition the molding and use the other slot to saw the second miter.

Lay off a nailing line along the top edge of the molding, 1 inch from the edge and drill pilot

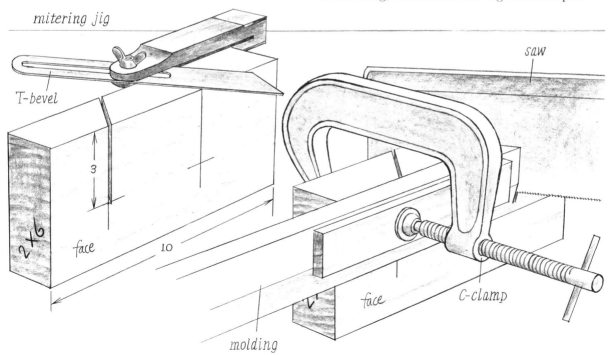

mitering jig

saw

T-bevel

3

2×6

face

10

face

molding

C-clamp

holes clear through, spaced about 4 inches apart. Hold the molding in place, aligned flush with the top of the cupboard and at both ends, and nail it in place.

Cut a 6-inch length of molding for each of the small corner pieces. Miter one end and pare it with a 1/2-inch chisel to fit the miter of the long front molding already nailed in place. Hold it in place against the cupboard and mark its length flush with the back of the cupboard. Then saw it to length, using the backsaw and miter box.

fastening small corner molding pieces

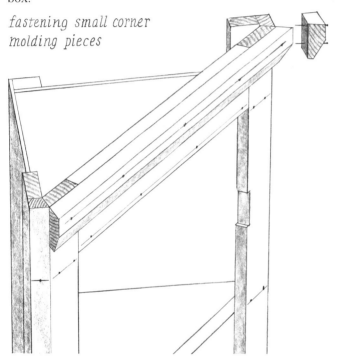

When nailing these corner pieces in place, work carefully as they are likely to split. Drill two 1/16-inch pilot holes in each one. Hold the molding flat on the bench and tap 4d finish nails partway into the holes. Then spread glue on the back side, on the mitered end, and on the miter of the long front molding, as well as on the top end of the pilaster. When the glue is tacky, hold the molding piece firmly in place and gently tap in the nails. Wipe off any excess glue with a damp sponge.

attaching the door cleats

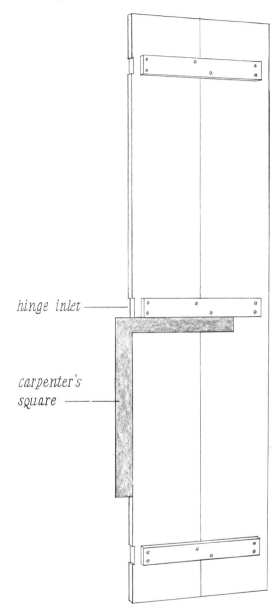

hinge inlet ————

carpenter's
square ————

DOOR

Make up the door from two boards joined with either an edge-butt or a tongue and groove joint (see *Making Joints*, p. 46, p. 88). Make the door 1/8 inch wider than the opening to allow extra wood for fitting. Fit the door to the opening and locate and cut the three hinge inlets (see *Hanging Doors*, p. 123). Sand the inside of the door to final smoothness (see *Sanding*, p. 132).

Cut the door cleats to size and drill and countersink the screw holes no closer than 1 inch to their ends or to the glued joint of the door. Clamp the cleats in place with C-clamps, using the carpenter's square to line them up even with the hinge inlets. Then drive the screws. Hang the door, again referring to page 123.

Install the two-piece door latch lined up with the middle hinge. Lay the button piece of the latch against the stile, set back from the edge about 1/16 inch. Mark its position by drawing inside the screw holes. Then use the awl to punch holes in the centers of these marks. Lay the latch in place again and drive the screws. Attach the striker plate in the same way, set back 1/16 inch from the edge of the door.

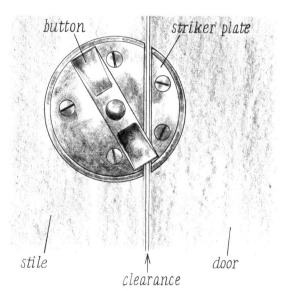

button   striker plate

stile   clearance   door

Slant-back Dresser

HEIGHT 76¼   WIDTH 35   DEPTH 16

Slant-back Dresser

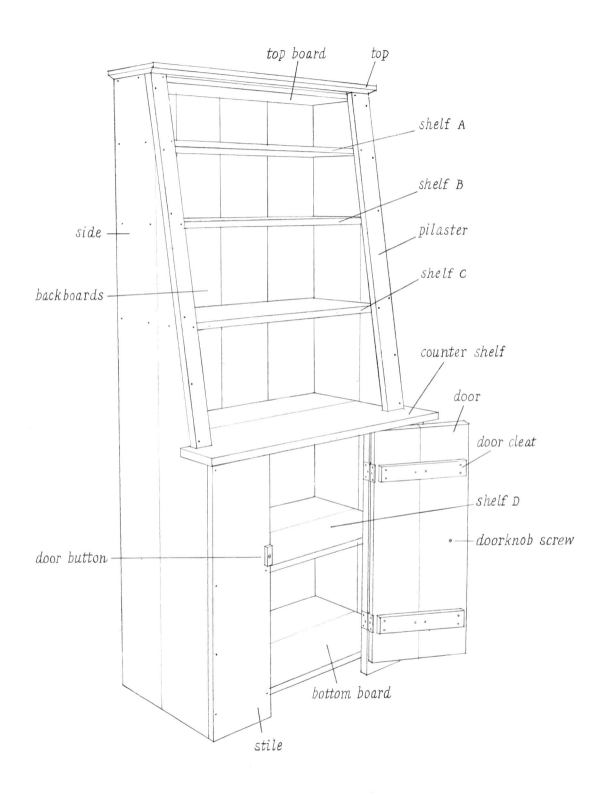

top board

top

shelf A

shelf B

pilaster

shelf C

side

backboards

counter shelf

door

door cleat

shelf D

doorknob screw

door button

bottom board

stile

LUMBER REQUIRED

No. Pcs.	Nominal Dimensions
2	1 × 8 × 12'
1	1 × 10 × 10'
1	1 × 10 × 12'
1	1 × 8 × 12'
1	1 × 12 × 12'
1	5/4 × 10 × 10'
1	1 × 8 × 3'
4	1 × 10 × 8' milled to 1/2″ thick

MATERIALS

No. Pcs.	Part	Dimensions
2	sides	3/4 × 15 1/4 × 75 1/4
2	counter cleats	1 × 1 × 14 3/4
4	shelf cleats	3/4 × 1 1/4 × 14 3/4
1	bottom board	3/4 × 14 3/4 × 31 1/2
1	shelf D	3/4 × 14 3/4 × 31 1/2
1	shelf A	3/4 × 6 3/4 × 32
1	shelf B	3/4 × 8 3/8 × 32
1	shelf C	3/4 × 10 × 32
1	construction brace	1/4 × 2' × 3' fir plywood
1	top board	3/4 × 5 3/4 × 32 1/4
2	stiles	3/4 × 8 1/2 × 31
2	stile cleats	1 × 1 × 5 3/4
1	counter shelf	1 × 16 1/2 × 35
4	backboards	1/2 × 8 1/2 × 73 1/2 *
2	deadmen	1 × 4 × 28 rough lumber
2	pilasters	3/4 × 2 × 45
1	top	1 × 8 × 35
1	door	3/4 × 15 7/8 × 28 3/4
2	door cleats	3/4 × 2 × 14 3/8
1	doorknob	1″ round hardwood drawer pull
1	door button	1/2 × 3/4 × 2 hardwood
12	screws	1 1/4 × No. 6 flathead *door cleats*
19	screws	1 1/4 × No. 7 flathead *counter shelf cleats, shelf D, bottom board, door button*
16	screws	1 1/2 × No. 8 flathead *stile cleats, counter shelf, top to top board*
quant	nails	4d finish *backboards*
quant	nails	6d finish *bottom board, top board, shelf D, stiles, pilasters*
2	hinges	2 × 1 3/8 brass butts

*or 1 pc. 1/4 × 3' × 8' hardwood plywood

cutting diagram

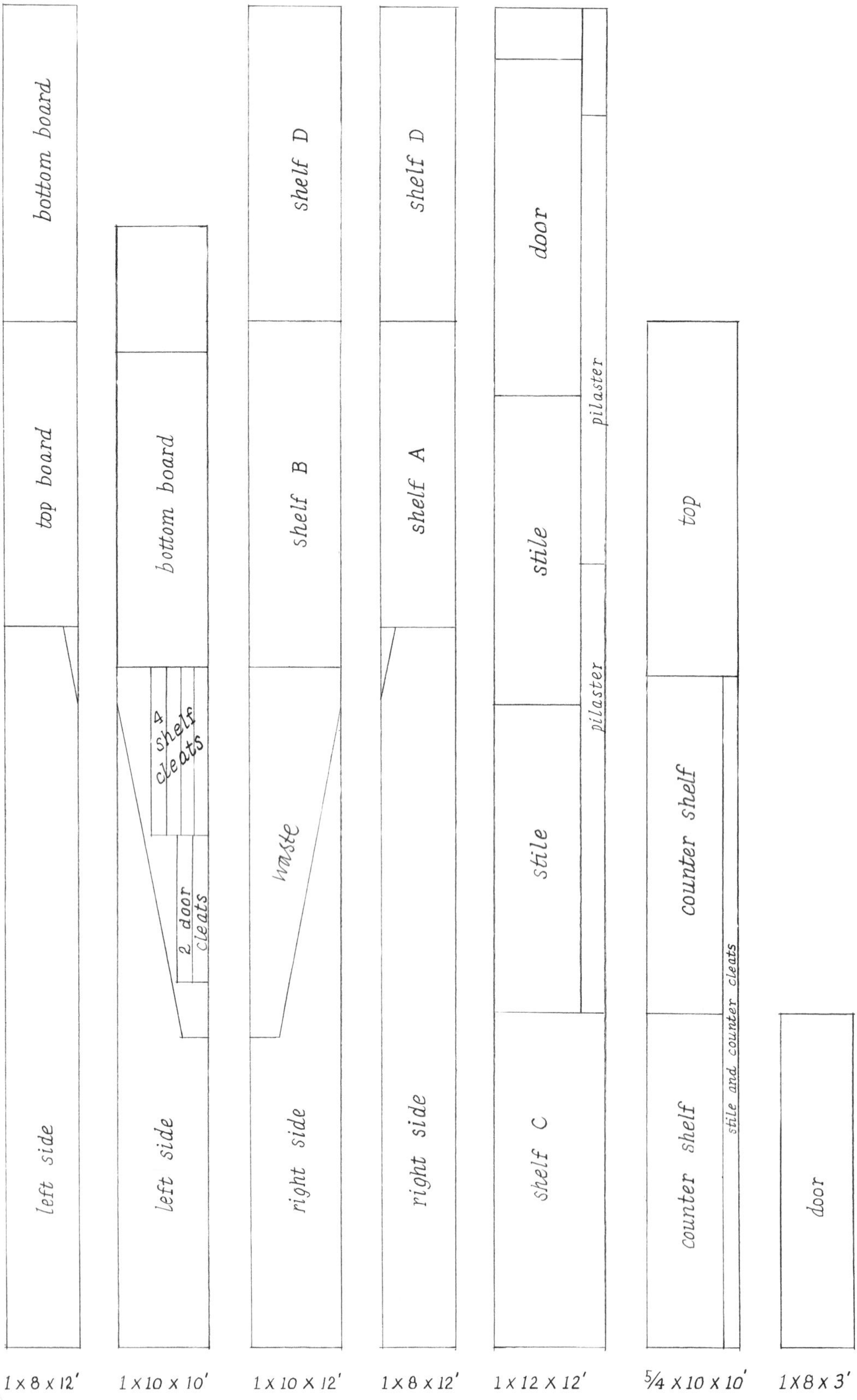

bottom board	bottom board	shelf D	shelf D	door		
top board	shelf B		shelf A	stile	top	
	4 shelf cleats			pilaster		
		waste			counter shelf	
	2 door cleats			stile		
				pilaster		
left side	left side	right side	right side	shelf C	counter shelf	door
					stile and counter cleats	

| 1 x 8 x 12' | 1 x 10 x 10' | 1 x 10 x 12' | 1 x 8 x 12' | 1 x 12 x 12' | 5/4 x 10 x 10' | 1 x 8 x 3' |

204

cutting diagram / backboards

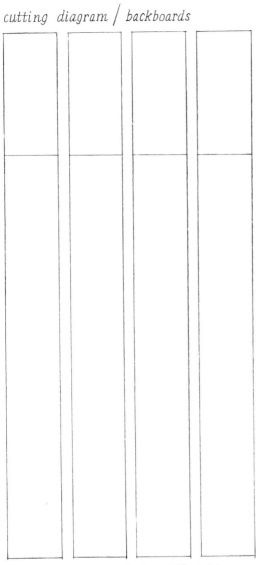

4 pcs 1 x 10 x 8' milled to ½" thick

*diagram for
gluing-up
side sections*

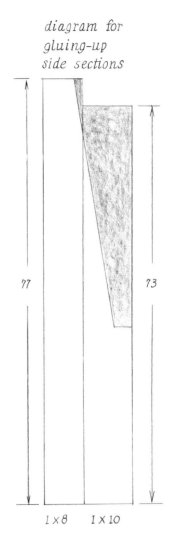

77   73

1 x 8   1 x 10

marking positions of shelves and cleats

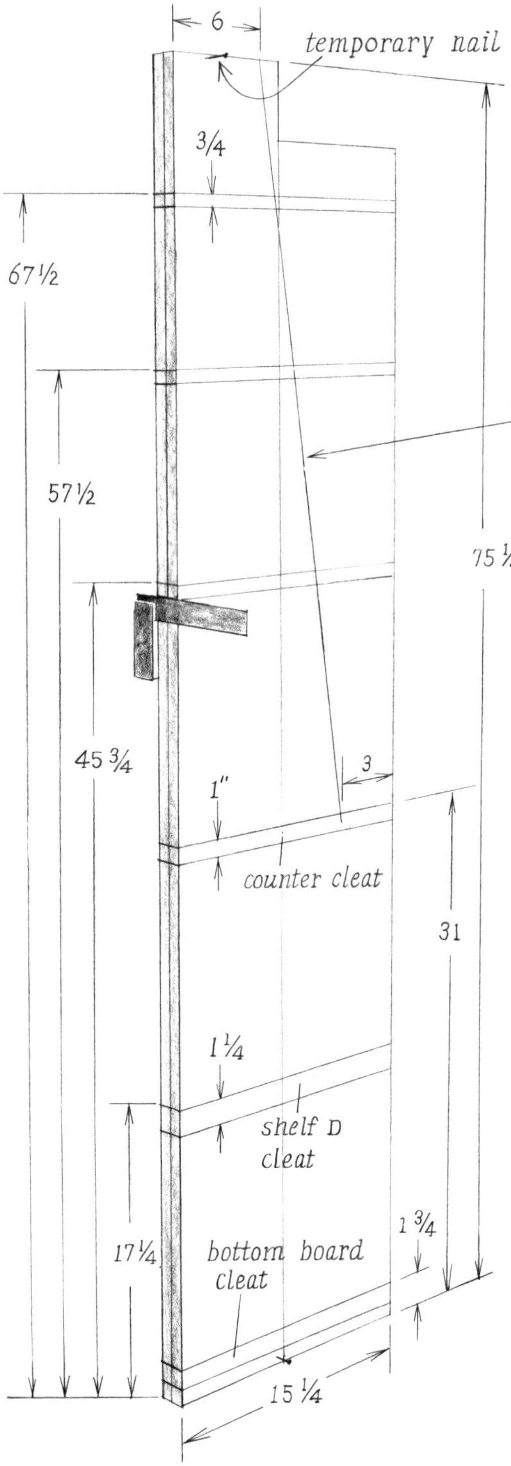

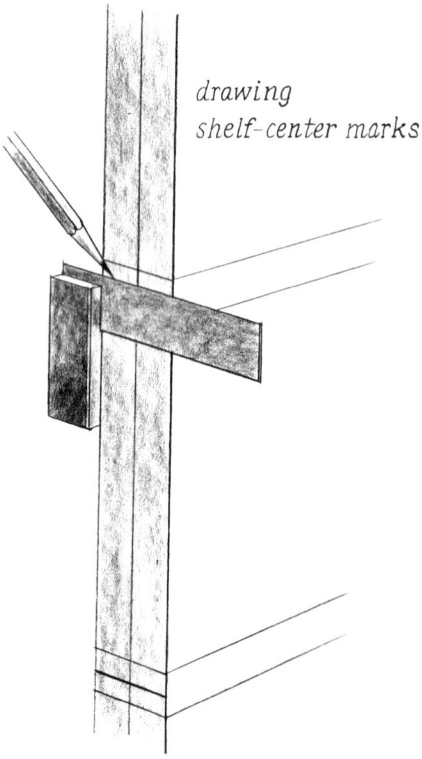

← 6 →

temporary nail

3/4

67 1/2

57 1/2

slant line

75 1/4

45 3/4

3

1"

counter cleat

31

1 1/4

shelf D
cleat

17 1/4

bottom board
cleat

1 3/4

15 1/4

*drawing
shelf-center marks*

DRESSER SIDES

Make up the two sides using either an edge-butt or tongue and groove joint to join the boards (see *Making Joints*, p. 46, p. 88). Plane their edges and ends smooth and square. Use a jack or jointer plane for the edges, and a block plane for the end grain (see *Woodworking Practices*, p. 28, p. 29).

Tack the sides together back to back with temporary nails top and bottom. Then across the back edges mark the positions of the three upper shelves A, B, and C and the cleats for the counter shelf, shelf D, and the bottom board, using the dimensions given in the illustration. Use the carpenter's square to carry these marks over onto the inside faces. These reference lines are used in cutting the housed joints for the three upper shelves, and to attach the cleats for the counter shelf, shelf D, and the bottom board. Use the try square to make center marks between each pair of these lines—on the back edges only. These center marks will be used later for drawing nailing lines when fastening the shelves and backboards in place. Lay off the slant line on both side sections as shown in the illustration.

Remove the temporary nails and take the sides apart. Then use the grooving or combination plane to shoot rabbets along the inside back edges of both side sections (see *Making Joints*, p. 83), to the dimensions given in the illustration. The backboards will fit down into these rabbets.

Cut the slant lines with a ripsaw—a bit wide of the mark—making the long rip cuts first and the 3-inch crosscuts last, to form the notches that the counter shelf rests on (see *Making Joints*, p. 80). Be careful not to saw beyond the inside corner. True up and smooth the slant edges, using the block plane for most of this work, and the chisel to clean out the sharp, inside corner of the notches. Then cut the rabbet across the inside top of each side section into which the top board fits (see *Making Joints*, p. 83).

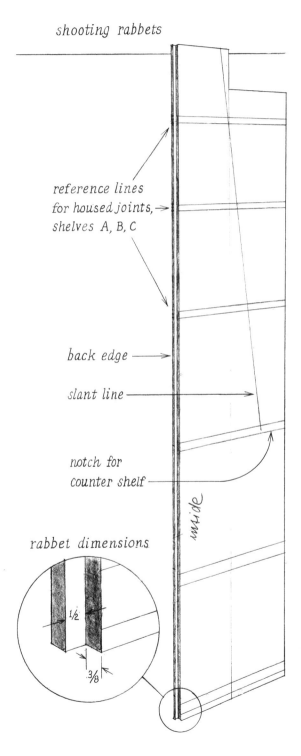

shooting rabbets

reference lines
for housed joints,→
shelves A, B, C

back edge →

slant line

notch for
counter shelf

inside

rabbet dimensions

½

⅜

Then use the backsaw to make pairs of parallel crosscuts for the three housed joints for shelves A, B, and C, and clean out the waste with a 1/2-inch chisel (see *Making Joints*, p. 66).

Cut the two counter cleats and the four shelf cleats (shelf D and bottom board) to size. Drill and countersink 3 screw holes in the shelf D and bottom board cleats, and 5 screw holes in the counter cleats as shown in the illustration. Locate the screw holes no closer than 1 inch to the ends or to the glued joints. Screw the cleats in place. Then lay the carpenter's square on the center marks on the back edges of the side sections and draw nailing lines for shelves A, B, and C across the outside faces of both sides. These nailing lines mark the centers of the housed joints.

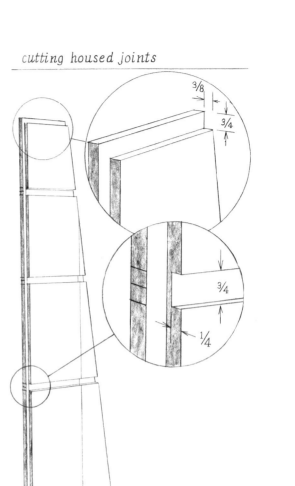

cutting housed joints

3/8

3/4

3/4

1/4

counter cleat

shelf D cleat

bottom board cleat

counter cleat

up into counter

SHELVES

Make up the bottom board and shelf D, using either an edge-butt or tongue and groove joint to join the boards (see *Making Joints*, p. 46, p. 88). Lay off nailing lines across the ends of the bottom board and shelf D, located 3/8 inch in from the edges, as shown in the diagram. Locate and drill pilot holes for all the nails.

Also cut out shelves A, B, and C, making them a bit full in width. This surplus is necessary because the front edges of these shelves are planed off at a bevel to conform to the slant of the dresser, but not until the shelves have been installed. Plane the back edges of all three shelves square and smooth, and plane their ends square and true as well (see *Woodworking Practices*, p. 28).

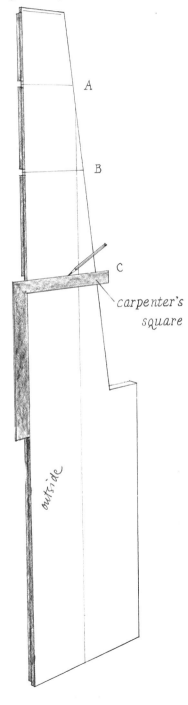

drawing nailing lines

A

B

C

carpenter's square

outside

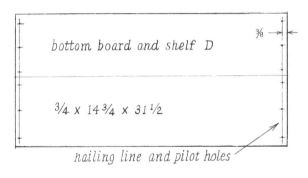

bottom board and shelf D

3/8

¾ x 14¾ x 31½

nailing line and pilot holes

shelf A   ¾ x 6¾ x 32

shelf B   ¾ x 8 3/8 x 32

shelf C   ¾ x 10 x 32

ASSEMBLING THE DRESSER

Lay one side section flat on the floor or a pair of sawhorses, and nail one end of the bottom board to the cleat, using 6d finish nails. Then stand shelves A, B, and C in their housings one at a time to try them for fit. They should be a snug push fit, but if too tight, shave a slight bevel on their under edges—across the grain—with the block plane (see *Making Joints*, p. 66).

The next operation must be done with dispatch before the glue begins to set up, so have everything laid out ready—glue, mallet, and a piece of scrap wood. Wipe glue sparingly *along the edges* of one end of a shelf—not in the housing. Stand the glued end of the shelf in the housing, flush with the inside of the rabbet at

the back. Lay a piece of scrap wood on the free end of the shelf and tap it down into the housing with the mallet. See that it is down tight front and back. Wipe off any excess glue with a damp sponge. Glue and put in the other two shelves in the same way.

Attach the other side section as follows. Glue the upended ends of shelves A, B, and C as before (but not the bottom board). Then pick up the other side section and lay it on top of the upended shelves, starting them into their housings. Be sure that the back edges of the shelves and the bottom board are flush with the inside of the rabbet at the back of the side section. This is important because the backboards lie against the shelves and are nailed to their back edges. Now hold the scrap wood over each

assembling the dresser

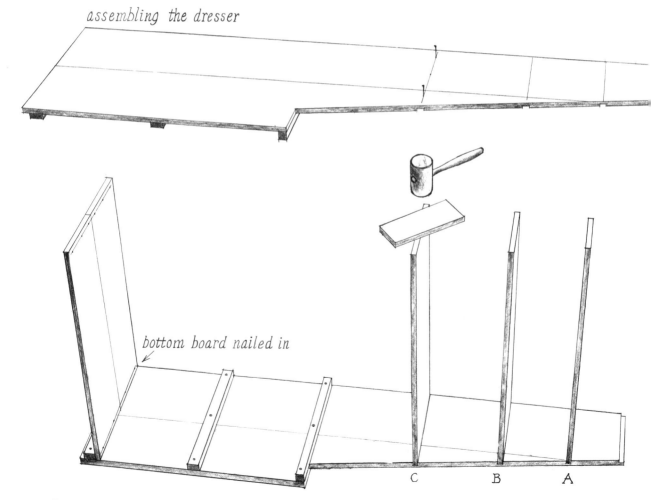

bottom board nailed in

C B A

housing in turn and tap the joints down tight with the mallet. Immediately wipe off any excess glue with a damp sponge.

Working as quickly as possible, lay the dresser on its back and put a pair of clamps across the assembly to maintain end pressure on the shelves. Furniture clamps are best, but it can be done with simple clamp boards as shown in the illustration (see *Woodworking Practices*, p. 35). This jig when tightened with a couple of wedges will hold things good and firm. Now drill 1-inch deep pilot holes on the nailing lines and drive 6d finish nails through the dresser side and into the ends of the shelves—3 nails into shelf C, and 2 each into shelves A and B. Go to the other side of the dresser, drill corresponding pilot holes and drive nails into the other ends of the three shelves.

Then use the carpenter's square to adjust the whole assembly square, and tack the ply-

wood construction brace across the lower section of the dresser, as shown in the illustration. Leave the work to dry overnight.

When the glue is thoroughly dry, remove the construction brace in order to finish nailing in the bottom board. Shift the middle clamp board down to the very bottom of the dresser and wedge it tight to squeeze the dresser side tight against the end of the bottom board. Then drive 6d finish nails through the pilot holes already drilled, into the bottom board cleat.

Cut the top board to size and plane its edges and ends (end grain) smooth and square (see *Woodworking Practices*, p. 29). Drill 2 pilot holes through each side of the dresser on the nailing lines at the very top. Set the top board in place in the rabbets, with its back edge exactly flush with the inside of the rabbets. Then tighten the wedges of the clamp board and drive the 4 nails.

nailing shelves A, B, and C

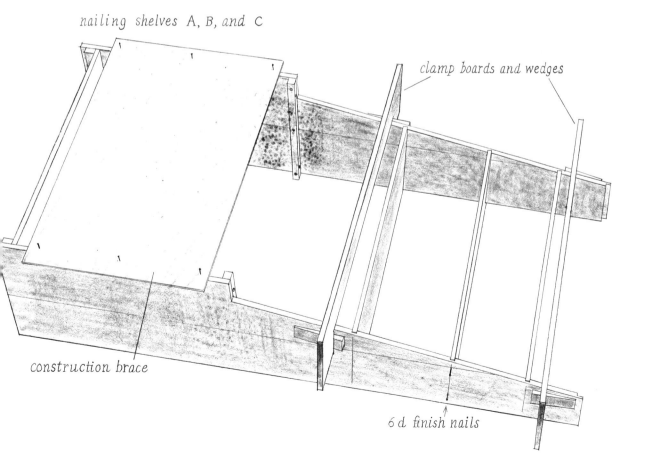

clamp boards and wedges

construction brace

6 d finish nails

STILES AND SHELF D

Cut the stiles to size, and cut the hinge inlets in the right-hand stile (see *Hanging Doors*, p. 123). Lay out nailing lines along the outside edges of both stiles 3/8 inch in from the edge. Drill a single pilot hole on the line, 1 1/2 inches from the top of the stile and clear through. Make up the stile cleats and drill and countersink the

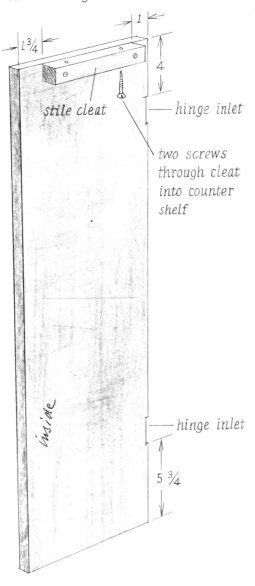

inside of right-hand stile

1

1 3/4

4

stile cleat

— hinge inlet

two screws
through cleat
into counter
shelf

inside

— hinge inlet

5 3/4

screw holes. Then clamp them to the inside of the stiles in the position shown in the illustration—flush at the top—and drive the 2 screws.

Stand shelf D in place resting on the two cleats, and wedge one of the clamp boards across the dresser just below the cleats to hold the shelf firmly. Check to see that the back edge of the shelf comes flush with the inside rabbet line at the back. Then drive 6d finish nails through the pilot holes already drilled at both ends of the shelf. Remove the clamp board.

Next, attach the stiles. As they help to stiffen the dresser and hold it square, take care when nailing them in place. Start a 6d finish nail (nail 1 in the illustration) into the pilot hole of one stile and lay it in place, its long edge flush with the side of the dresser and its top flush with that of the counter cleat. Tack this nail partway in. Use the carpenter's square to make sure the dresser has not shucked out of shape, as shown in the illustration. Use the carpenter's square to draw nailing lines across the face of the stile, centered on shelf D and on the bottom board. Check the alignment again, then drill a 1-inch deep pilot hole for nail 2 and tack this nail partway in. Drill another pilot hole at 3 and drive a nail partway. Then drive these 3 nails home. Check with the carpenter's square again, drill a 1-inch deep pilot hole at 4 and drive the nail. Then drill pilot holes and drive the other 4 nails in the locations shown in the illustration.

Fasten the second stile in the same way, checking to see that the door opening (measured across from stile to stile) is the same top and bottom. If this second stile hangs out past the dresser side a fraction, it can be planed flush later. Stand the dresser upright.

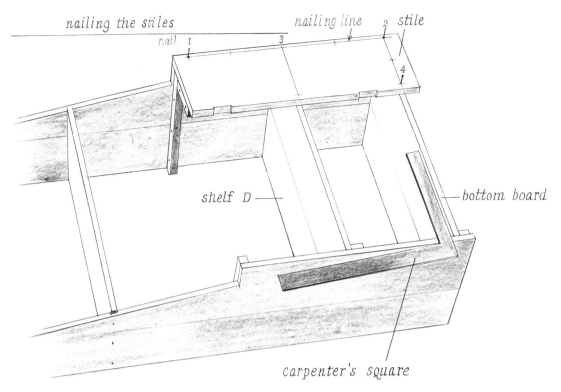

nailing the stiles · nail 1 · 3 · nailing line · 2 · stile · 4

shelf D

bottom board

carpenter's square

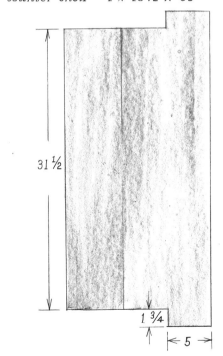

Counter shelf 1 x 16 ½ x 35

31 ½

1 ¾

5

COUNTER SHELF

Make the counter shelf, using either an edge-butt or tongue and groove joint to join the boards (see *Making Joints*, p. 46, p. 88). Then notch out the ends (see *Making Joints*, p. 80) to the dimensions given in the diagram. Sand the short ends (end grain) to final finish (see *Woodworking Practices*, p. 40). Slide the counter shelf in place resting on the counter cleats, and push it tight against the front edges of the dresser sides. Have someone hold it there. Working from the back of the dresser, drive screws up through the counter cleats into the shelf. Drive 2 more up through each stile cleat.

BACKBOARDS

The back of the dresser is covered with several thin boards rabbeted, lapped, and nailed in dry (without glue) to allow for expansion and contraction. Cut the four backboards to size, making the two outside ones (boards 1 and 4) about 1/8 inch full in width. Joint their edges, then shoot all the rabbets at one session after adjusting and testing the plane (see *Making Joints*, p. 83). Note that boards 1 and 4 are rabbeted on the inside edge only. Then number the boards 1, 2, 3, and 4. Sand their inside surfaces to final smoothness (see *Sanding*, p. 132).

Have someone help you turn the dresser facedown in order to nail in the backboards. Support its top end with a pair of deadmen tacked to the top board, and block up the bottom as shown in the illustration. Lay the backboards in place and bring them tight against one another. Together they should be a trifle too wide for the space between rabbets. Plane a bit off the outside edges of 1 and 4 until they lie flat with all the seams tight. Tap their top ends down flush with the top board. Then lay off nailing lines across all the backboards, using the carpenter's square aligned with the shelf center marks already drawn on the back edges of the dresser sides. Also lay off vertical nailing lines 3/16 inch in from the outside edges of boards 1 and 4.

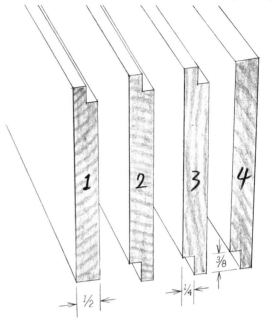

backboards 1 and 4 rabbeted one edge only

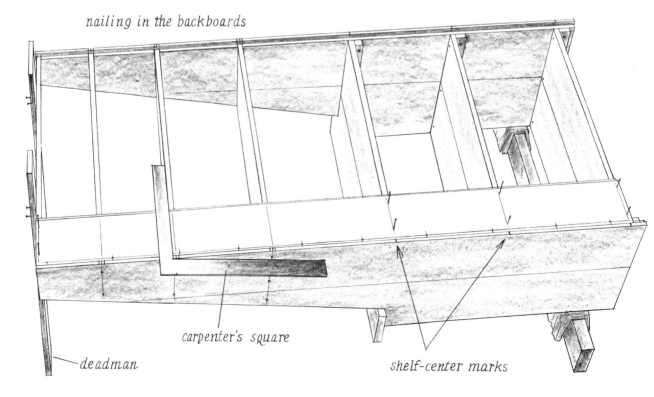

nailing in the backboards

carpenter's square

deadman

shelf-center marks

Lay board 1 in place with the open side of the rabbet up. Drill a 3/4-inch-deep pilot hole on the vertical nailing line about 1 1/2 inches from the top, and another near the bottom. Cant the holes into the rabbet a bit to prevent the nails stabbing through inside. Drive 4d finish nails in these holes. Then drive 8 more nails, spacing them about 7 inches apart along the same nailing line, as shown in the illustration.

Lay the carpenter's square against the side of the dresser and shuck the dresser if neces-

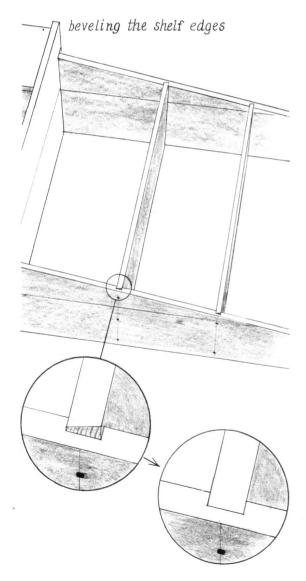

beveling the shelf edges

sary to get a square alignment with one of the shelves. Then drill pilot holes and drive 2 nails (on the horizontal nailing line) into the bottom board, and another 2 into the top board. Drill holes and drive 2 nails into each of the other shelves, staying on the nailing lines.

Lay the next board in place, squeeze the joint tight, and drive nails in the same order—first into the top, then the bottom, and finally into the remaining shelves. Continue in this fashion, nailing in all the other boards. Turn the dresser over on its back and remove the deadmen.

BEVELING THE SHELF EDGES

Use a sharp block plane set for a fine cut to bevel the front edges of shelves A, B, and C flush with the angle of the slanting dresser sides, as shown in the illustration. Plane lightly from the sides toward the middle, taking care not to splinter the wood where the shelves meet the dresser sides.

PILASTERS

Cut the pilasters to size, adding 2 inches to the length for beveling and fitting. First bevel the lower end that rests on the counter shelf. To find the correct angle, hold a scrap of 3/4-inch wood alongside the edge of the pilaster and draw a pencil line, as shown in the illustration. Saw the angle with a backsaw and smooth the cut if necessary with a 1/2-inch chisel. Lay out nailing lines 3/8 inch in from the outside edges of both pilasters, and drill 2 pilot holes clear through—one hole about 1 1/2 inches from the top, and another the same distance from the bottom.

Start a 6d finish nail into each hole. Lay the pilaster in place, flush with the dresser side and the angled end held down tight against the counter shelf. Drive these 2 nails all the way in. Use the try square and pencil to draw light nail-

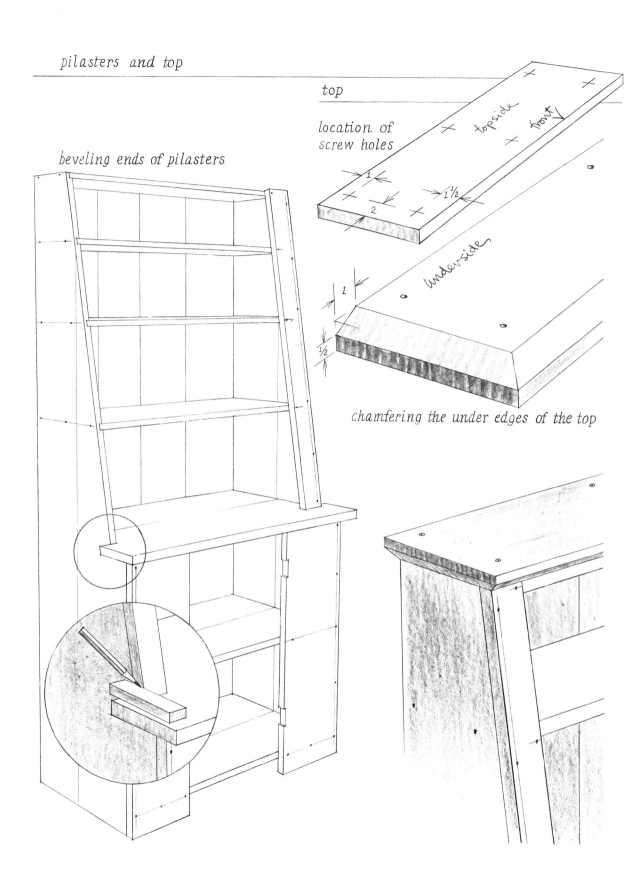

top

*location of
screw holes*

beveling ends of pilasters

chamfering the under edges of the top

ing lines across the face of the pilaster, centered on shelves A, B, and C. Then drill 8 more
1-inch deep pilot holes—one each into the front
edge of the top board and shelves A, B, and C,
and 4 into the edge of the dresser side. Drive
these 8 nails. Fasten the other pilaster in the
same way. Then use the block plane to shave
the top ends of the pilasters flush with the top
board of the dresser.

TOP

Cut the top to size and plane its edges and ends
(end grain) square and smooth (see *Woodworking Practices*, p. 29). Lay off the chamfering lines on its underside—front and sides only—
to the dimensions shown in the illustration. As
the top is flush at the back, there is no chamfer
on the back edge. Use a jack or jointer plane

door, cleats, knob, and button

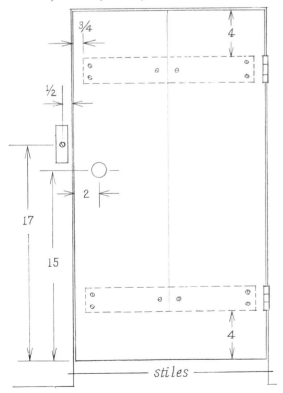

for the long chamfer and a block plane for the
ends. Cut the chamfers just to the layout lines,
then sand them smooth. Drill and countersink
the 6 screw holes from the top side. Lay the
top in place flush along the back of the dresser
and with an equal amount of overhang at the
ends. Drive one screw at each end, check the
alignment again, then drive the rest of the
screws.

DOOR

Measure the width of the door opening and make
the door about 3/16 inch wider than this measurement to allow wood for fitting. Join the
boards with either an edge-butt or tongue and
groove joint (see *Making Joints*, p. 46, p. 88).
Fit the door to the opening and locate and cut
the hinge inlets as described in *Hanging Doors*,
page 123. Then sand the inside surface of the
door to final smoothness (see *Sanding*, p. 132).

Cut the door cleats to size and drill and
countersink the screw holes, locating them no
closer than 3/4 inch to the ends or to the glued
joint. Clamp the cleats to the inside of the door,
using the carpenter's square to line them up
even with the hinge inlets. Drive a screw at one
end of each cleat, check the alignment again
with the square, then drive a screw at the other
end. Remove the clamps and drive the remaining screws. Hang the door, again referring to
Hanging Doors, page 123.

Install the doorknob and make and attach
the door button (see *Hanging Doors*, p. 128).
Adjust the screw of the door button so that it
turns easily without dropping away and allowing the door to pop open.

Pine Dressing Table

HEIGHT 33¼ WIDTH 31¾ DEPTH 15½

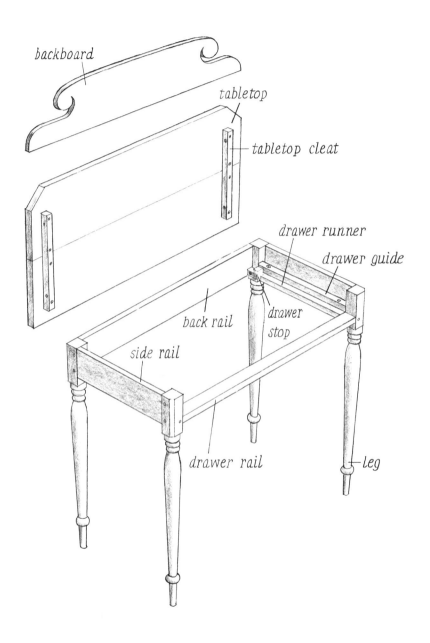

backboard

tabletop

tabletop cleat

drawer runner

drawer guide

back rail

drawer stop

side rail

drawer rail

leg

LUMBER REQUIRED

No. Pcs.	Nominal Dimensions
1	$1 \times 12 \times 10'$
1	$1 \times 10 \times 8'$
1	$9/4 \times 6 \times 6'$
1	$1/4 \times 14 \times 3'$ hardwood plywood
1	$1/4 \times 3'$ hardwood dowel

MATERIALS

No. Pcs.	Part	Dimensions
4	legs	$1\ 7/8 \times 1\ 7/8 \times 26\ 3/4$
1	back rail	$3/4 \times 4\ 1/4 \times 28$
2	side rails	$3/4 \times 4\ 1/4 \times 12\ 1/2$
1	drawer rail	$3/4 \times 1\ 7/8 \times 28$
12	drawbore pins	$1/4 \times 1\ 1/4$ hardwood dowel
2	drawbore pins	$1/4 \times 2$ hardwood dowel *drawer rail*
2	drawer runners	$3/4 \times 1\ 1/2 \times 13$
2	drawer guides	$3/4 \times 3/4 \times 11$
1	drawer front	$3/4 \times 3\ 1/2 \times 26\ 1/2$
1	drawer back	$3/4 \times 3 \times 25\ 1/2$
2	drawer sides	$1/2 \times 3\ 1/2 \times 11\ 3/4$
6	dowel pins	$1/4 \times 1\ 1/2$ hardwood dowel *drawer back joints*
1	drawer bottom	$1/4 \times 11\ 1/2 \times 26$ hardwood plywood
2	drawer pulls	$1\ 1/2''$ round hardwood
2	drawer stops	$3/4 \times 3/4 \times 1\ 1/2$
1	tabletop	$3/4 \times 15 \times 31\ 3/4$
2	tabletop cleats	$3/4 \times 3/4 \times 11$
1	backboard	$1/2 \times 6\ 1/2 \times 31\ 3/4$
2	backboard cleats	$1/2 \times 1\ 1/4 \times 6$
2	screws	$1/2 \times$ No. 4 flathead *front of drawer runners*
12	screws	$1\ 1/4 \times$ No. 6 flathead *back of drawer runners, drawer guides, tabletop cleats*
11	screws	$3/4 \times$ No. 6 flathead *backboard, backboard cleats, drawer stops*
4	screws	$1\ 1/2 \times$ No. 7 flathead *tabletop cleats to side rails*
8	nails	$1 \times$ No. 18 wire *back edge of drawer bottom*

Pine Dressing Table

cutting diagram

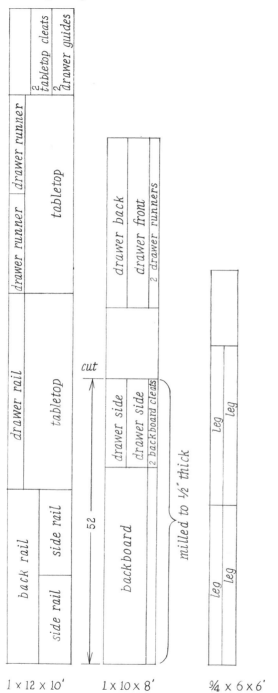

1 × 12 × 10'   1 × 10 × 8'   ¾ × 6 × 6'

location of drawbores / front legs

outside view

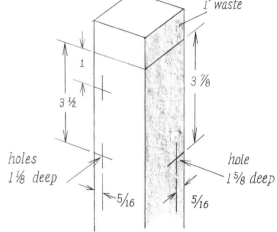

1" waste

1

3 ½

3 ⅞

holes
1 ⅛ deep

hole
1 ⅝ deep

5/16   5/16

TABLE FRAME

Cut the four legs, adding 2 inches to the length for waste. Use a jack or jointer plane to dress all four sides smooth and square. Mark out the centers of the drawbores on the outside faces of all four legs (see *Making Joints*, p. 72), using the square and marking gauge. Then drill 1/4-inch holes for the drawbore pins to the depths given in the illustrations. Lay out and cut the mortises in the front and back legs using the dimensions given in the diagrams.

Cut the back, drawer, and two side rails to size. Then lay out and cut all the tenons, using the dimensions given in the illustration. Make them a bit full in thickness, then shave each one to fit its own mortise. They should be a tight-push fit. As each tenon is fitted, mark it and its mortise with the same letter (see *Woodworking Practices*, p. 33). These reference marks guarantee that each tenon will go where it belongs when the frame is finally assembled. Now locate and drill the drawbores in the tenons. All these procedures are described in *Making Joints*, page 72.

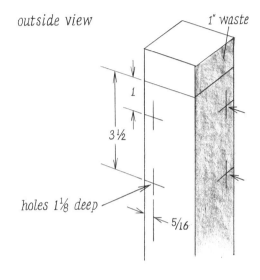

location of drawbores | back legs

outside view

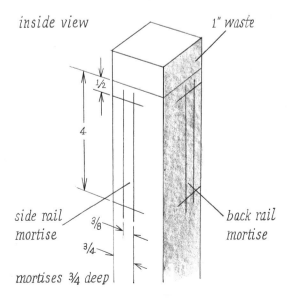

mortise dimensions | back legs

inside view

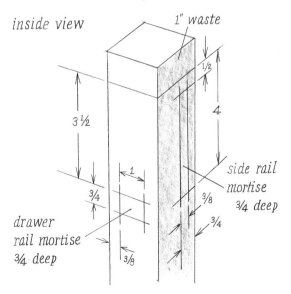

mortise dimensions | front legs

inside view

tenon dimensions for back, side, and drawer rails

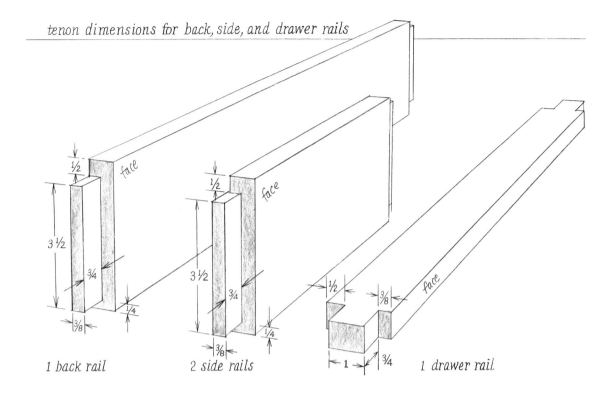

1 back rail   2 side rails   1 drawer rail

halved joints in ends of drawer rail

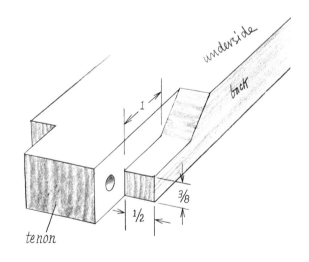

tenon

dimensions for leg pattern

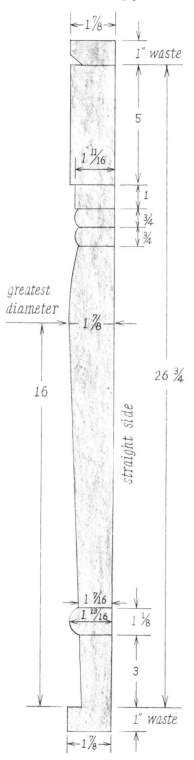

Next, cut the halved joints on the underside of the drawer rail, one at each end (see *Making Joints*, p. 62). The front ends of the drawer runners will be fitted into these joints later.

Lay out and cut a pattern for the leg to the dimensions given in the diagram. Transfer to the pattern all the reference marks. Then follow the directions in *Turned Legs*, page 95, for tracing the pattern and for using the lathebox to round-turn and shape the legs.

Bevel the outside top corners of the front legs as shown in the illustration. Cut off the 1 inch of waste from the tops and bottoms of the legs, using the backsaw and miter box. Cut the drawbore pins and slightly taper their entering ends so they can be driven more easily.

*dimensions for beveling
the outside corners of front legs*

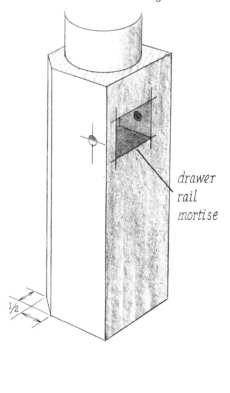

drawer
rail
mortise

ASSEMBLING THE FRAME

First put together the side units, each of which consists of a front and a back leg and a side rail. Lay the back leg on a piece of carpet or an old towel on the workbench to protect the leg turnings. Stand the side rail on end with its tenon starting into the mortise of the leg. Then push it firmly into place to close the joint. Lay the front leg on top of the upended rail and start the mortise and tenon joint together. Then tap the leg down to close the joint.

Lay the side unit flat on the bench and put a clamp across the assembly from leg to leg. A furniture clamp is best, but it can be done with a simple clamp board as shown in the illustration (see *Woodworking Practices*, p. 35). This jig when tightened with a couple of wedges will hold things good and firm. Tap the wedges up tight. Start the tapered ends of 2 drawbore pins into one leg joint and drive them home with the hammer, tapping first one and then the other to draw the joint up evenly. Tighten the clamp board wedge again, then drive the pins into the other leg joint. Trim the projecting drawbore pins flush (see *Making Joints*, p. 79). Then assemble the other side unit in the same way.

assembling the frame

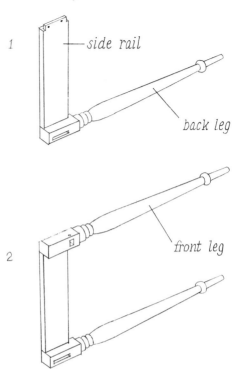

1 —side rail

back leg

2 front leg

3 *driving drawbore pins into the leg joints*

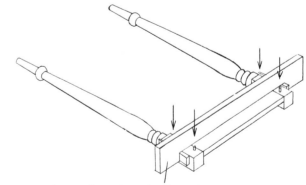

clamp board wedged across side unit

4

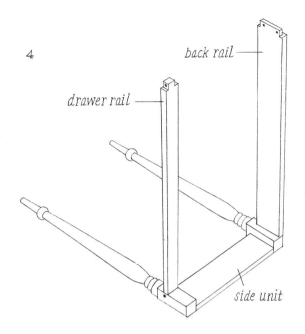

back rail

drawer rail

side unit

The back rail and drawer rail are now joined to the side units. Lay one side unit flat on the bench. Stand the back rail on end, start its tenon into the back leg mortise, then push it firmly in place to close the joint. Push the drawer rail joint together in the same way. Pick up the other side unit and lay it on top of the upended rails, starting both joints together at the same time. Make a fist or use a mallet to tap the legs alternately to close both joints evenly.

5

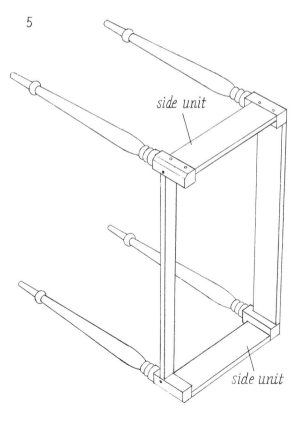

side unit

side unit

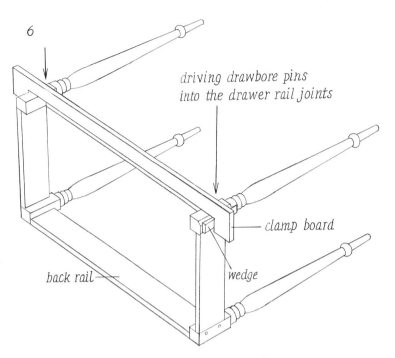

*driving drawbore pins
into the drawer rail joints*

clamp board

back rail

wedge

Lay the table frame on its back, put a clamp board across the front of the assembly and wedge it up tight. Then drive a drawbore pin into each of the drawer rail joints. Trim the drawbore pins flush (see *Making Joints*, p. 79). Remove the clamp board, turn the table frame over on its front, and wedge the clamp board across the back. Then drive 2 drawbore pins into each of the back leg joints, and trim them flush as before. Remove the clamp board.

DRAWER RUNNERS AND GUIDES

Cut the drawer runners to size, cut the halved joints in their front ends, and cut the notches in their back ends (see *Making Joints*, p. 62, p. 80), using the dimensions given in the illustration. Drill and countersink the screw holes. Lay the table bottom-side up and fasten the runners in place with screws front and back. Stand the table on its legs.

Cut the drawer guides to size and drill and countersink the screw holes. Clamp them to the runners, making sure that their inside edges are aligned flush with the inside faces of the front legs. Drive the screws with the clamps in place.

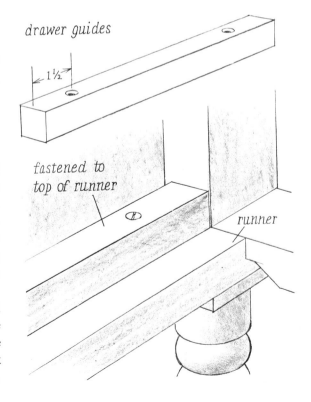

drawer guides

1½

*fastened to
top of runner*

runner

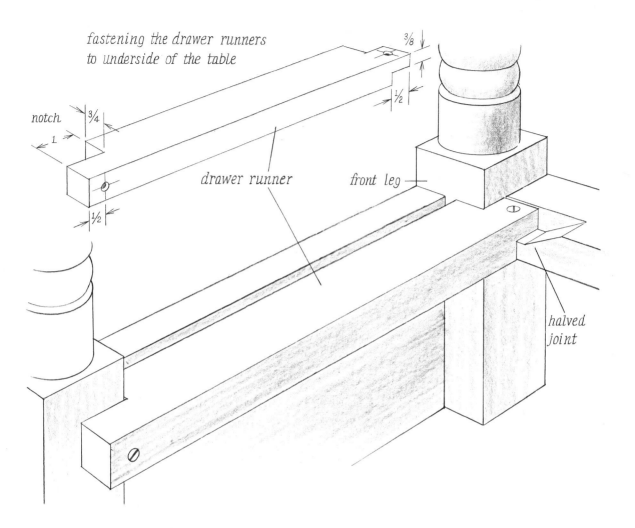

fastening the drawer runners
to underside of the table

³⁄₈

½

notch

¾

1

½

drawer runner

front leg

halved
joint

DRAWER

The drawer is joined with dovetails at the front and dowel pins at the back. Use the dimensions given in the illustrations to lay out the dovetails, the location of the dowel pinhole centers, and the grooves in the drawer front and drawer sides. Then build and fit the drawer according to the procedures in *Making Joints*, page 52, and in *Drawer Construction*, page 112. Note that there is no groove in the drawer back. The bottom is simply nailed to its under edge.

Cut the drawer bottom to fit and sand its inside surface to final smoothness (see *Sanding*, p. 132) before assembling the drawer.

*dimensions for dovetails
and drawer bottom groove*

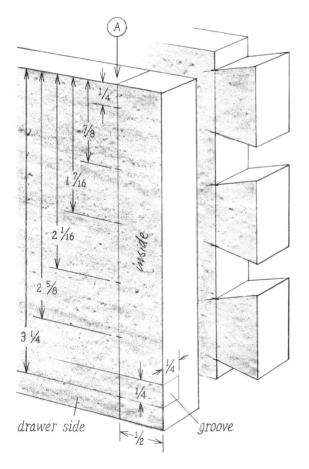

drawer side   *groove*

*back end of drawer side:
location of dowel pinhole centers*

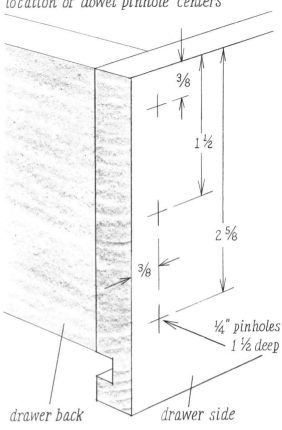

drawer back   *drawer side*

DRAWER PULLS AND STOPS

Lay out the position of the drawer pulls, centered on the drawer front 4 1/2 inches from each side. Drill the screw holes and attach the pulls. Make the drawer stops with the wood grain following the long dimension. Drill and countersink the screw holes in the location shown in the illustration. Push the drawer into place so that its front is exactly flush with the front edge of the drawer rail. Then, without moving the drawer, make pencil marks on the runners at the back of the drawer. Take the drawer out, align the stops with the pencil marks, and screw the stops to the sides of the runners.

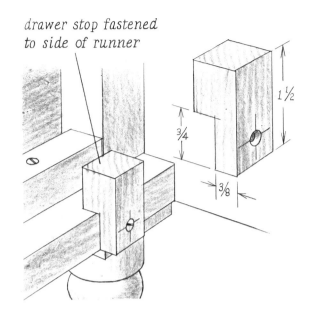

drawer stop fastened
to side of runner

TABLETOP

Make up the top from two boards joined with either an edge-butt or tongue and groove joint (see *Making Joints*, p. 46, p. 88). Cut 45-degree angles on the front corners to the dimensions given in the illustration. Make the tabletop cleats and drill and countersink the screw holes, locating them no closer than 1 inch to the glued joint of the tabletop. Sand the ends of the table-top (end grain) to final smoothness (see *Wood-working Practices*, p. 40, and *Sanding*, p. 132).

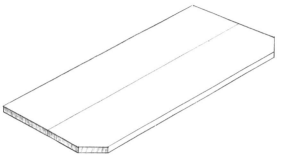

45° *angles on front corners of tabletop*

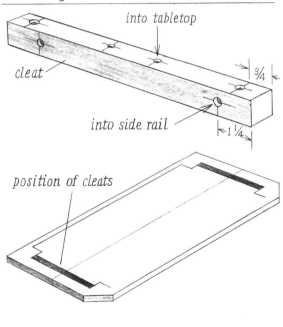

attaching cleats to the tabletop

into tabletop

cleat

into side rail

position of cleats

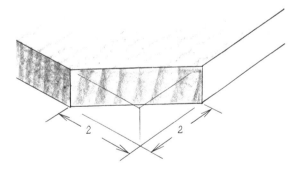

To attach the tabletop to the frame, lay the top facedown on the workbench. Set the table frame bottom-side up on top of it, and adjust its position so that there is a uniform overhang at the front and both ends, and a 1/2-inch gap at the back into which the backboard will be fitted. Then mark the position of the tabletop cleats on the tabletop by drawing a line around the inside of the table frame. Remove the table

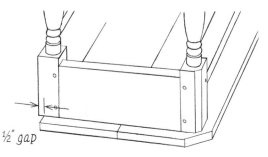

½" gap

231

half-pattern for backboard | 1" squares

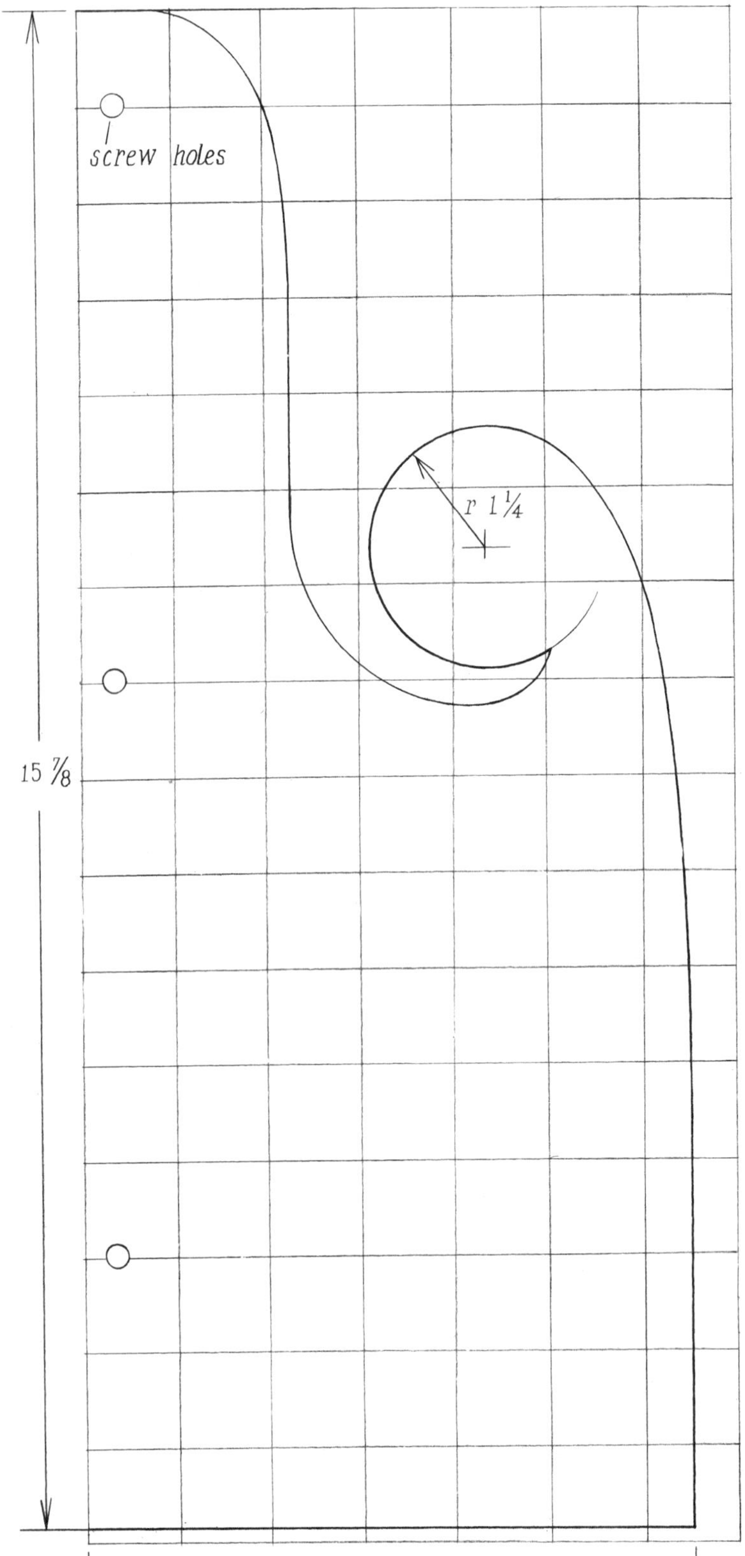

screw holes

$r\ 1\frac{1}{4}$

$15\frac{7}{8}$

$6\frac{1}{2}$

frame, align the cleats inside these marks, and screw them in place. Again, set the table frame bottom-side up, down over the cleats, and drive 2 screws through each cleat into the side rails. Stand the table on its legs.

BACKBOARD

Cut the backboard to size, make the scroll pattern from the diagram, and then trace it onto the work. Cut the scrolls with a coping saw, and smooth and fair up the curves with the file, spokeshave, and sandpaper. Drill and countersink the screw holes in the positions shown on the pattern. Fasten the backboard to the back edge of the tabletop. Make the two backboard cleats and fasten them in place. Put in the drawer.

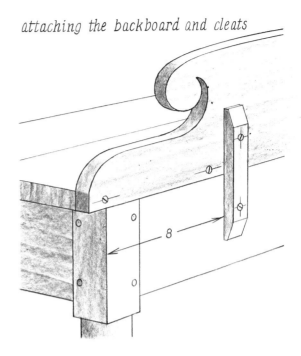

attaching the backboard and cleats

One-drawer Stand

HEIGHT 27⅝   WIDTH 18   DEPTH 16⅞

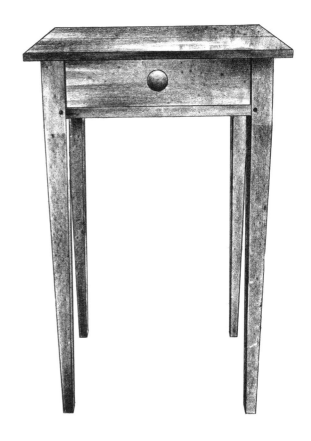

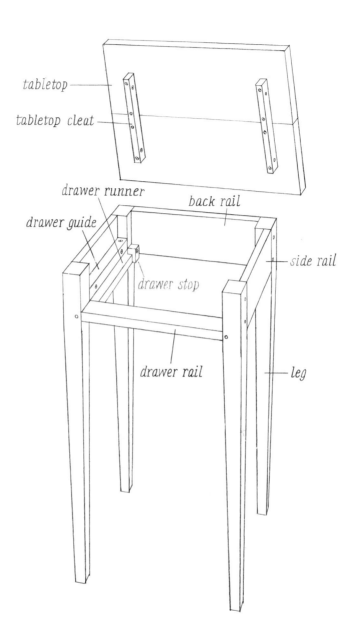

tabletop

tabletop cleat

drawer runner

drawer guide

back rail

drawer stop

side rail

drawer rail

leg

LUMBER REQUIRED

No. Pcs.	Nominal Dimensions
1	$1 \times 6 \times 12'$
1	$5/4 \times 12 \times 4'$
1	$8/4 \times 8 \times 3'$
1	$3/16 \times 3'$ hardwood dowel
1	$1/4 \times 14 \times 14$ hardwood plywood

MATERIALS

No. Pcs.	Part	Dimensions
4	legs	$1\ 1/2 \times 1\ 1/2 \times 26\ 3/4$
1	back rail	$3/4 \times 4 \times 14$
2	side rails	$3/4 \times 4 \times 12\ 7/8$
1	drawer rail	$7/8 \times 1\ 1/2 \times 14$
12	drawbore pins	$3/16 \times 1$ hardwood dowel
2	drawbore pins	$3/16 \times 1\ 5/8$ hardwood dowel *drawer rail*
2	drawer runners	$3/4 \times 1\ 1/2 \times 12\ 1/8$
2	drawer guides	$3/4 \times 3/4 \times 11\ 3/8$
1	drawer front	$3/4 \times 3 \times 12\ 7/16$
4	dowel pins	$3/16 \times 1\ 1/4$ hardwood dowel *drawer back joints*
2	drawer sides	$3/8 \times 3 \times 11\ 1/8$
1	drawer back	$3/8 \times 2\ 1/2 \times 11\ 11/16$
1	drawer bottom	$1/4 \times 12 \times 11$ hardwood plywood
1	drawer pull	$1\ 1/4''$ round hardwood
2	drawer stops	$3/4 \times 1\ 1/4 \times 1\ 1/2$
1	tabletop	$7/8 \times 16\ 7/8 \times 18$
2	tabletop cleats	$3/4 \times 1 \times 11\ 3/8$
14	screws	$1\ 1/4 \times$ No. 7 flathead *drawer guides to runners and side rails, tabletop cleats to side rails, and drawer guides to back legs*
8	screws	$1\ 1/2 \times$ No. 7 flathead *cleats to tabletop*
2	screws	$1 \times$ No. 6 flathead *drawer stops to runners*
quant	nails	$1 \times$ No. 17 wire *bottom board to drawer back*

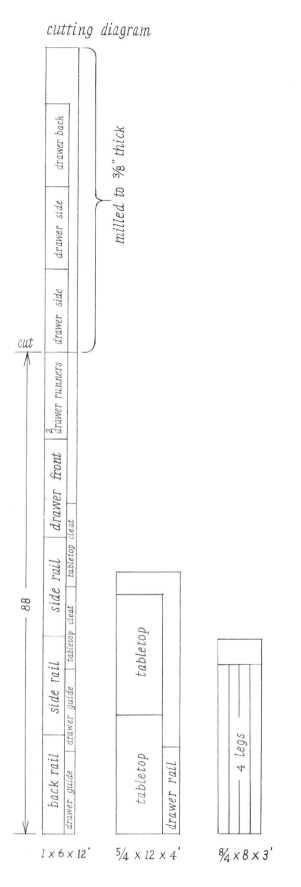

cutting diagram

milled to ⅜" thick

cut

drawer back

drawer side

drawer side

drawer runners 2

drawer front

tabletop cleat

side rail

tabletop cleat

side rail

drawer guide

back rail

drawer guide

88

1 x 6 x 12'

tabletop

tabletop

drawer rail

⁵⁄₄ x 12 x 4'

4 legs

⁸⁄₄ x 8 x 3'

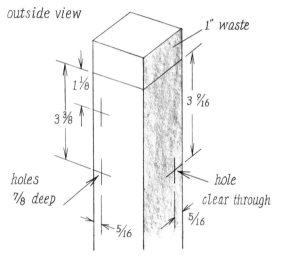

location of drawbores / front legs

outside view

1" waste

1⅛

3 ⁹⁄₁₆

3 ⅜

holes
⅞ deep

hole
clear through

⁵⁄₁₆

⁵⁄₁₆

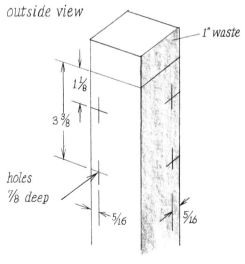

location of drawbores / back legs

outside view

1" waste

1⅛

3 ⅜

holes
⅞ deep

⁵⁄₁₆

⁵⁄₁₆

TABLE FRAME

Cut the four legs, adding 2 inches to the length for waste. Use a jack or jointer plane to dress all four sides smooth and square. Mark out the centers of the drawbores on the outside faces of all four legs (see *Making Joints*, p. 72) in the locations shown in the illustration, using the

square and jackknife and the marking gauge. Next, drill 3/16-inch holes for the drawbore pins to the depths specified in the illustrations. Lay out and cut the mortises in the front and back legs, using the dimensions given.

Cut the back rail, drawer rail, and two side rails to size. Then lay out and cut all the tenons, using the dimensions given in the illustration.

mortise dimensions | front legs

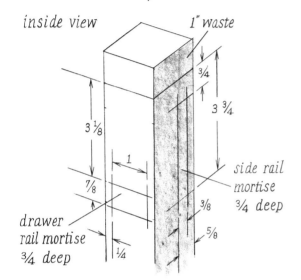

mortise dimensions | back legs

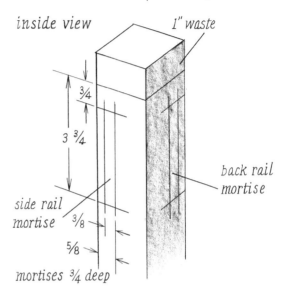

tenon dimensions for back, side, and drawer rails

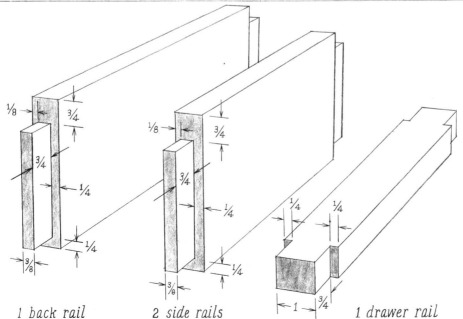

1 back rail   *2 side rails*   *1 drawer rail*   239

One-drawer Stand

Make them a bit full in thickness, then shave each one individually to fit its own mortise. They should be a tight-push fit. As each tenon is fitted, mark it and its mortise with the same letter (see *Woodworking Practices*, p. 33). These reference marks guarantee that each tenon will go where it belongs when the table frame is finally assembled. Then locate and drill the drawbores in the tenons. All these procedures are described in *Making Joints*, page 72.

Lay out and make a pattern for the leg to the dimensions given. Transfer to the pattern all the reference marks shown in the diagram. Then follow the directions in *Turned Legs*, pages 95, 110, for tracing the pattern and for using the lathebox to taper the legs. After that, cut off the surplus 1 inch of waste from the tops and bottoms of the legs, using the backsaw and miter box. Cut the drawbore pins and slightly taper their entering ends so that they can be driven more easily.

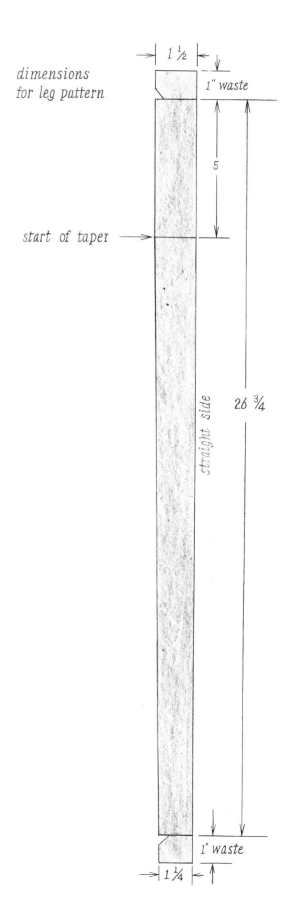

dimensions for leg pattern

1½

1" waste

5

start of taper

straight side

26 ¾

1" waste

1¼

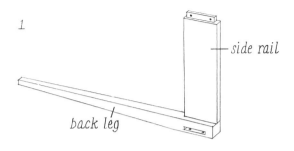

assembling the frame

1

side rail

back leg

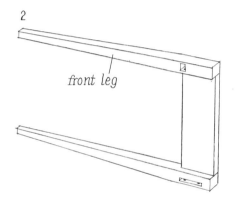

2

front leg

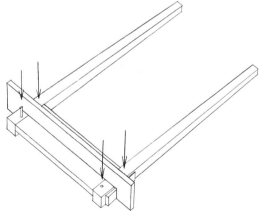

3 *driving drawbore pins into the leg joints*

clamp board wedged across side unit

ASSEMBLING THE FRAME

First put together the side units, each of which consists of a front and a back leg and a side rail. Lay the back leg on a piece of carpet or an old towel on the workbench to protect the work. Stand the side rail on end with its tenon starting into the mortise of the leg. Then push it firmly into place to close the joint. Lay the front leg on top of the upended rail and start the mortise and tenon joint together. Then tap the leg down to close the joint.

Lay the side unit flat on the bench and place a clamp across the assembly from leg to leg. A furniture clamp is best, but it can be done with a simple clamp board as shown in the illustration (see *Woodworking Practices*, p. 35). This jig when tightened with a wedge will hold things good and firm. Start the tapered ends of 2 drawbore pins into one leg and then drive them home with the hammer, tapping first one and then the other to draw the joint up evenly. Tighten the clamp board wedge again, then drive the pins into the other leg joint. Trim the projecting drawbore pins flush. Remove the clamp board. Then assemble the other side unit in the same way.

To complete the assembly of the table frame, the back rail and the drawer rail are now joined to the side units. Lay one side unit flat on the bench. Stand the back rail on end, starting its

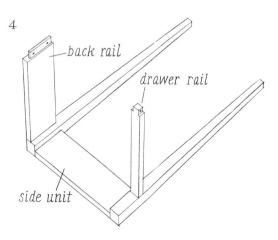

4

back rail

drawer rail

side unit

tenon into the back leg mortise. Then push it firmly into place to close the joint. Push the drawer rail joint together in the same way. Pick up the other side unit and lay it on top of the upended rails and start both joints together at the same time. Make a fist or use a mallet to tap the legs alternately to close both joints evenly.

Lay the table frame on its back, put a clamp board across the front of the frame, and wedge it up tight. Then drive a drawbore pin into each joint of the drawer rail. Trim the drawbore pins flush. Remove the clamp board, turn the table over on its front, and wedge the clamp board across the back side. Then drive 2 drawbore pins into each of the back leg joints and trim them flush as before. Remove the clamp board.

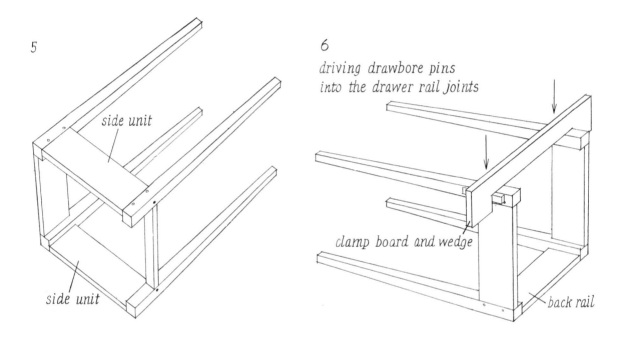

5

side unit

side unit

6

driving drawbore pins into the drawer rail joints

clamp board and wedge

back rail

drawer runners and guides

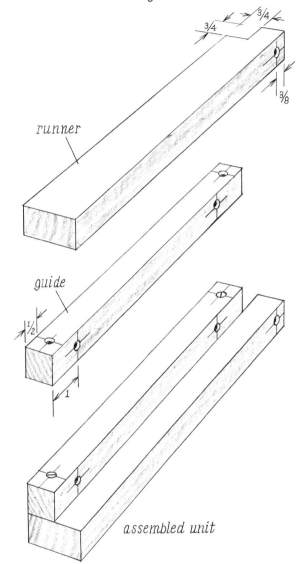

runner

guide

assembled unit

DRAWER RUNNERS AND GUIDES

Cut the runners to size and cut the notches in their back ends (see *Making Joints*, p. 80), using the dimensions given in the illustration. Then cut the guides to size. Drill and countersink the screw holes in the runners and guides. Screw the guides to the top of the runners in the position shown. Then fasten these units in place by driving 2 screws through the guide into the side rail, and another screw through the back end of the runner into the back leg. Make sure that the top surfaces of the runners are flush with the top of the drawer rail, so that the drawer will run smoothly.

attaching drawer runner and guide units to side rails and back legs

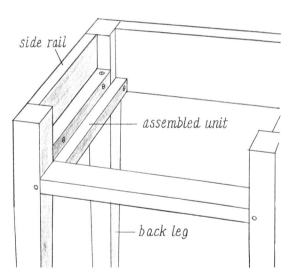

side rail

assembled unit

back leg

243

DRAWER

The drawer is joined with dovetails at the front and dowel pins at the back. Use the dimensions in the illustrations to lay out the dovetails, the location of the dowel pinhole centers, and the grooves in the drawer front and sides. Then build and fit the drawer according to the procedures described in *Making Joints*, page 52, and in *Drawer Construction*, page 112. Note that there is no groove in the drawer back—the bottom is simply nailed to its under edge. Cut the drawer bottom to fit and sand its inside surface to final smoothness (see *Sanding*, p. 132) before assembling the drawer.

back end of drawer side :
location of dowel pinhole centers

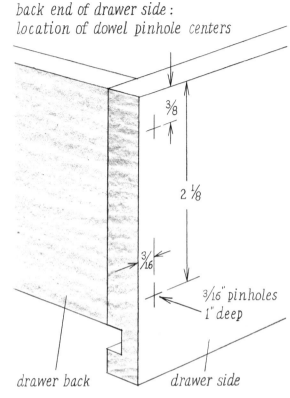

3/8

2 1/8

3/16

3/16" pinholes
1" deep

drawer back   drawer side

dimensions for dovetails
and drawer bottom groove

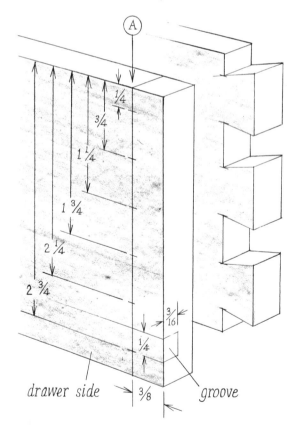

(A)

1/4

3/4

1 1/4

1 3/4

2 1/4

2 3/4

3/16

1/4

drawer side   3/8   groove

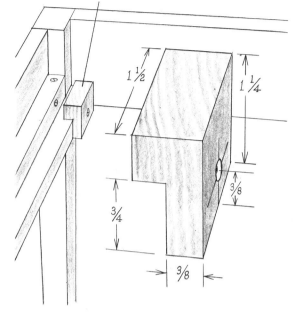

drawer stop fastened to side of runner

1 1/2
1 1/4
3/4
3/8
3/8

attaching cleats to the tabletop

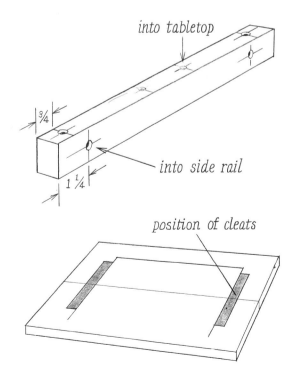

into tabletop
into side rail
3/4
1 1/4

position of cleats

DRAWER PULL AND STOPS

Lay out the position of the drawer pull centered both ways on the drawer front (see *Drawer Construction*, p. 120). Drill the screw hole and attach the pull. Make the drawer stops with the wood grain following the long dimension. Drill and countersink the screw holes as shown. Then push the drawer in place so that its front is flush with the outside edge of the drawer rail. Without moving the drawer, make pencil marks on the runners at the back of the drawer. Take the drawer out, align the stops with the pencil marks, and screw the stops to the side of the runners.

TABLETOP

Make up the top from two boards joined with either an edge-butt or tongue and groove joint (see *Making Joints*, p. 46, p. 88). Cut the tabletop cleats to size and drill and countersink the screw holes, keeping the center ones clear of the glued joint. Sand the ends of the tabletop (end grain) to final smoothness (see *Woodworking Practices*, p. 40, and *Sanding*, p. 132).

To attach the tabletop to the frame, lay the top facedown on the bench on a piece of carpet or an old towel to protect the work. Set the frame bottom-side up on top of it, and adjust its position so that there is a uniform amount of overhang on all four sides. Then mark the position of the cleats on the tabletop by tracing a line around the inside of the table frame. Remove the table frame, align the cleats inside these marks, and screw them in place. Again set the table frame bottom-side up, and down over the cleats. Drive 2 screws through each cleat into the side rails. Stand the table on its legs and put in the drawer.

Breadboard-top Table

HEIGHT 29   WIDTH 44½   DEPTH 25

Breadboard-top Table

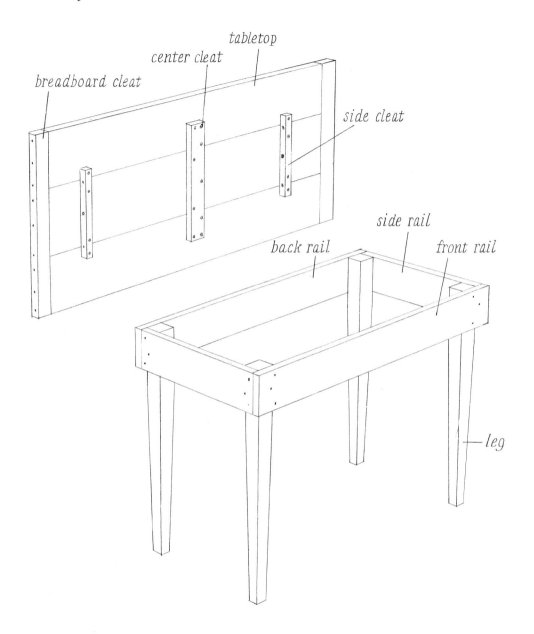

breadboard cleat

center cleat

tabletop

side cleat

side rail

back rail

front rail

leg

LUMBER REQUIRED

No. Pcs.	Nominal Dimensions
1	$1 \times 6 \times 10'$
1	$5/4 \times 10 \times 12'$
1	$9/4 \times 6 \times 6'$

MATERIALS

No. Pcs.	Part	Dimensions
4	legs	$2 \times 2 \times 28$
2	side rails	$3/4 \times 4\ 3/4 \times 16\ 3/4$
2	deadmen	$2 \times 4 \times 12$
1	front rail	$3/4 \times 4\ 3/4 \times 33$
1	back rail	$3/4 \times 4\ 3/4 \times 33$
1	construction brace	$1 \times 10 \times 48$ rough lumber
1	tabletop	$1 \times 25 \times 40\ 1/2$
2	breadboard cleats	$1 \times 2 \times 25$
1	center cleat	$1 \times 1\ 3/4 \times 16\ 3/4$
2	side cleats	$1 \times 1 \times 12\ 3/4$
18	screws	$1\ 1/2 \times$ No. 8 flathead *side cleats to side rails, center and side cleats to tabletop*
quant	nails	7d old-fashioned fine finish *rails to legs*
quant	nails	10d galvanized finish *breadboard cleats to tabletop*

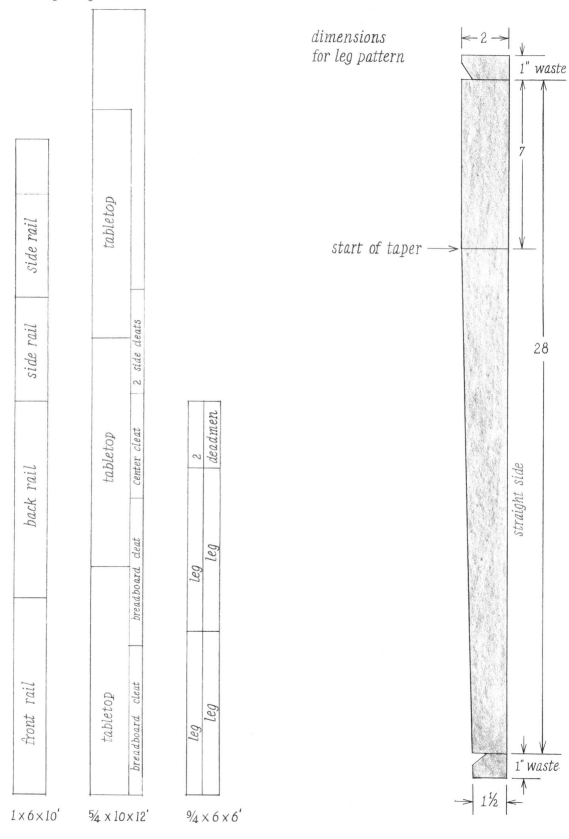

cutting diagram

front rail

side rail

side rail

back rail

$1 \times 6 \times 10'$

tabletop

tabletop

tabletop

breadboard cleat

breadboard cleat

center cleat

2 side cleats

$\frac{5}{4} \times 10 \times 12'$

leg

leg

leg

leg

2 deadmen

$\frac{9}{4} \times 6 \times 6'$

dimensions
for leg pattern

2

1" waste

7

start of taper

28

straight side

$1\frac{1}{2}$

1" waste

side rails: marking out the centers of nail pilot holes

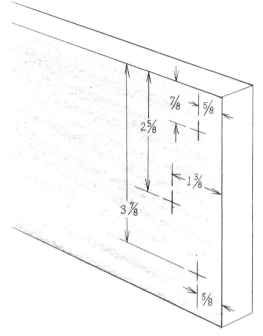

drilling nail pilot holes

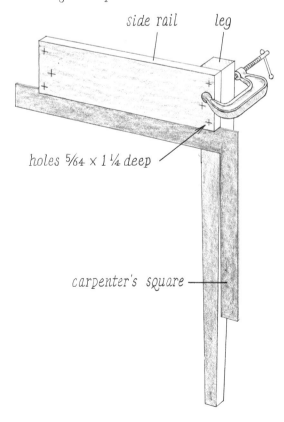

side rail   leg

holes 5⁄64 × 1¼ deep

carpenter's square

TABLE FRAME

Cut the four legs, adding 2 inches to the length for waste. Use a jack or jointer plane to dress all four sides smooth and square. Lay out and cut a pattern for the leg to the dimensions given in the illustration. Transfer to the pattern all the reference marks. Then follow the directions given in *Turned Legs*, pages 95, 110 for tracing the pattern and for using the lathebox to taper all four sides of the legs. Cut off the surplus 1 inch of waste from the tops and bottoms of the legs, using the backsaw and miter box.

Next make up the two side units. Cut the side rails to size, taking special care to plane their ends smooth and square. Do not sandpaper these end-grain surfaces: the outer edges should be clean and sharp in order to make a tight seam with the side rails. Use the try square to mark out the centers of the nail pilot holes to the dimensions shown. Then clamp the end of one side rail to the top of one leg. Check to see that the rail is flush with the side and top end of the leg. Use the carpenter's square to check the alignment. Tighten the clamp. Then drill 2 pilot holes 5/64 inch in diameter and 1 1/4 inches deep. The third hole is drilled later. Remove the clamp and drive 7d nails partway into the holes in the rail, letting their points come through 1/8 inch. Then spread glue on the meeting surfaces of the leg and rail. Lay the rail in place on the leg, starting the nail points into the pilot holes.

These square-cut nails require fairly heavy hammer blows. If your workbench is not good and solid, clamp the side rail to the leg and hold the work on an anvil, as shown in the illustration. Lacking that, use a heavy hardwood block or a cement block covered with a scrap of 2 x 4. Use strong, sure hammer blows. Drive the nails not quite flush, then use a heavy nail set to set their heads just barely below the surface. Wipe off any excess glue with a damp sponge. Leave the work to dry overnight. Then drill the middle

side rail clamped to leg for nailing

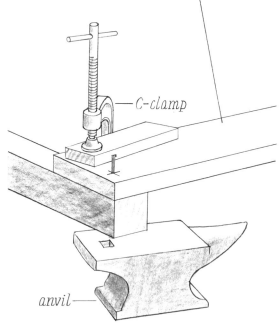

C-clamp

anvil

nail pilot hole and drive the nail. Glue and nail the other leg. Make up the other side unit in the same way.

Then cut the two deadmen and wedge them tight into the side units as shown in the illustration. They support the heavy pounding of driving the nails which otherwise would loosen the joints already finished.

FRONT AND BACK RAILS

Cut the front and back rails to size, taking special care to make them exactly the same length and to plane their ends smooth and square. Do not sandpaper these end-grain surfaces: here again the outer edges should be clean and sharp in order to make a tight seam with the side rails. Use the try square to mark out the centers of the nail pilot holes in both ends of both rails as shown.

deadman wedged into side unit

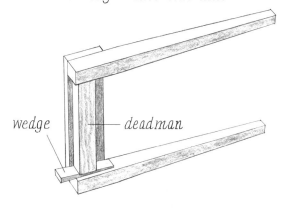

wedge — deadman

front and back rails: marking out the centers of nail pilot holes

$\frac{5}{8}$

$1\frac{5}{8}$

$2\frac{1}{8}$

$1\frac{3}{8}$

$4\frac{1}{8}$

$1\frac{5}{8}$

ASSEMBLING THE FRAME

The awkward job of fastening the front and back rails to the side units can be managed as shown in the illustrations. Mark off the length of the front and back rails on the edge of a wide piece of rough lumber to be used as a construction brace. Stand the side units on edge and block up their legs to keep the work level. Stand the brace on edge and tack it to the side units with the marks aligned as shown. Clamp both ends of the front rail to the side units, flush at the top and at the ends. Drill 2 nail pilot holes 5/64 inch in diameter and 1 1/4 inches deep in both ends of the rail. The third hole is drilled later. Remove the clamps.

To fasten the front rail in place, drive 7d nails partway into the 2 pilot holes at both ends, letting their points come through 1/8 inch. Then

assembling the frame

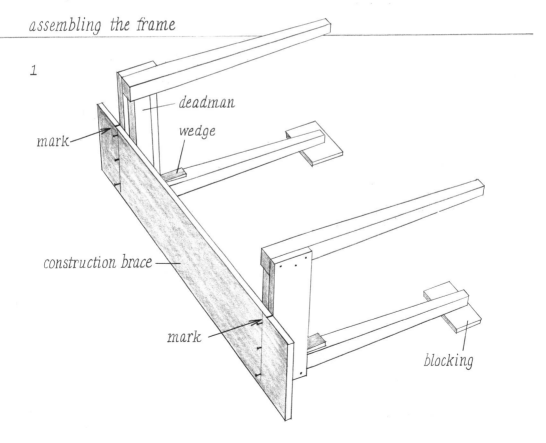

1

mark

deadman

wedge

construction brace

mark

blocking

spread glue thinly on the meeting surfaces of the leg and rail joints. Now lay the rail in place on top of the side units, starting the nail points into the pilot holes. Put a clamp on each end, check the alignment, and tighten the wedges under the deadmen. Then drive the nails. Wipe off any excess glue with a damp sponge. Drill the middle pilot holes and drive the nails. Leave the work to dry overnight.

To fasten the back rail, remove the brace and turn the table frame the other side up. Block up under the tapered legs as before and be sure the deadmen are wedged tight. Clamp the back rail in place, flush at the top and ends, and attach it in the same way.

TABLETOP

Make up the top from three boards joined with either edge-butt or tongue and groove joints (see *Making Joints*, p. 46, p. 88). Plane their edges smooth and square. If you use tongue and groove joints, leave the outside edges of the two outside boards square.

Cut the breadboard cleats, adding an extra 1/8 inch to the length for trimming. Joint their long edges square (see *Woodworking Prac-*

fastening the front rail

nail pilot holes ⁵⁄₆₄ × 1¼ deep

blocking

front rail

deadman

wedge

nailing breadboard cleats to tabletop

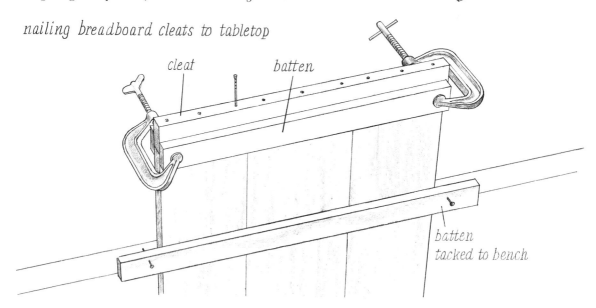

cleat *batten*

batten tacked to bench

attaching cleats to the tabletop

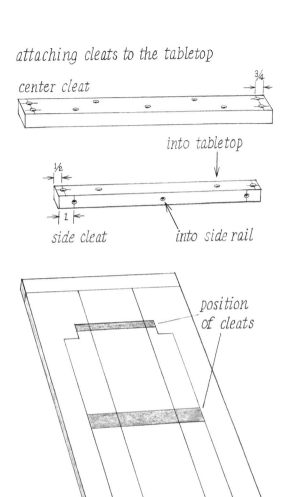

center cleat

¾

into tabletop

½

side cleat

1

into side rail

position of cleats

tices, p. 28). Stand the tabletop against the bench with one edge held in the vise for support, or hold it with a batten tacked to the edge of the workbench as shown. Clamp a batten on either side of the tabletop with the breadboard cleat sandwiched between them. Drill pilot holes for the 10d nails, being careful to locate them no closer than 1 inch to the ends or the glued joints. Drive and set the nails just barely below the surface. Attach the other breadboard cleat in the same way. Turn the tabletop on its side and plane the ends of the cleats down flush with the long edge of the tabletop, planing toward the middle from both ends. Then turn the tabletop over and trim the other end of the cleats flush in the same way.

To fasten the tabletop to the frame, lay it facedown and set the frame bottom-side up on top of it. Adjust the position of the frame so that it is centered in both directions on the tabletop. Then mark the position of the cleats by tracing a line around the inside of the table frame. Remove the table frame. Cut the center and two side cleats to size and drill and countersink the screw holes, locating them no closer than 1 inch to the ends and the glued joints of the tabletop. Screw the cleats in place. Then set the table frame bottom-side up over the cleats. Drive 3 screws through each side cleat into the side rails. Stand the table on its legs.

Pencil-post Bed

HEIGHT 70   WIDTH 58   DEPTH 80½

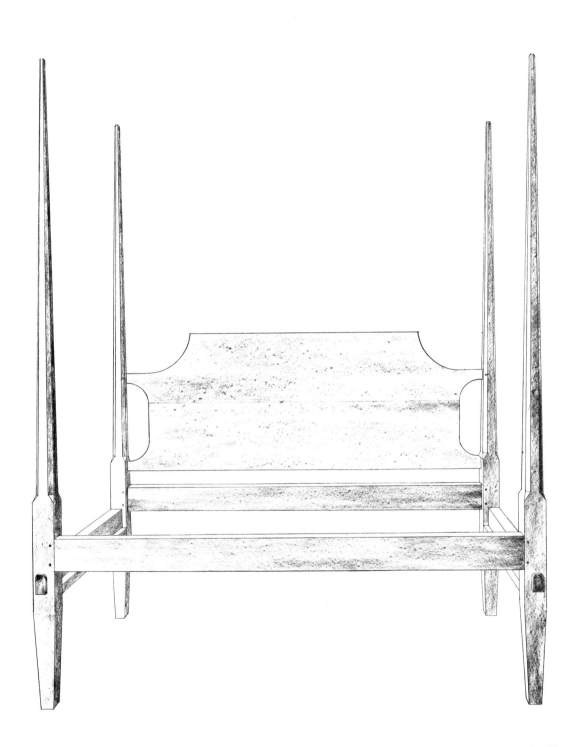

Pencil-post Bed

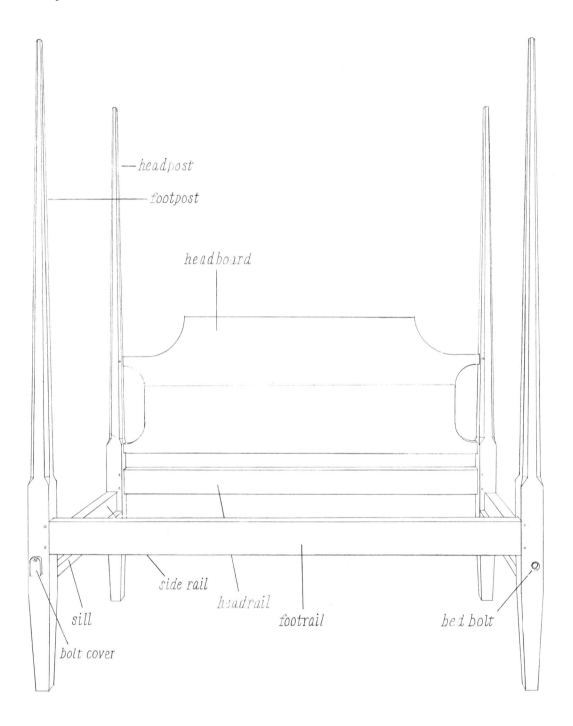

headpost

footpost

headboard

side rail

headrail

footrail

bed bolt

sill

bolt cover

258

LUMBER REQUIRED

No. Pcs.	Nominal Dimensions
1	$1 \times 12 \times 10'$
1	$5/4 \times 6 \times 8'$ hardwood
1	$8/4 \times 10 \times 12'$
1	$3 \times 6 \times 12'$
1	$1/4 \times 3'$ hardwood dowel

MATERIALS

No. Pcs.	Part	Dimensions
4	posts	$2\ 1/2 \times 2\ 1/2 \times 70$
1	headrail	$1\ 3/4 \times 3\ 3/4 \times 55\ 1/2$
1	footrail	$1\ 3/4 \times 3\ 3/4 \times 55\ 1/2$
2	side rails	$1\ 3/4 \times 3\ 3/4 \times 77$
2	sills	$1 \times 1 \times 75\ 1/2$ hardwood
1	notched deadman	$1 \times 4 \times 3'$
1	headboard	$3/4 \times 20\ 1/2 \times 55\ 1/2$
1	spreader	$1 \times 2 \times 54\ 1/2$
2	headboard cleats	$3/4 \times 2 \times 17\ 1/2$
10	drawbore pins	$1/4 \times 1\ 3/4$ hardwood dowel
4	bolt covers	$1/4 \times 1\ 1/2 \times 2\ 1/2$ hardwood
16	screws	$2 \times$ No. 9 flathead *sills*
8	screws	$1\ 1/4 \times$ No. 7 flathead *headboard cleats*
4	bed bolts	$3/8 \times 6$ machine
8	flat washers	$3/8$ inside diameter
4	screws	$3/4 \times$ No. 6 flathead brass *bolt covers*
2	screws	$3/4 \times$ No. 7 flathead *spreader*

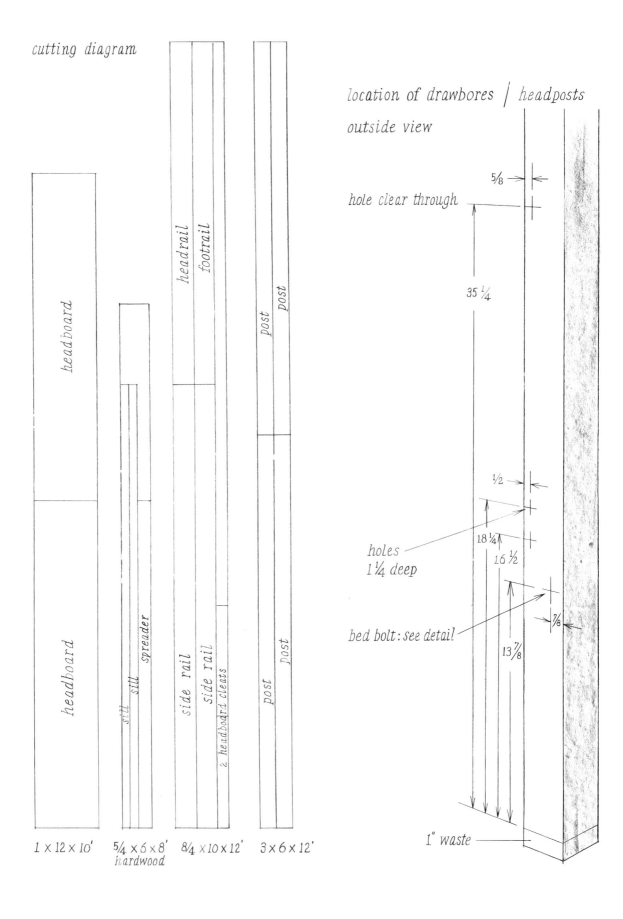

cutting diagram

headboard

headboard

1 × 12 × 10'

sill
sill
spreader

5/4 × 6 × 8'
hardwood

headrail
footrail

side rail
side rail
2 headboard cleats

8/4 × 10 × 12'

post
post

post
post

3 × 6 × 12'

location of drawbores / headposts

outside view

5/8

hole clear through

35 1/4

1/2

holes
1 1/4 deep

18 1/4

16 1/2

bed bolt: see detail

13 7/8

7/8

1" waste

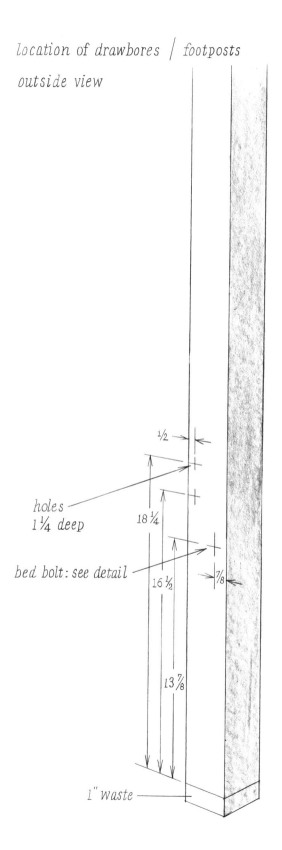

location of drawbores / *footposts*

outside view

½

holes
1 ¼ *deep*

18 ¼

bed bolt: see detail

16 ½

⅞

13 ⅞

1" *waste*

Although this bed can be made entirely of pine, the use of a hardwood such as cherry, beech, or walnut will provide for good crisp edges on the tapered octagonal sections of the posts.

POSTS

Cut the four posts, adding 2 inches to the length for waste. Use a jack or jointer plane to dress all four sides smooth and square. Mark out the centers of the drawbores on the outside faces of all four legs (see *Making Joints*, p. 72), using the try square, jackknife, and marking gauge. Then drill 1/4-inch holes for the drawbore pins to the depths given in the illustration. Use a depth stop slipped over the drill to ensure accuracy (see *Woodworking Practices*, p. 38). Note that the lower mortise and tenon joints of the headboard are loose, with no drawbore pins. Next, mark out the centers of the bed bolt holes—one in each post—and use the brace and a 1-inch auger bit to bore counterbores 7/16 inch deep. Then use a 7/16-inch bit to bore the bolt holes clear through.

detail:
bed bolt holes

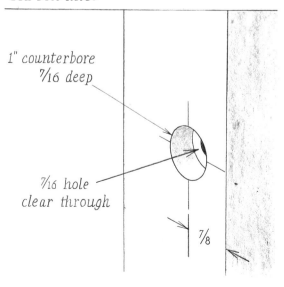

1" *counterbore*
7/16 *deep*

7/16 *hole*
clear through

⅞

Pencil-post Bed

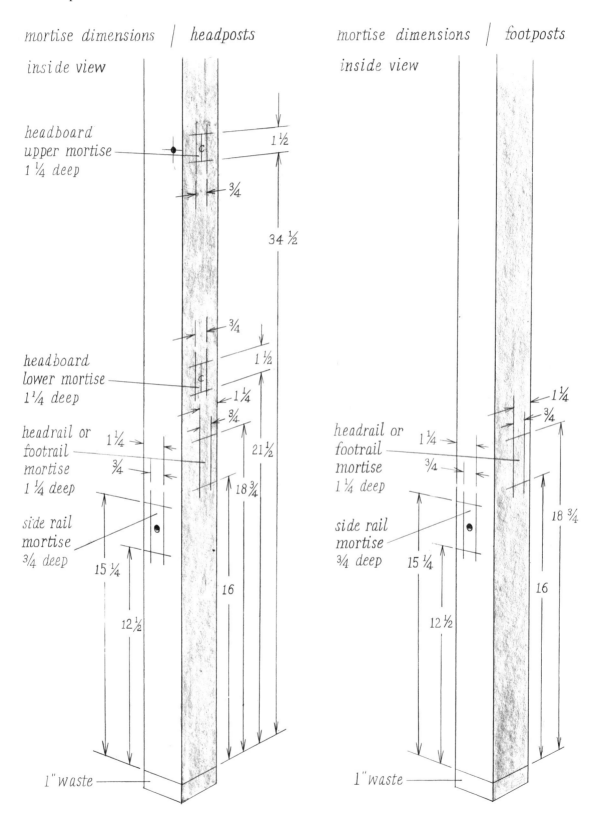

mortise dimensions / headposts

inside view

headboard
upper mortise
1 ¼ deep

1 ½

¾

34 ½

¾

1 ½

headboard
lower mortise
1 ¼ deep

1 ¼

¾

21 ½

headrail or
footrail
mortise
1 ¼ deep

1 ¼

¾

18 ¾

side rail
mortise
¾ deep

15 ¼

16

12 ½

1" waste

mortise dimensions / footposts

inside view

1 ¼

¾

headrail or
footrail
mortise
1 ¼ deep

1 ¼

¾

18 ¾

side rail
mortise
¾ deep

15 ¼

16

12 ½

1" waste

tenon dimensions for rails

headrail and footrail

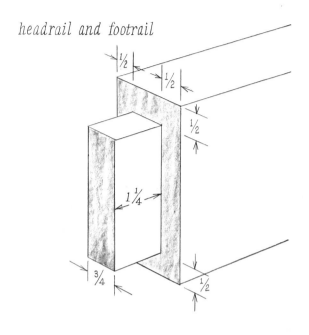

side rails

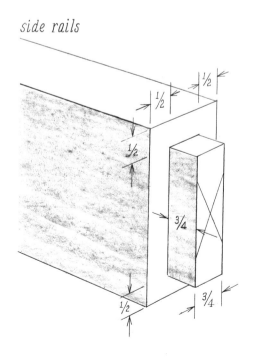

Lay out and cut the mortises for the head- and footposts (see *Making Joints*, p. 72), using the dimensions shown in the diagrams. Use a mallet and a 3/4-inch chisel for the bulk of this work and a 1/2-inch chisel to finish the bottoms of the mortises.

RAILS

Cut the headrail, footrail, and side rails to size. On the ends of the side rails mark their centers by drawing diagonal lines. Then lay out and cut all the tenons, using the dimensions in the illustration. Make them a bit full in thickness, then shave each one to fit its own mortise. They should be a tight-push fit. As each tenon is fitted, mark it and its mortise with the same letter (see *Woodworking Practices*, p. 33). These reference marks guarantee that the tenons will go where they belong when the frame is finally assembled. Now locate and drill the drawbores in the tenons. All these procedures are described in *Making Joints*, page 72.

Lay out and cut the box cavities for the bed bolt nuts on the inside of both side rails—one at each end—to the dimensions given in the illustration. Then with the brace and a 7/16-inch auger bit, bore holes into the ends of the side rail tenons clear through into the box cavities. Run a 3/8-inch bolt through to clean out the shavings. Then put a washer and nut into each cavity to see that the bolt freely engages and screws into the nut. Pare the cavity a bit if needed.

SILLS

Cut the sills to size and drill and countersink the screw holes. Then cut a halved joint in the center of each one (see *Making Joints*, p. 62) to the dimensions shown in the illustration. The halved ends of the spreader fit down into these joints. Clamp the sills to the side rails flush with their lower edges and screw them in place.

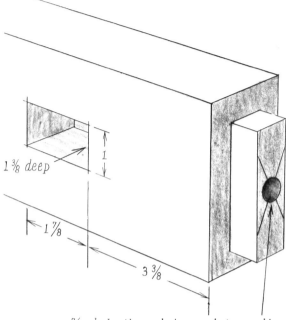

side rails:
dimensions for box cavities

1 ⅜ *deep*

1

1 ⅞

3 ⅜

⁷⁄₁₆ *hole through tenon into cavity*

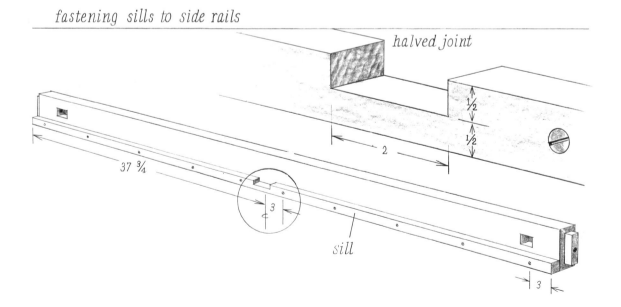

fastening sills to side rails

halved joint

½

½

2

37 ¾

3

sill

3

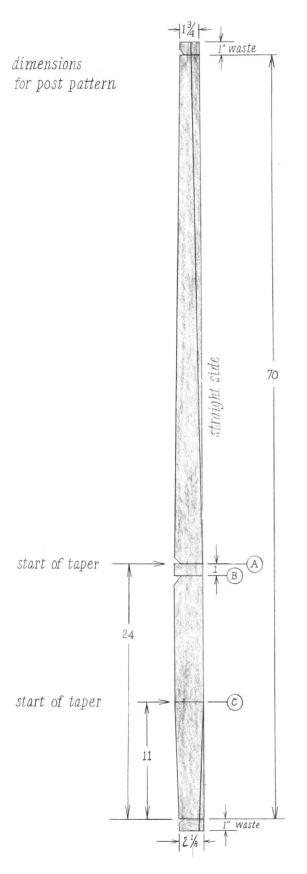

dimensions
for post pattern

→|1¾|←

1" waste

straight side

70

start of taper

1
———
1

Ⓐ
Ⓑ

24

start of taper

Ⓒ

11

1" waste

→|2⅛|←

SHAPING THE POSTS

Lay out and cut a pattern for the posts to the dimensions in the diagram. Transfer to the pattern all the reference marks. Note that the bed-posts are tapered square in section below the rails and octagonal above. Follow the directions in *Turned Legs*, pages 95, 110 for tracing the pattern and for square-tapering the lower 11 inches of the posts, as well as for square-tapering their upper sections from A to the top. When these upper sections have been square-tapered, they are then made octagonal in section by chamfering off the four edges as follows. Using the octagon dimensions in the diagrams, tick off pencil marks at point A, 3/4 inch in from

octagon dimensions

section of post at point Ⓐ

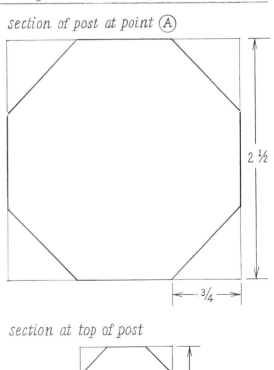

2½

←—¾—→

section at top of post

1

→|⁹⁄₃₂|←

265

Pencil-post Bed

both edges on all four sides of the post. Tick off similar marks at the top of the post, 9/32 inch in from the edges on all four sides. Then draw pencil lines connecting the marks at point A with those at the top of the post, using a 48-inch straightedge, or a length of 1 x 2 lumber which has been jointed straight and true on one edge. Carefully align the straightedge with both tick marks and hold it securely in place with two or three C-clamps while you draw the line. Repeat this same operation on all four sides of the post. Then lay out the angled lines from A to B that mark the triangular stops.

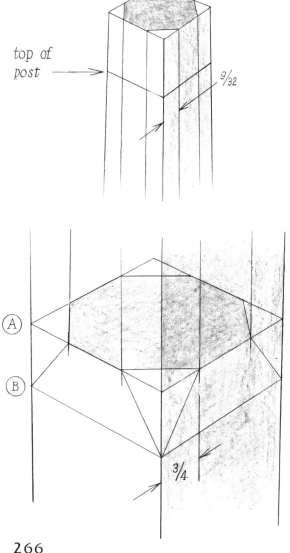

top of post

9/32

A

B

3/4

laying out octagon taper lines

top of post

9/32

straightedge

C-clamp

blocking

3/4

A

B

To cut the chamfers, clamp the post in the vise between a pair of V-blocks and support its top end on the notched deadman resting on the floor. First use the backsaw to cut down at point A, sawing on the waste side of the mark and not quite down to the octagon lines. Use the drawknife or a 1-inch chisel to pare out a box about 8 inches long. Take off wood little by little, keeping the cut surface as flat as possible. Don't chamfer clear to the lines: some wood must be left for the final finishing. When the box has been cut, use the block plane to chamfer the rest of the edge clear to the top of the post, again leaving extra wood for finishing.

cutting the chamfers

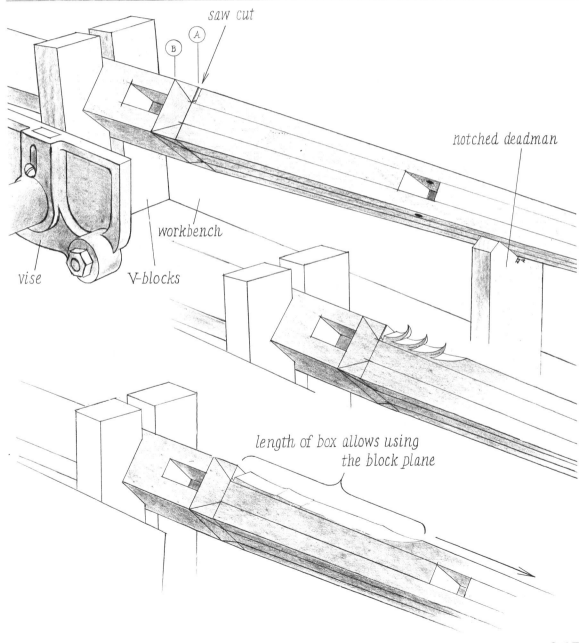

saw cut

B   A

notched deadman

vise   V-blocks   workbench

length of box allows using
the block plane

Next cut the beveled stop, as shown in the illustration. Use a sharp 1-inch chisel and pare only a little wood at a time. Be careful not to cut too close to the chamfer. Leave this junction to be finished later.

Then rotate the post in the V-blocks and cut the other three sides in succession. As the work is rotated, lay a folded cloth in the notch of the deadman to protect the work.

To finish the chamfers, use a freshly sharpened block plane set for the finest cut possible. Hold it level with the flat of the chamfer and make long, nonstop passes from the stop to the top of the post, keeping a sharp eye on the taper lines. Then use the 1-inch chisel to shave the bottom end of the chamfers, and to trim the angled stops exactly to the marks. To remove any irregularities where the planed chamfer meets the chisel work, use a 10-inch double-cut file, stroking it at a slight angle to smooth this section. Do not sandpaper the chamfers or the crisp edges will be destroyed. Chamfer and finish the other posts in the same way. Then cut off the 1-inch waste sections. The

V-blocks made from scrap lumber

cutting the beveled stop

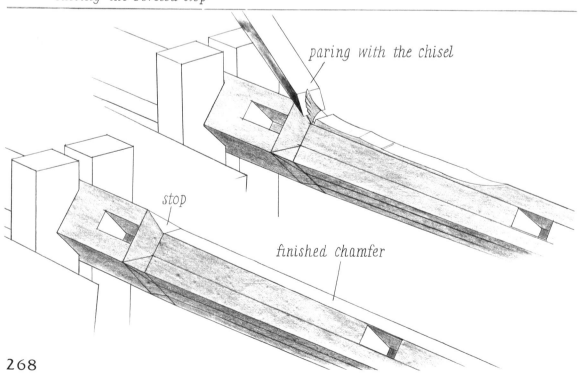

paring with the chisel

stop

finished chamfer

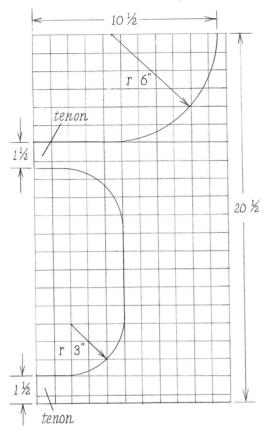

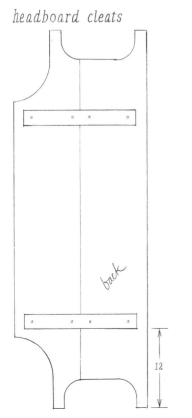

headboard cleats

foot of the posts can be sawn off in the miter box, using the backsaw, and the top end sawn freehand with the post resting in the notched deadman on folded cloth.

HEADBOARD

Make up the headboard from two boards joined with either an edge-butt or tongue and groove joint (see *Making Joints*, p. 46, p. 88). Check the exact position of the headboard mortises, then make a pattern for the scrollwork from the diagram. Trace the scrolls onto the headboard and cut them with a coping saw. Saw the tenons a bit full in width. Use a round rasp and a sanding block to fair up the scrolled sections. Then fit the tenons to the mortises in the headposts, and mark them with pairs of letters (see *Woodworking Practices*, p. 33). Sand both sides of the headboard to final smoothness (see *Sanding*, p. 132), and mark its back side with an X so that when the head of the bed is assembled, the tenons will go into the proper mortises.

Cut the headboard cleats to size and drill and countersink the screw holes, locating them no closer than 1 inch to the ends or to the glued joint of the headboard. Then clamp them to the back of the headboard, check their alignment with the carpenter's square, and fasten them in place.

ASSEMBLING THE BED

Assemble the foot of the bed first. Lay the two footposts flat on an old blanket on the floor to protect the work. Lay the footrail in position between them and start the tenons into the mortises. Use a mallet and a scrap of wood to tap the joints shut. Place a clamp across the assembly from post to post. A furniture clamp is best but it can be done with a simple clamp board as shown in the illustration (see *Woodworking Practices*, p. 35). This jig when tightened with a couple of wedges will hold things good and firm. Now locate the position of the tenon drawbores by marking through the holes in the posts. Remove the clamp board, take the joints apart and drill the drawbores in both foot-rail tenons (see *Making Joints*, p. 78). Cut the drawbore pins and slightly taper their entering ends. This allows them to be driven more easily. Again clamp the assembly together and tap the wedges up tight. Then drive 2 drawbore pins into each joint and trim the pins flush (see *Making Joints*, p. 79).

Use the same method to assemble the head of the bed. Lay the headposts flat on the floor and lay the headrail and headboard in position between them. You may need some help here to start all six tenons into the mortises at once. Use a mallet and a scrap of wood to tap the joints shut. Wedge a clamp board across the assembly just above the headrail. Check to see that the headrail-to-post joints close tight. If they don't, the tenons of the headboard are probably too long and will have to be trimmed. Tighten the clamp board wedge again and mark the position of the tenon drawbores as before. Remove the clamp board, take the pieces apart, and drill the tenon drawbores. Then put all the pieces together again, wedge the clamp board across

the assembly, and drive 2 drawbore pins into each headrail joint, and one into each of the upper headboard joints. Trim the drawbore pins flush, being especially careful not to damage the chamfered upper section of the headposts.

The side rails are now joined to the head- and footposts as shown in the illustration. Start a side rail tenon into the post mortise. Slide a washer onto a bed bolt and push the bolt through the post, through the tenon and into the box cavity. Put another washer on the end of the bolt and thread on a nut. Have someone steady the foot-section (or head-section as the case may be) while you tighten the head of the bolt with a socket wrench. Bolt the corresponding end of the other side rail in place in the same way. To join the head-section of the bed (or the foot-section as the case may be) to the side rails, prop up their loose ends on boxes and have someone help start the joints together. Then tighten all the bed bolts.

BOLT COVERS

Make the four bolt covers, using the dimensions given in the illustration. Drill and countersink the screw holes. To locate the position of the bolt cover, lay it over one of the bed bolt

driving drawbore pins into the footpost joints

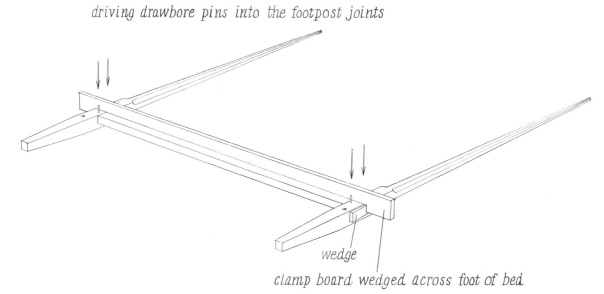

wedge

clamp board wedged across foot of bed

assembling bed bolt joints

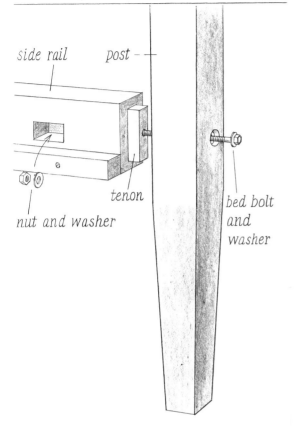

side rail

post

tenon

nut and washer

bed bolt and washer

heads centered horizontally on the bolt and with its lower end overlapping the bolt hole about 1/8 inch. Mark the center of the screw hole by marking through it with a pencil. Remove the bolt cover and drill a pilot hole in the bedpost, having first made a trial pilot hole to fit the 3/4 x No. 6 brass screw. Then measure the location of the pilot hole, transfer the measurements to the other three posts, and drill similar pilot holes. Fasten the bolt covers in place.

SPREADER

Cut the spreader, making it the same length as the *inside width* of the bed as measured from the inside of one side rail to the other, in the middle of the bed. Then work the halved joints in its ends (see *Making Joints*, p. 62). Drill and countersink a screw hole in each end, as shown in the illustration. Lay the spreader across the bed and into the halved joints of the sills. If necessary, pare the joints of the spreader so that its top surface comes flush with that of the sills. Then fasten it in place with a screw at each end.

bolt cover

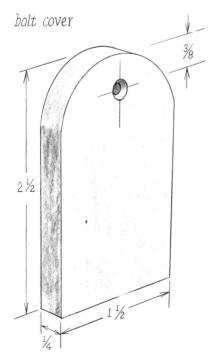

$3/8$

$2 1/2$

$1 1/2$

$1/4$

spreader

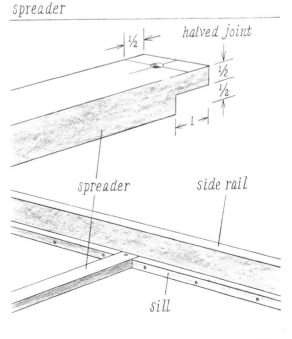

halved joint

$1/2$

$1/2$

$1/2$

1

spreader

side rail

sill

Writing Table

HEIGHT 29   WIDTH 45   DEPTH 28

Writing Table

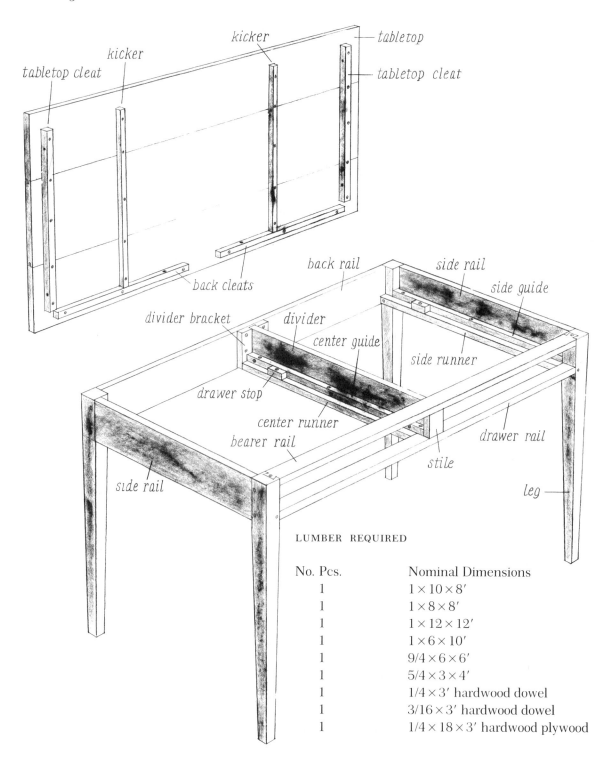

LUMBER REQUIRED

No. Pcs.	Nominal Dimensions
1	$1 \times 10 \times 8'$
1	$1 \times 8 \times 8'$
1	$1 \times 12 \times 12'$
1	$1 \times 6 \times 10'$
1	$9/4 \times 6 \times 6'$
1	$5/4 \times 3 \times 4'$
1	$1/4 \times 3'$ hardwood dowel
1	$3/16 \times 3'$ hardwood dowel
1	$1/4 \times 18 \times 3'$ hardwood plywood

MATERIALS

No. Pcs.	Part	Dimensions
4	legs	2 1/8 × 2 1/8 × 28 1/4
2	side rails	3/4 × 4 3/4 × 24 1/4
1	back rail	3/4 × 4 3/4 × 41 1/4
1	drawer rail	3/4 × 2 1/8 × 41 1/4
1	bearer rail	3/4 × 2 1/8 × 40 3/4
1	stile	3/4 × 2 1/4 × 3 1/4
1	divider bracket	3/4 × 4 × 4 3/4
2	side runners	3/4 × 1 1/2 × 24 1/8
2	side guides	3/4 × 3/4 × 22 1/4
1	divider	3/4 × 4 × 24 3/4
1	center runner	3/4 × 3 3/4 × 22 7/8
2	center drawer guides	3/4 × 3/4 × 24 1/4
1	tabletop	3/4 × 28 × 45
2	tabletop cleats	1 × 1 × 22 1/4 hardwood
2	back cleats	1 × 1 × 17 1/2 hardwood
2	kickers	3/4 × 3/4 × 22 1/4
12	drawbore pins	1/4 × 1 1/4 hardwood dowel
2	drawbore pins	1/4 × 2 hardwood dowel *drawer rail*
2	drawer fronts	3/4 × 3 1/4 × 18 1/2
4	drawer sides	1/2 × 3 1/4 × 17 3/4
2	drawer backs	1/2 × 2 3/4 × 17 3/8
12	dowel pins	3/16 × 1 1/2 hardwood dowel, *drawer back joints*
2	drawer bottoms	1/4 × 17 7/8 × 17 1/2 hardwood plywood
4	drawer stops	3/4 × 3/4 × 2 1/2
2	screws	5/8 × No. 6 flathead *side runner halved joints*
4	screws	1 × No. 6 flathead *drawer stops*
26	screws	1 1/4 × No. 7 flathead *backs of side runners, guides, divider bracket, kickers*
3	screws	1 1/2 × No. 6 flathead *bearer rail*
22	screws	1 1/2 × No. 8 flathead *tabletop and back cleats to top, tabletop and back cleats to side and back rails*
5	screws	1 3/4 × No. 7 flathead *center runner and drawer rail to divider*
2	drawer pulls	1 3/8″ round brass pulls
quant	nails	8d galvanized finish *drawer and bearer rails and divider bracket*
quant	nails	1 1/4 × No. 17 wire *drawer bottoms to drawer backs*

cutting diagram

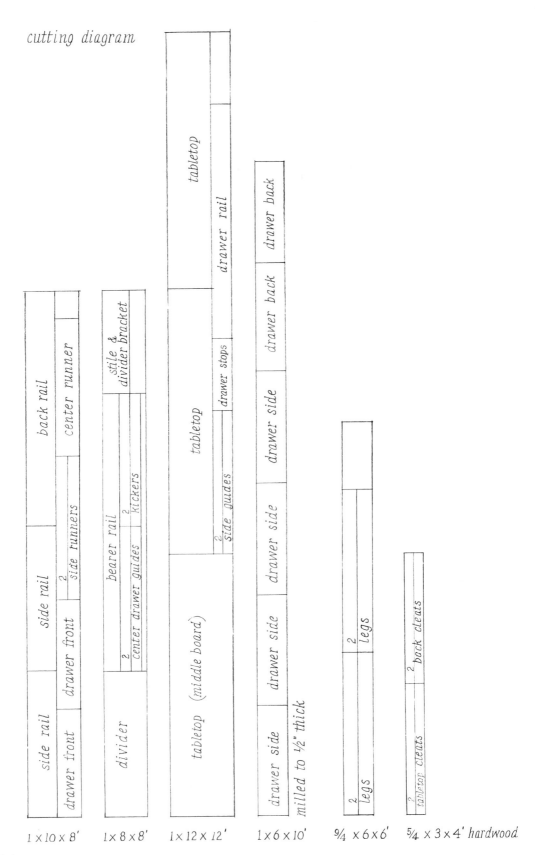

side rail

side rail

drawer front

drawer front

back rail

center runner

2 side runners

$1 \times 10 \times 8'$

divider

bearer rail

2 center drawer guides

2 kickers

stile &
divider bracket

$1 \times 8 \times 8'$

tabletop (middle board)

tabletop

tabletop

drawer rail

2 side guides

drawer stops

$1 \times 12 \times 12'$

drawer side

drawer side

drawer side

drawer side

drawer side

drawer back

drawer back

$1 \times 6 \times 10'$

milled to ½" thick

2 legs

2 legs

¾ × 6 × 6'

2 tabletop cleats

2 back cleats

⁵⁄₄ × 3 × 4' hardwood

TABLE FRAME

Cut the legs, adding 2 inches to the length for waste. Use a jack or jointer plane to dress all four sides smooth and square. Mark out the centers of the drawbores on the outside faces of all four legs (see *Making Joints*, p. 72), using the square and jackknife and the marking gauge. Then drill 1/4-inch holes for the drawbore pins

to the depths given in the illustrations. Lay out and cut the mortises in the front and back legs, using the dimensions shown in the illustrations.

Cut the back rail, the drawer rail, and the two side rails to size. Then lay out and cut all the tenons, to the dimensions given in the illustration. Make them a bit full in thickness, then shave each one individually to fit its own mor-

location of drawbores / front legs

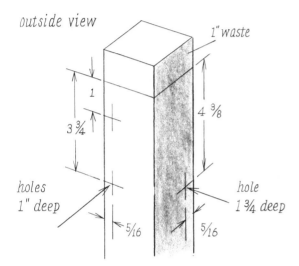

location of drawbores / back legs

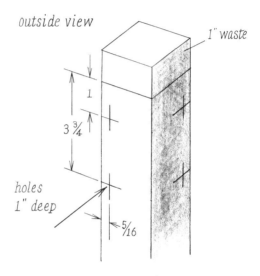

mortise dimensions / front legs

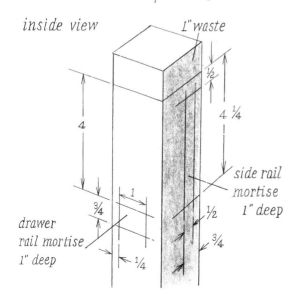

mortise dimensions / back legs

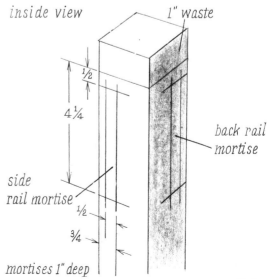

tise. They should be a tight-push fit. As each tenon is fitted, mark it and its mortise with the same letter (see *Woodworking Practices*, p. 33). These reference marks guarantee that each tenon will go where it belongs when the frame is finally assembled. Now locate and drill the drawbores in the tenons. All these procedures are described in *Making Joints*, page 72.

Next, cut the halved joints on the underside of the drawer rail—one at each end (see *Making Joints*, p. 62). The front ends of the drawer runners will be fitted into these joints.

STILE AND DIVIDER BRACKET

Make the stile and divider bracket. Since they both have center grooves of the same dimensions, the practical way is to shoot a groove in one length of wood, then cut it into two pieces. Shoot the groove with a grooving or combination plane (see *Making Joints*, p. 60), using the dimensions given in the illustration. Use the miter box and backsaw to cut the divider bracket to exact length. Then trim the stile part to size, removing the waste from the ends and sides, as

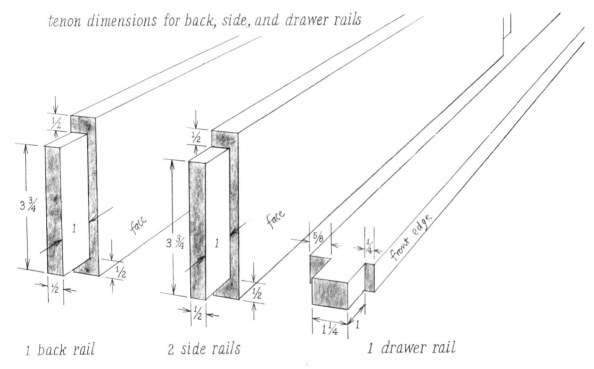

tenon dimensions for back, side, and drawer rails

1 back rail   2 side rails   1 drawer rail

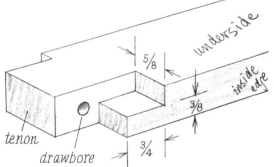

halved joints in ends of drawer rail

tenon   drawbore

shown in the illustration. Drill and countersink 4 screw holes in the divider bracket and set it aside until later.

Lay the drawer rail bottom-side up on the bench and mark its center point. Lay the try square against the rail and carry the center mark clear across and down over the front edge. Drill and countersink a 1/8-inch screw pilot hole on this line as shown in the illustration. A screw will later be driven up through this hole into the divider. Mark the position of the 2 nail pilot holes,

stile and divider bracket

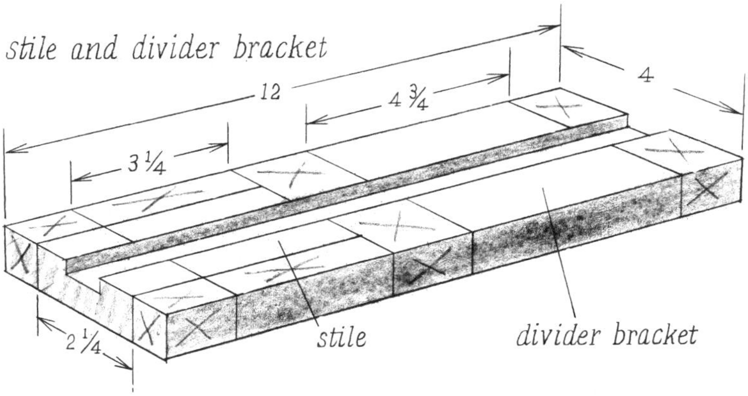
12
4 3/4
4
3 1/4
2 1/4
stile
divider bracket

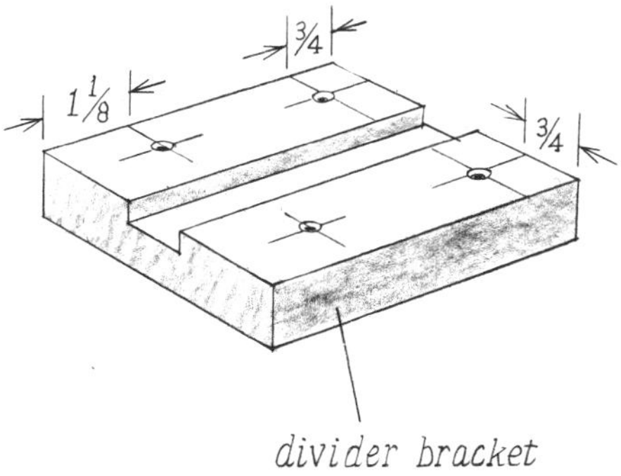
3/4
1 1/8
3/4
divider bracket

underside of drawer rail:
location of screw and nail pilot holes

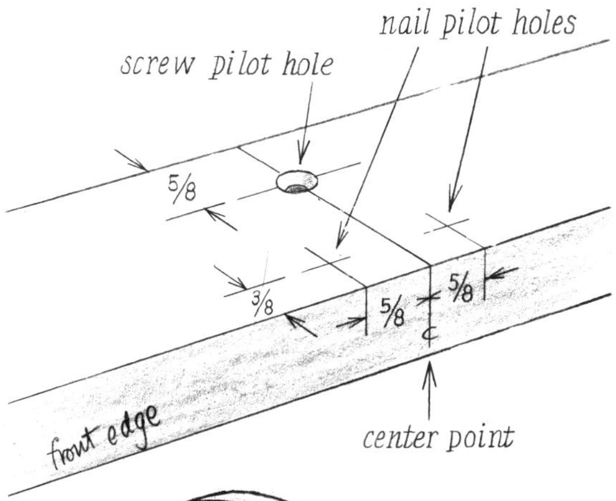
nail pilot holes
screw pilot hole
5/8
3/8
5/8
5/8
front edge
center point

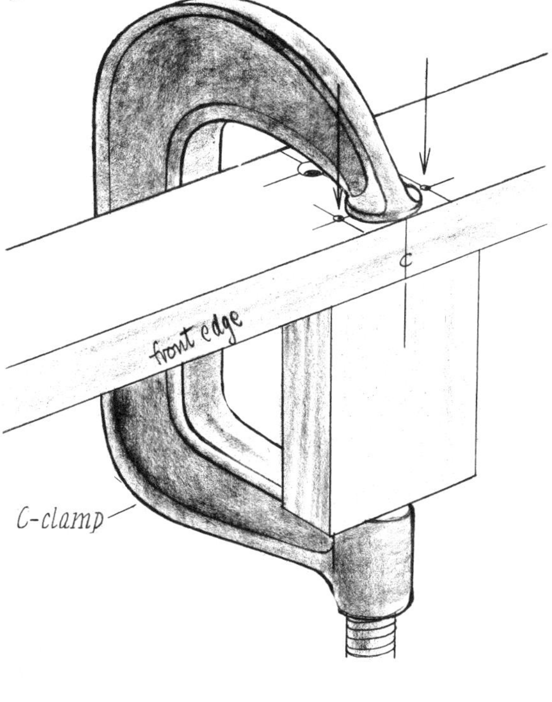
front edge
C-clamp

as shown in the illustration. Now clamp the stile to the rail, centered on the center point and flush with the front edge of the rail. Drill 2 pilot holes 7/64 x 1 3/4″ through the rail and into the stile. Remove the clamp and start 8d galvanized finish nails into the holes, letting their points come through about 1/4 inch. Clamp the stile end-up in the vise. Lay the drawer rail on top of it, starting the nail points into the pilot holes. Drive the nails.

nailing the drawer rail to the stile

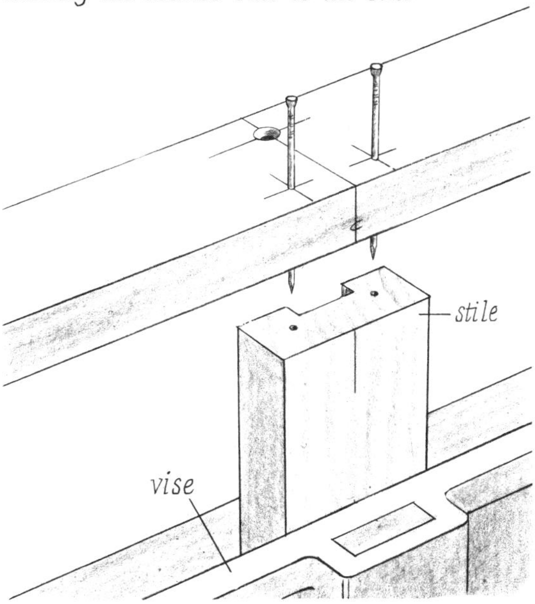
stile
vise

TAPERING THE LEGS

Lay out and make a pattern for the leg to the dimensions given in the illustration. Transfer to the pattern all the reference marks. Then follow the directions in *Turned Legs*, pages 95, 108 for tracing the pattern and for using the lathe-box to taper the inside faces of the legs. Cut off the surplus 1 inch of waste from the tops and bottoms of the legs, using the backsaw and miter box. Now cut the drawbore pins and slightly taper their entering ends to allow them to be driven more easily.

BEARER RAIL

At this time cut the bearer rail to size and lay out and cut the dovetails on both its ends (see *Making Joints*, p. 52), to the dimensions given in the illustration. Then, locate, drill, and countersink the screw holes—one in each dovetail. These holes are drilled clear through. Lay out the mortises on the top ends of the front legs, using the dovetails as patterns. Scribe their outlines with an awl and mark the width and depth of the mortises on the inside faces of both legs. Then cut the mortises (see *Making Joints*, p. 59).

dimensions for bearer rail dovetails

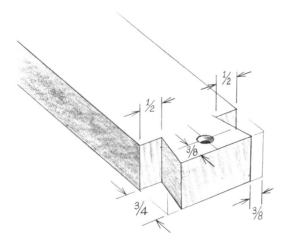

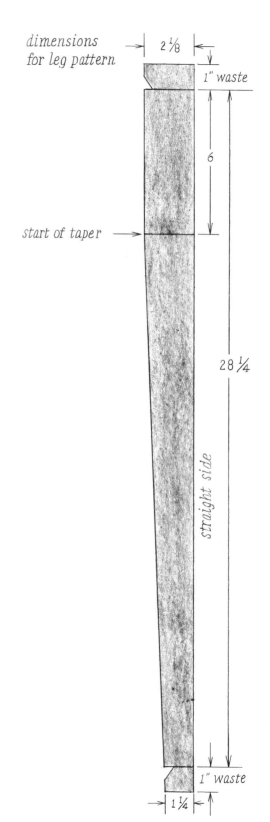

dimensions for leg pattern

2 ⅛

1" waste

6

start of taper

28 ¼

straight side

1" waste

1 ¼

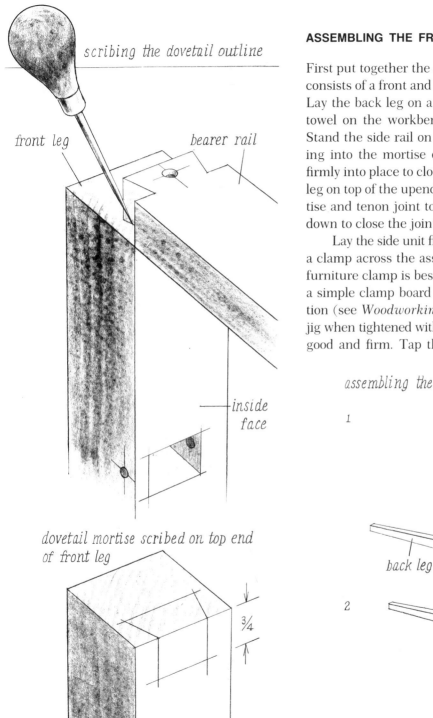

scribing the dovetail outline

front leg

bearer rail

inside face

dovetail mortise scribed on top end of front leg

¾

inside face

ASSEMBLING THE FRAME

First put together the side units, each of which consists of a front and a back leg and a side rail. Lay the back leg on a piece of carpet or an old towel on the workbench to protect the work. Stand the side rail on end with its tenon starting into the mortise of the leg. Then push it firmly into place to close the joint. Lay the front leg on top of the upended rail and start the mortise and tenon joint together. Then tap the leg down to close the joint.

Lay the side unit flat on the bench and place a clamp across the assembly from leg to leg. A furniture clamp is best, but it can be done with a simple clamp board as shown in the illustration (see *Woodworking Practices*, p. 35). This jig when tightened with a wedge will hold things good and firm. Tap the wedge up tight. Start

assembling the frame

1

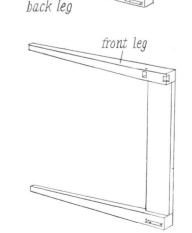

side rail

back leg

2

front leg

the tapered ends of 2 drawbore pins into one leg and then drive them home with the hammer, tapping first one and then the other to draw the joint up evenly. Tighten the clamp board wedge again, then drive the pins into the other leg joint. Trim the projecting drawbore pins flush. Remove the clamp board. Assemble the other side unit in the same way.

To complete the assembly of the table frame, the back rail and drawer rail are now joined to the side units. Lay one side unit down flat. Stand the back rail on end, starting its tenon into the back leg mortise. Then push it firmly into place to close the joint. Push the drawer rail joint together in the same way. Pick up the other side unit and lay it on top of the upended rails and

3 *driving drawbore pins into the leg joints*

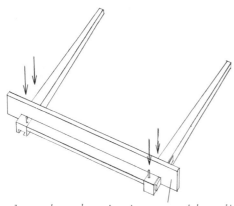

clamp board wedged across side unit

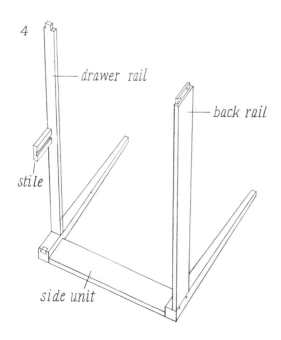

drawer rail

back rail

stile

side unit

5

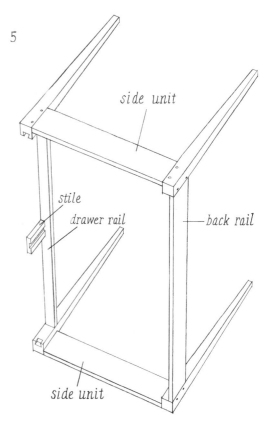

side unit

stile

drawer rail

back rail

side unit

start both joints together at the same time. Make a fist or use a mallet to tap the legs alternately to close both joints evenly.

Lay the table frame on its back, put a clamp board across the front of the frame and wedge it up tight. Then drive a drawbore pin into each joint of the drawer rail. Trim the drawbore pins flush. Remove the clamp board, turn the frame over on its front and wedge the clamp board across the back side. Then drive 2 drawbore pins into each of the back leg joints, and trim the pins flush as before. Remove the clamp board.

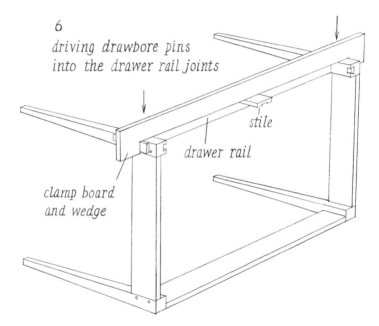

6
driving drawbore pins into the drawer rail joints

stile

drawer rail

clamp board and wedge

DIVIDER AND CENTER RUNNER

The divider, divider bracket, and center runner are assembled as a unit and then fastened into the table frame. Cut the center runner to size, draw a line down its center, and drill and countersink 3 screw holes from the underside as shown in the illustration. Cut the divider to size and cut the notch in its front end (see *Making Joints*, p. 80), to the dimensions given. Clamp the divider to the center of the runner as shown, with a 1/4-inch overhang at the back, and the notch aligned with the front end of the runner.

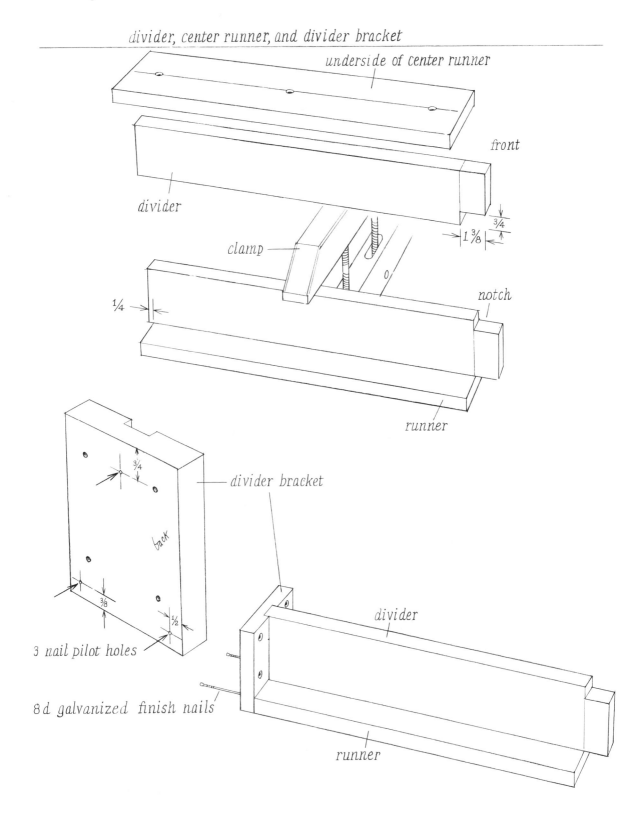

divider, center runner, and divider bracket

underside of center runner

front

divider

clamp

notch

1/4

3/4

1 3/8

0

runner

divider bracket

back

3/4

3/8

1/2

3 nail pilot holes

8d galvanized finish nails

divider

runner

Make sure that the divider is centered on the runner, then tighten the clamps and drive the screws.

On the back of the divider bracket locate and drill pilot holes for 3 nails as shown. Wipe a little glue on the back end of the divider, then fit the groove of the bracket over it and nail it

CENTER DRAWER GUIDES

Cut the two guides to size and drill and countersink the screw holes. Glue the guides and screw them to the runner and to the divider— one on either side of the divider—as shown in the illustration on the following page.

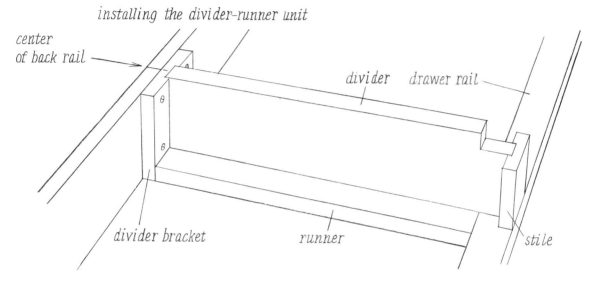

installing the divider-runner unit

center of back rail — divider · drawer rail · · divider bracket · runner · stile

SIDE RUNNERS AND GUIDES

in place flush with the top of the divider. Wipe off any excess glue with a damp sponge.

Fasten the whole unit in place as shown in the illustration. Mark the center of the back rail. Wipe glue on the notched end of the divider and start it into the groove of the stile. Push the assembly down evenly so that the notched end of the divider rests on the drawer rail. Lightly clamp the divider bracket to the back rail, lined up with the center mark and flush with the top of the rail. As quickly as possible before the glue sets up, put a clamp or clamp board across the table frame from front to back to hold the stile groove joint together. Crawl underneath and drive the screw up through the drawer rail into the end of the divider. Then drive the 4 screws through the bracket into the back rail. Wipe off any excess glue with a damp sponge. Leave the clamp on and set the work aside to dry.

These are made up as two units and then fastened in place. Cut the runners to size and work the halved joints on their front ends (see *Making Joints*, p. 62) to the dimensions given in the illustration. Then cut the notches front and back (see *Making Joints*, p. 80). Drill and countersink the screw holes. Cut the guides, drill and countersink the screw holes, and fasten them to the tops of the runners.

To install these units, lay the table frame bottom-side up. Touch a little glue on the halved joints and fit them into those in the underside of the drawer rail. Drive the front screws partway in to hold things temporarily. Go to the back and align the units flush with the bottom edge of the back rail. Drive a screw through the back of the runners into the back legs. Then tighten both screws. Wipe off any excess glue with a damp sponge. Stand the table frame on its legs.

center drawer guides

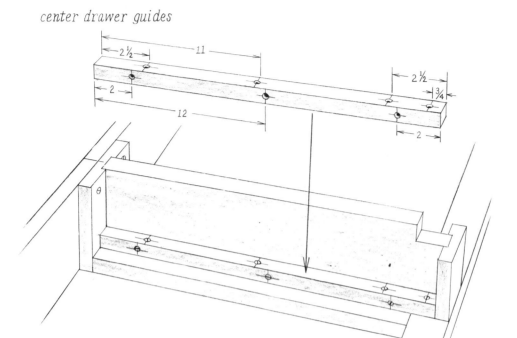

side runner-guide unit

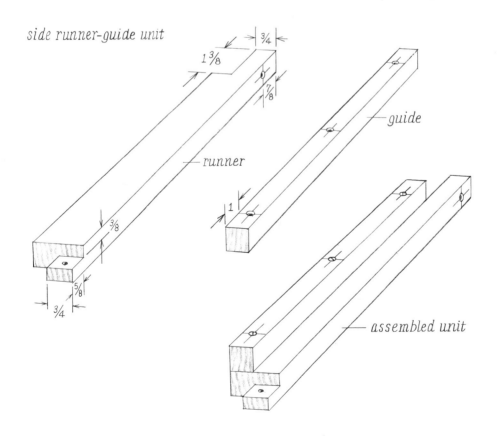

runner

guide

assembled unit

INSTALLING THE BEARER RAIL

Lay the bearer rail in place across the front of
the table to see if any fitting of the dovetail joints
is needed. If so, carefully shave the sides of the
dovetails until the joints will close about halfway with hand pressure alone. Then take the
rail out, touch glue onto the sides of both dovetails as well as into the notch of the divider, and
replace the rail over the mortises. Use a mallet
to tap the joints alternately to close them evenly.
Then drive a screw through each dovetail into
the leg. Finally, drill and countersink a screw
hole 1 1/8-inch deep in the center of the rail
and drive the screw down into the divider, as
shown.

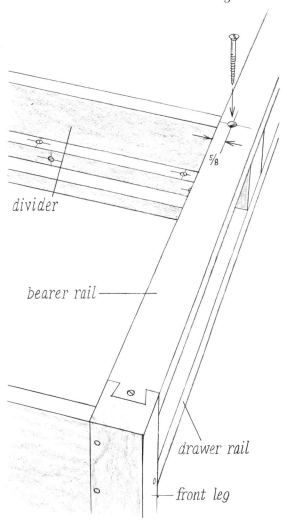

divider

bearer rail

5/8

drawer rail

front leg

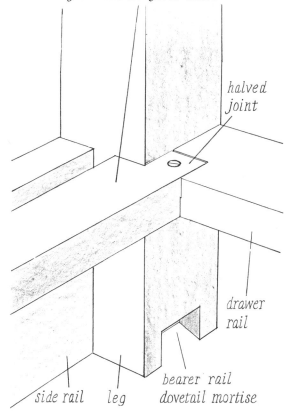

*underside of table:
installing the runner-guide units*

*halved
joint*

*drawer
rail*

side rail   *leg*   *bearer rail
dovetail mortise*

DRAWERS

The drawers are joined with dovetails in the front
and dowel pins at the back. Use the dimensions
in the illustrations to lay out the dovetails, the
location of the dowel pinhole centers, and the
grooves in the drawer fronts and sides. Then
build and fit the drawers according to the procedures described in *Making Joints*, page 52,
and in *Drawer Construction*, page 112. Note
that there are no grooves in the drawer backs.
The bottoms are simply nailed to their under
edges. Cut the drawer bottoms to fit, and sand
their inside surfaces to final smoothness (see
Sanding, p. 132) before assembling the drawers.

DRAWER PULLS AND STOPS

Lay out the position of the drawer pulls centered both ways on the drawer fronts. Then drill the screw holes and attach the pulls. Make the drawer stops with the wood grain following the long dimension. Drill and countersink the screw holes as shown. Push the drawers into the table so that their fronts are flush with the outside edge of the drawer rail. Without moving the drawers, make pencil marks on the runners at the back of the drawers. Take out the drawers, align the stops with the pencil marks, and screw them to the runners.

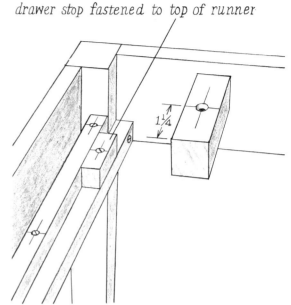

drawer stop fastened to top of runner

dimensions for dovetails and drawer bottom groove

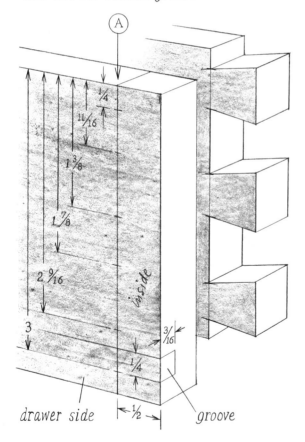

drawer side   groove

back end of drawer side: location of dowel pinhole centers

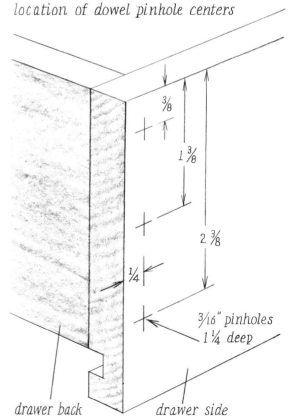

drawer back   drawer side

TABLETOP

Make up the top from three boards joined with either an edge-butt or tongue and groove joint (see *Making Joints,* p. 46, p. 88). Sand the ends of the tabletop (end grain) to final smoothness (see *Woodworking Practices,* p. 40, and *Sanding,* p. 132). Cut the tabletop cleats, back cleats, and kickers to size. Drill and countersink the screw holes.

To attach the tabletop to the frame, lay the top facedown on the floor or a pair of sawhorses. Set the table frame bottom-side up on top of it. Adjust its position so there is a uniform amount of overhang on all four sides. Then mark the position of the cleats on the tabletop by tracing a line around the inside of the frame. Remove the table frame, align the cleats and kickers in the positions shown in the illustration, and screw them in place. Again set the table frame bottom-side up, and down over the cleats. Drive 2 screws through each tabletop cleat into the side rails, and one screw through each back cleat into the back rail. Stand the writing table on its legs and put in the drawers.

attaching cleats and kickers to the tabletop

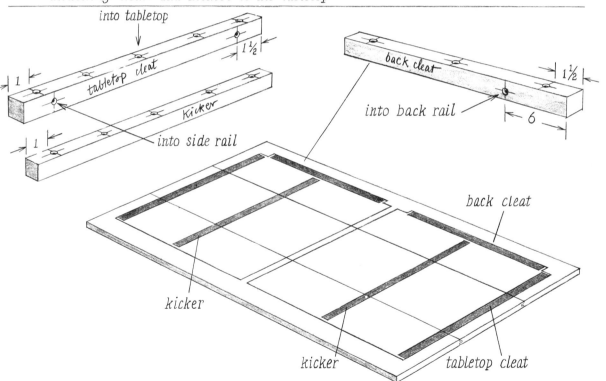

into tabletop

tabletop cleat

$1\frac{1}{2}$

1

kicker

into side rail

1

back cleat

$1\frac{1}{2}$

into back rail

6

back cleat

kicker

kicker

tabletop cleat

Blanket Chest

HEIGHT 21½   WIDTH 42½   DEPTH 21½

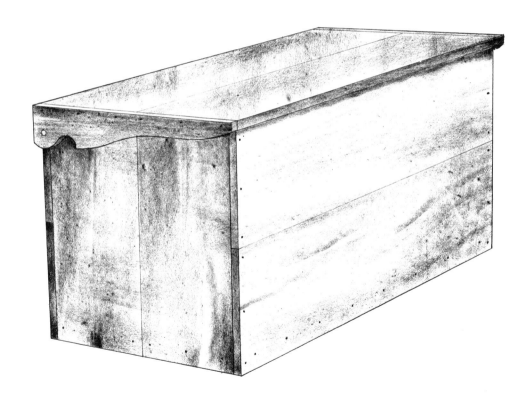

Blanket Chest

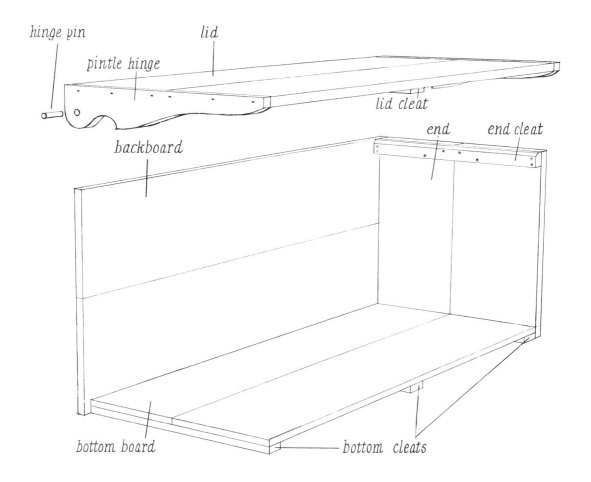

hinge pin

pintle hinge

lid

lid cleat

backboard

end

end cleat

bottom board

bottom cleats

LUMBER REQUIRED

No. Pcs.	Nominal Dimensions
3	$1 \times 12 \times 12'$
1	$5/4 \times 12 \times 8'$
1	$5/8 \times 3'$ hardwood dowel

MATERIALS

No. Pcs.	Part	Dimensions
1	bottom	$3/4 \times 19 \ 1/2 \times 41$
2	ends	$3/4 \times 19 \ 1/2 \times 20 \ 5/8$
1	back	$3/4 \times 20 \ 5/8 \times 42 \ 1/2$
1	front	$3/4 \times 20 \ 5/8 \times 42 \ 1/2$
1	lid	$7/8 \times 21 \ 1/2 \times 42 \ 3/4$
3	bottom cleats	$3/4 \times 1 \ 1/2 \times 19 \ 1/2$
2	end cleats	$3/4 \times 2 \times 19 \ 1/2$
1	lid cleat	$3/4 \times 1 \ 1/2 \times 18 \ 1/2$
2	pintle hinges	$3/4 \times 4 \times 21 \ 1/2$
2	hinge pins	$5/8 \times 1 \ 5/8$ hardwood dowel
quant	nails	7d old-fashioned fine finish *ends to bottom, front and back to ends and bottom, pintle hinges to lid*
18	screws	$1 \ 1/4 \times$ No. 8 flathead *bottom cleats*
18	screws	$1 \ 1/4 \times$ No. 8 flathead brass *end and lid cleats*

cutting diagram

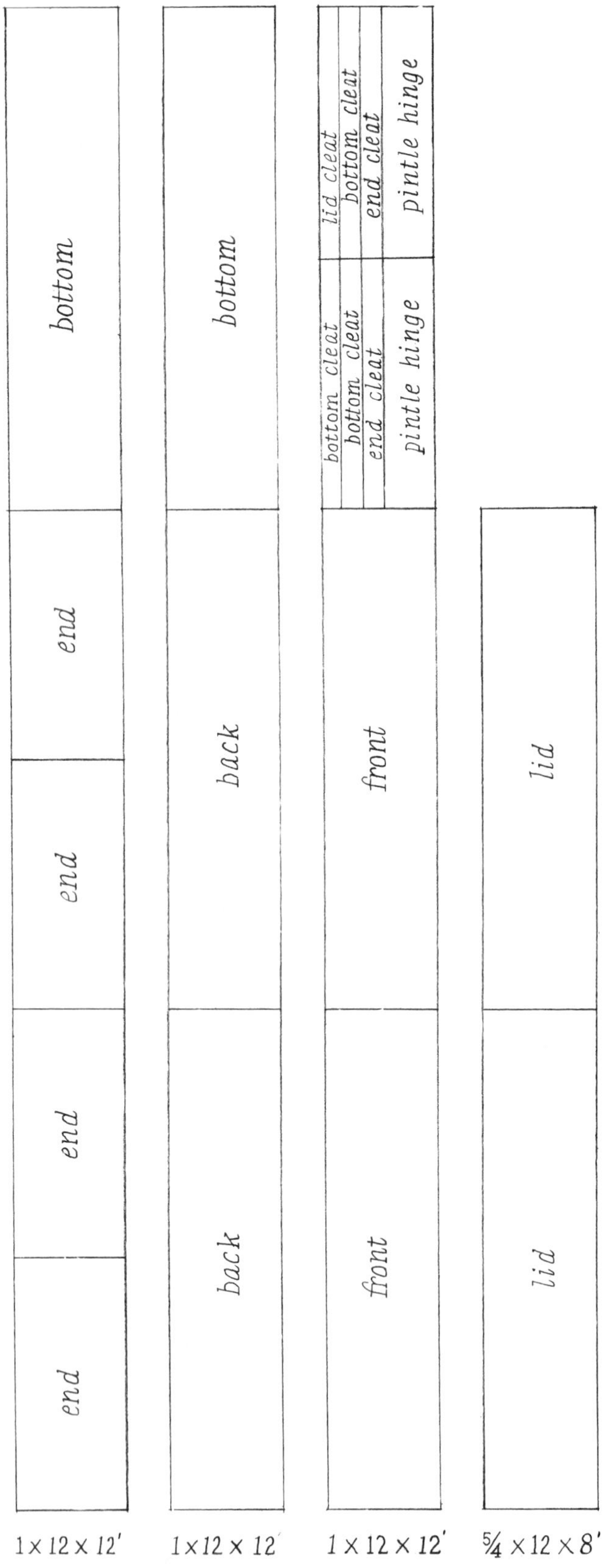

bottom

end

end

end

1 × 12 × 12'

bottom

back

back

1 × 12 × 12'

lid cleat
bottom cleat
end cleat

pintle hinge

bottom cleat
bottom cleat
end cleat

pintle hinge

front

front

1 × 12 × 12'

lid

lid

⅝ × 12 × 8'

attaching cleats to underside of bottom

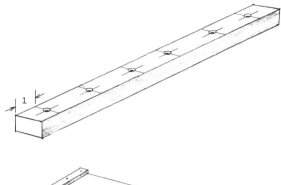

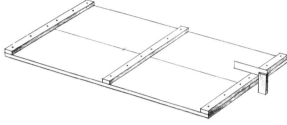

chamfered end cleats

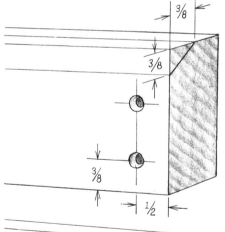

This chest is of the six-board type, each of the six being made up of two boards. Make up the bottom, ends, back, front, and lid, joining the boards with either edge-butt or tongue and groove joints (see *Making Joints,* p. 46, p. 88). Also at this time sand their inside surfaces to final smoothness (see *Sanding,* p. 132). Note in the list of materials that the lid is 1/4-inch longer than the chest itself in order to allow clearance for easy movement of the lid.

Cut the three bottom cleats and locate, drill, and countersink the screw holes, locating them no closer than 1 inch to their ends or to the glued joint. Lay the bottom board facedown on the floor or a pair of sawhorses. Clamp one cleat in the center, using the carpenter's square to align it at right angles to the long edge of the bottom board. Next, clamp a cleat at each end, making them flush with the ends of the bottom board. Then drive the screws.

Cut the two end cleats to size, then mark out and plane chamfers on their inside upper edges to the dimensions shown in the illustration. Drill and countersink the screw holes, locating the middle screws no closer than 1 inch to the glued joint. Clamp the cleats in place on the ends, making them exactly flush at the top. Then drive the brass screws.

Use the carpenter's square to lay off nailing lines across the outside of the bottom of both end sections to the dimensions given in the illustration. These lines should be centered accurately on the edges of the bottom boards. Then mark off the centers of 6 nail pilot holes spaced about 4 inches apart, but no closer than 1 inch to the outside edges or to the glued joints. Drill the pilot holes clear through.

end boards: laying off nailing lines and nail pilot hole centers

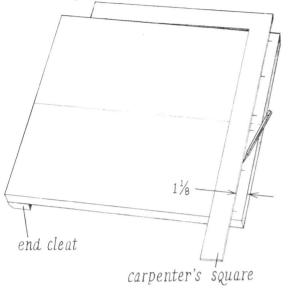

end cleat

$1\frac{1}{8}$

carpenter's square

ASSEMBLY

Stand the bottom board on the floor against the workbench with one edge in the vise for support, or with a batten nailed across it as shown in the illustration. Start nails into 2 of the pilot holes of one end unit, tapping them in until their points barely come through. Lay the end unit on top of the upended bottom board and align it flush at both sides and along the bottom edge. You will probably need some help to do this. Drive both nails in about 1/2 inch. Check the alignment of the sides and bottom edge again. Then, keeping the end unit level, drive these nails all the way. Then drive the other nails. Stand the work on its other end and nail the second end unit in place in the same way.

Lay off nailing lines along the bottom edge and ends of the backboard to the dimensions given. Then mark the centers of the nail pilot holes, spaced about 4 inches apart but no closer than 1 inch to the outside edges or to the glued joints. Note that the uppermost nails must be located carefully in order to stay clear of the hinge pinhole and the beveled top edge, as

assembling the chest

1

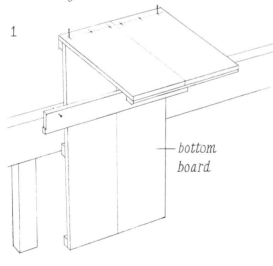

bottom board

2

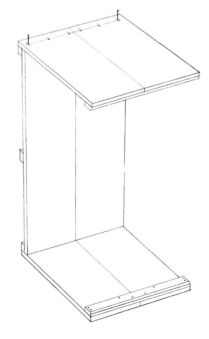

3

*backboard: laying off nailing lines
and nail pilot hole centers*

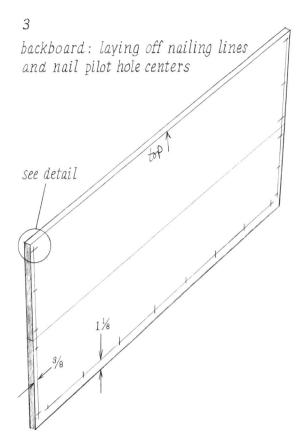

see detail

top

1⅛

³⁄₈

4

*detail:
location of uppermost nails*

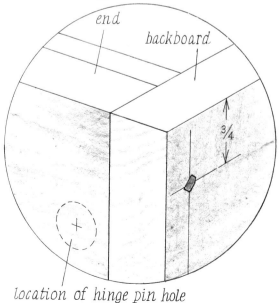

end

backboard

¾

location of hinge pin hole

5

backboard

6

front board

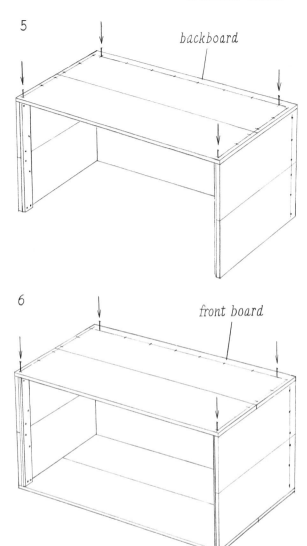

shown in the illustration. Drill all the pilot holes
clear through. Now start a nail into each of the
corner pilot holes, tapping them in until their
points barely come through. Then lay the backboard in place, aligned flush along the bottom
edge as shown in the illustration. Drive the 2
nails into the bottom board about 1/2 inch. Align
the top corners exactly flush, then drive the 2
top corner nails in about 1/2 inch. Make a final
check of the alignment all the way around, then
drive the 4 nails all the way. Then drive the other
nails. Turn the chest over and attach the front
board, using these same procedures.

Cut the lid cleat to size and drill and countersink the screw holes, again locating the middle ones no closer than 1 inch to the glued joint. Clamp the cleat to the underside of the lid, centered both ways as shown in the illustration. Drive the brass screws.

Cut the pintle hinges to size. Make a scroll pattern from the diagram and trace it onto both hinge pieces. Bore the 5/8-inch holes clear through for the hinge pins. Then cut the scrollwork with either a compass or coping saw, and smooth and fair up its curves with the round rasp, spokeshave, file, and sandpaper block. Drill nail pilot holes along the top edges of the hinges, spacing them as shown in the scroll pattern diagram.

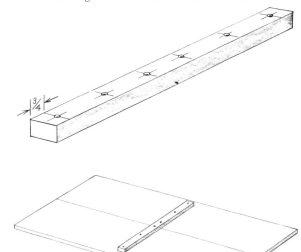

attaching cleat to underside of lid

$\frac{3}{4}$

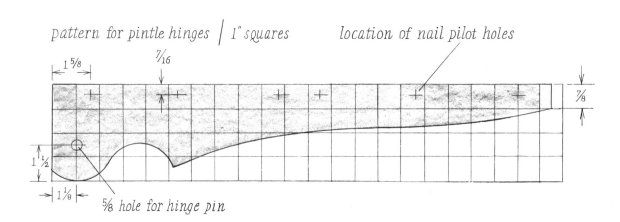

pattern for pintle hinges / 1" squares   *location of nail pilot holes*

1 $\frac{5}{8}$ $\frac{7}{16}$ $\frac{7}{8}$

1 $\frac{1}{2}$

1 $\frac{1}{8}$

$\frac{5}{8}$ *hole for hinge pin*

To attach the hinges, stand the lid on the floor against the workbench with one edge in the vise for support, or with a batten nailed across it as shown in the illustration. Start a nail into each end of the hinge, tapping them in until their points barely come through. Lay the hinge in place on the upended lid and align it flush front and back and along the top edge. Drive both nails in about 1/2 inch, check the alignment again, then drive them all the way. Drive the other nails, then attach the other hinge in the same way.

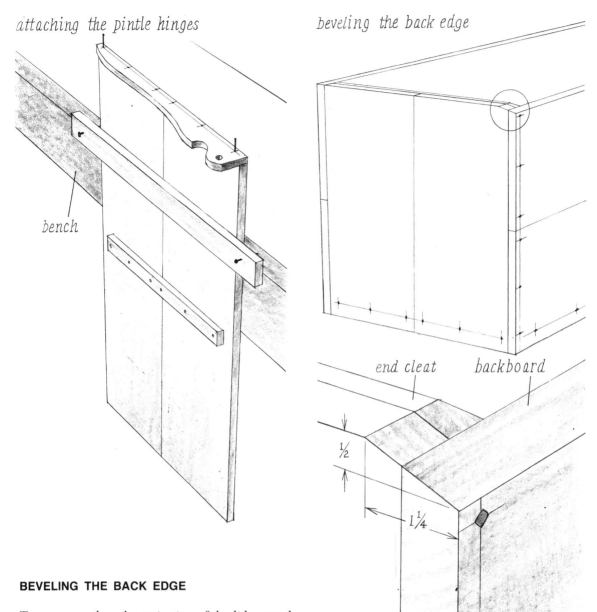

attaching the pintle hinges

bench

beveling the back edge

end cleat   backboard

½

1¼

BEVELING THE BACK EDGE

To accommodate the swinging of the lid around the axis of the hinge pins, it is necessary to bevel the outside top edge of the backboard as well as a bit of each end unit where they join the backboard. Lay off bevel lines on both ends and along the outside of the backboard to the dimensions given in the illustration. Then use a jack or jointer plane to bevel the backboard, keeping the plane tilted to the angle as marked on the ends. When the bevel nearly touches the wood of the end units, use a 1-inch chisel to pare the bevels on the end units and end cleats, and for a short distance into the backboard. Avoid simply planing across these corner junctions and splintering the wood. The final planing of the bevel should be done with a sharp block plane operated with good pressure and set for a very fine cut.

HINGE PINHOLES

Lay the lid on the chest with a shim at each end as shown in the illustration—a 3 x 5 filing card folded into thirds. The shims provide the necessary clearance between lid and chest to ensure easy closing. Adjust the lid so that it is flush with the back of the chest. Then tap a wedge between the hinge and the chest in order to draw the near hinge tight against the chest, as shown in the illustration. Using a 5/8-inch auger bit, rotate it by hand into the hinge hole until its point stabs a pinpoint mark in the wood of the chest. Remove the bit and the wedge, then repeat the process on the other end of the chest. Lift off the lid, then use the brace and an 11/16-inch auger bit to bore the pinholes, starting the point of the bit in the pinpoint marks. *Do not bore clear through.* When the point of the bit starts to prick through on the inside of the chest—stop. Withdraw the bit and clean out the shavings. This slightly larger hole allows the pin—which is glued only to the hinge—to turn freely.

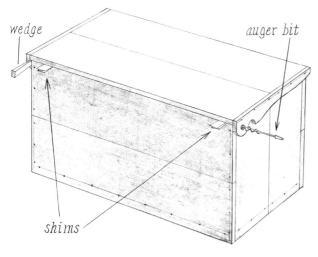

boring the hinge pinholes

wedge

auger bit

shims

INSTALLING HINGE PINS

With the lid in place again, cut two pieces of 5/8-inch dowel about 4 inches long and sand off the sharp edges at their entering ends. Push this end of the dowel through the hinge and into the hole in the chest until it stops. Make a pencil mark on the dowel, then pull it out. Wipe glue around the dowel—on the inner side of the pencil mark—in a band no wider than 1/2 inch. The dowel is glued to the hinge only. Twist the glued dowel into the hole until it stops. Wipe off any excess glue with a damp sponge. Glue in the other hinge pin in the same way, then leave the work to dry overnight.

Cut off both pins and trim them flush (see *Making Joints*, p. 79). When this is done, try lifting and closing the lid. If it rubs or growls at any point, use the block plane, file, or sandpaper to ease the offending section.

Sideboard

HEIGHT 29½   WIDTH 48   DEPTH 12¼

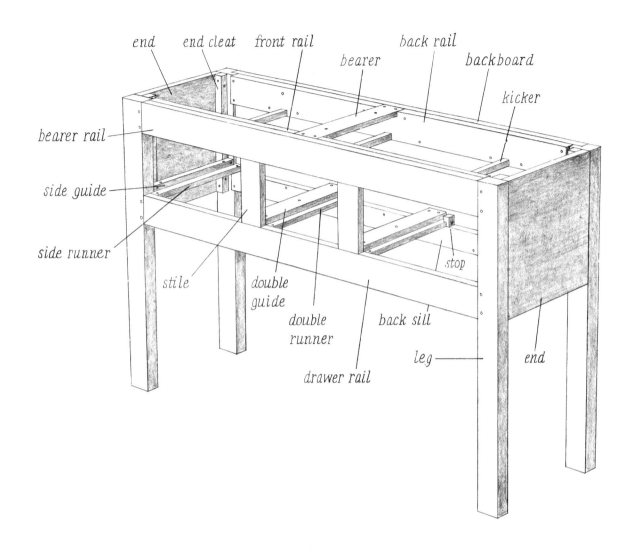

LUMBER REQUIRED

No. Pcs.	Nominal Dimensions
1	$2 \times 10 \times 6'$
1	$1 \times 12 \times 10'$
1	$1 \times 12 \times 12'$
1	$1 \times 14 \times 54''$
1	$1 \times 8 \times 8'$
1	$1/4 \times 12 \times 3'$ hardwood plywood
1	$5/4 \times 4 \times 1'$ hardwood
1	$1/4 \times 3'$ hardwood dowel
2	$3/16 \times 3'$ hardwood dowel

MATERIALS

No. Pcs.	Part	Dimensions
4	legs	1 1/4 × 2 1/4 × 28 3/4
1	bearer rail	3/4 × 3 × 41 3/8
1	drawer rail	3/4 × 2 3/4 × 41 3/8
8	drawbore pins	1/4 × 1 1/8 hardwood dowel
1	front rail	3/4 × 3 × 39 3/8
1	back rail	3/4 × 3 × 39 3/8
1	front sill	3/4 × 2 × 39 3/8
1	back sill	3/4 × 2 × 39 3/8
2	stiles	3/4 × 2 × 7 1/4
1	backboard	3/4 × 11 1/2 × 41 3/8
2	ends	3/4 × 8 3/4 × 11 1/2
4	end cleats	3/4 × 3/4 × 11 1/2
2	side runners	3/4 × 1 1/2 × 9 3/4
2	side guides	3/4 × 3/4 × 8 3/4
2	double runners	3/4 × 3 1/2 × 9 3/4
2	double guides	3/4 × 2 × 9 3/4
3	drawer kickers	3/4 × 3/4 × 9 3/4
1	bearer	3/4 × 2 × 9 3/4
2	drawer fronts	3/4 × 5 3/4 × 13
2	drawer backs	3/4 × 5 3/4 × 12 1/4
2	drawer bottoms	1/4 × 8 7/8 × 12 1/2 hardwood plywood
1	middle drawer front	3/4 × 5 3/4 × 9 3/8
1	middle drawer back	3/4 × 5 1/4 × 8 5/8
1	middle drawer bottom	1/4 × 8 7/8 × 9 hardwood plywood
6	drawer sides	3/8 × 5 3/4 × 9 1/4
36	dowel pins	3/16 × 1 1/8 hardwood dowel
3	drawer pulls	brass plate with drop
6	drawer stops	3/4 × 3/4 × 1 1/2
1	tabletop	3/4 × 12 1/4 × 48
2	tabletop cleats	1 × 1 × 7 1/4 hardwood
8	screws	5/8 × No. 5 flathead *stiles*
6	screws	1 × No. 5 flathead *drawer stops*
8	screws	1 × No. 7 flathead *backboard*
10	screws	1 1/4 × No. 6 flathead *kickers, bearer*
92	screws	1 1/4 × No. 7 flathead *rails, sills, cleats, guides, runners*
15	screws	1 1/4 × No. 8 flathead *end cleats to legs, bearer to tabletop*
10	screws	1 1/2 × No. 8 flathead *tabletop cleats to tabletop, and to ends*
quant	nails	1 1/4 × No. 16 wire *back edges of drawer bottoms*

cutting diagram

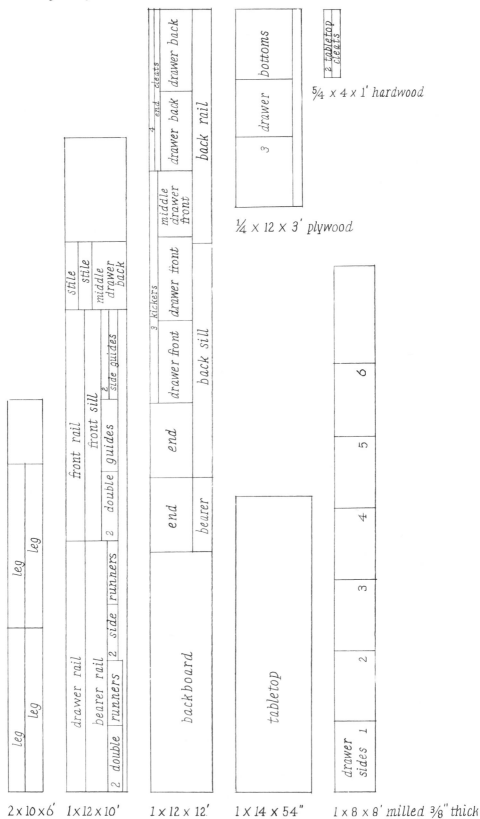

4 end cleats

drawer back

drawer back

back rail

bottoms

5/4 × 4 × 1' *hardwood*

stile

stile

middle
drawer
back

middle
drawer
front

3 drawer

1/4 × 12 × 3' *plywood*

front rail

front sill

2 side guides

3 kickers

drawer front

drawer front

back sill

2 double guides

end

end

bearer

drawer rail

bearer rail

2 side runners

2 double runners

leg

leg

leg

leg

backboard

tabletop

drawer
sides 1

2

3

4

5

6

2 × 10 × 6'   1 × 12 × 10'   1 × 12 × 12'   1 × 14 × 54"   1 × 8 × 8' *milled* 3/8" *thick*

FRONT UNIT

Cut the front legs, adding 2 inches to the length for waste. Plane them to uniform size and dress all four sides square and smooth. Mark out the centers of the drawbores on their outside faces (see *Making Joints*, p. 88), using the square and marking gauge. Next drill 1/4-inch holes for the drawbore pins to a depth of 1 inch. Lay out and cut the mortises, using the dimensions given in the diagram. Then use a backsaw and miter box to cut off the surplus 1 inch of waste from the tops and bottoms of the legs.

Cut the drawer rail and bearer rail to size. Then lay out and cut all the tenons, using the dimensions given in the illustration. Make them

location of drawbores / front legs

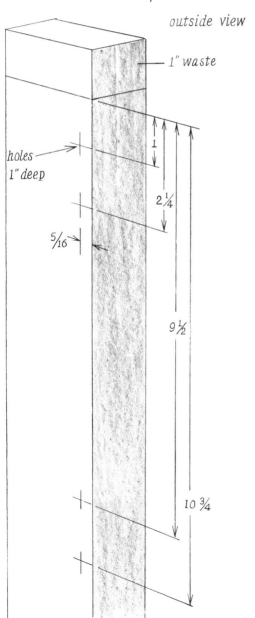

mortise dimensions / front legs

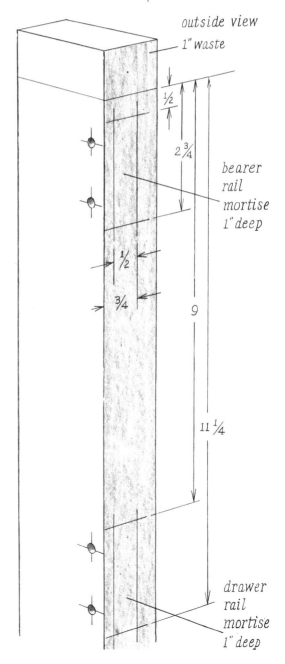

a bit full in thickness, then shave each one individually to fit its own mortise. They should be a tight-push fit. As each tenon is fitted, mark it and its mortise with the same letter (see *Woodworking Practices*, p. 33). These reference marks guarantee that each tenon will go where it belongs when the sideboard frame is finally assembled. Now locate and drill the drawbores in the tenons. All these procedures are described in *Making Joints*, page 72.

Next, cut the halved joints in both rails (see *Making Joints*, p. 62), in the locations and to the dimensions specified in the illustration. The stiles will be fitted into these joints later.

Cut the drawbore pins and slightly taper their entering ends. This allows them to be driven more easily.

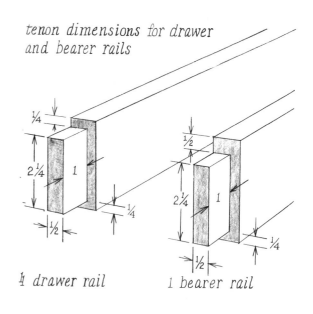

tenon dimensions for drawer and bearer rails

¼ drawer rail   1 bearer rail

halved joints in bearer and drawer rails

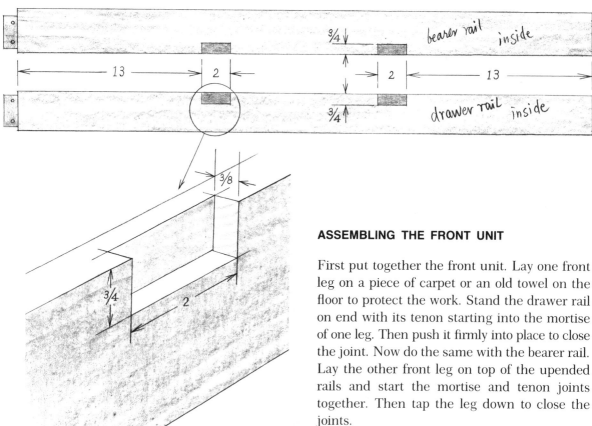

bearer rail inside

drawer rail inside

ASSEMBLING THE FRONT UNIT

First put together the front unit. Lay one front leg on a piece of carpet or an old towel on the floor to protect the work. Stand the drawer rail on end with its tenon starting into the mortise of one leg. Then push it firmly into place to close the joint. Now do the same with the bearer rail. Lay the other front leg on top of the upended rails and start the mortise and tenon joints together. Then tap the leg down to close the joints.

assembling the front unit

1

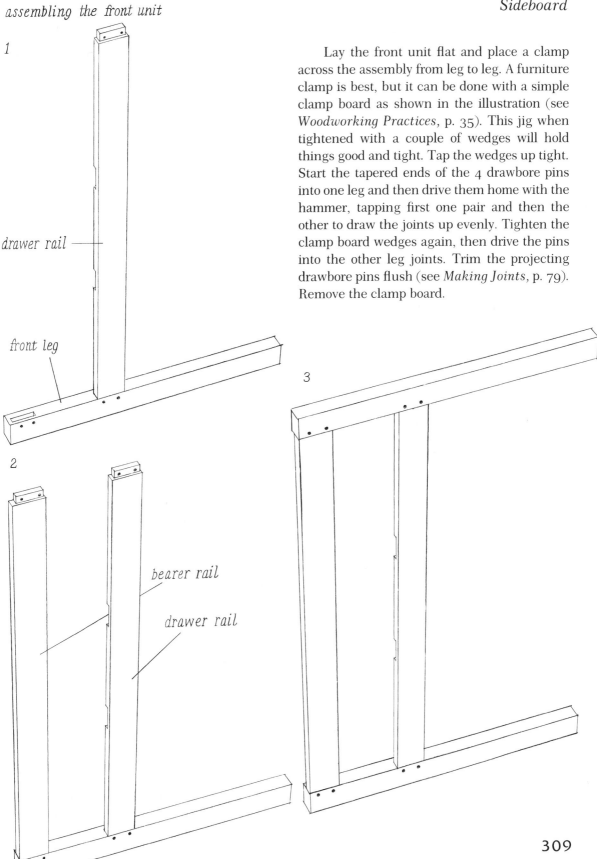

drawer rail

front leg

2

bearer rail

drawer rail

3

Lay the front unit flat and place a clamp across the assembly from leg to leg. A furniture clamp is best, but it can be done with a simple clamp board as shown in the illustration (see *Woodworking Practices,* p. 35). This jig when tightened with a couple of wedges will hold things good and tight. Tap the wedges up tight. Start the tapered ends of the 4 drawbore pins into one leg and then drive them home with the hammer, tapping first one pair and then the other to draw the joints up evenly. Tighten the clamp board wedges again, then drive the pins into the other leg joints. Trim the projecting drawbore pins flush (see *Making Joints,* p. 79). Remove the clamp board.

4

driving drawbore pins into the leg joints

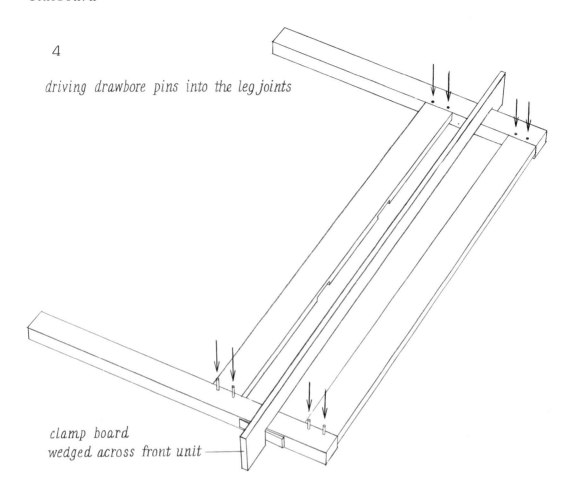

clamp board
wedged across front unit

front and back rails and sills :
notches for bearer and kickers | location of screw holes

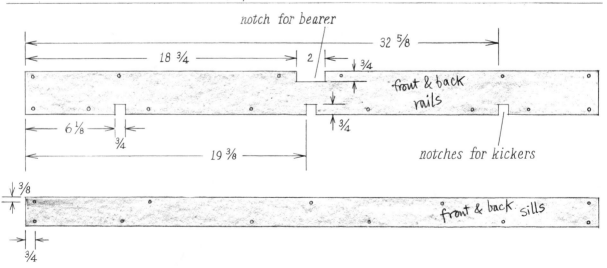

notch for bearer

18 ¾   2   32 ⅝

¾

front & back rails

6 ⅛

¾

19 ⅜

notches for kickers

⅜

front & back sills

¾

FRONT AND BACK RAILS AND SILLS

Cut the front and back rails to size. Then clamp them together and lay out the notches for the bearer and kickers (see *Making Joints,* p. 80) to the dimensions given in the illustration. Hold the clamped work in the vise and use a back-saw and chisel to cut all the notches. Locate, drill, and countersink the screw holes. Remove the clamps. Now cut the front and back sills to size. Clamp them together and locate, drill, and countersink the screw holes. Remove the clamps.

STILES

Turn the front unit on its face and measure the distance between the halved joints in the bearer and drawer rails, and cut the stiles to fit. Then cut the halved joints at both ends of the stiles (see *Making Joints,* p. 62) and number the joints (see *Woodworking Practices,* p. 33). Drill and countersink the screw holes in the locations shown. To fasten the stiles, spread glue thinly on both surfaces of the joints, lay the stiles in place, and drive the screws. Immediately clean off any excess glue with a damp sponge, and leave the work to dry.

stiles

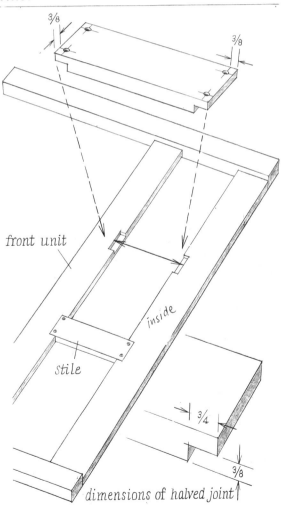

front unit

inside

stile

dimensions of halved joint

FASTENING FRONT RAIL AND SILL

Lay the front unit facedown. Lay the front rail on top of the bearer rail with the bearer notch at the top. The rail should just fit between the legs and come flush with both edges of the bearer rail. Drive one screw at each end, check the alignment again, then drive the rest of the screws.

Lay the front sill on top of the drawer rail, with their lower edges flush and a 3/4-inch lap as shown in the illustration. Drive one screw at each end, check the alignment, then drive the rest of the screws.

fastening front rail and sill

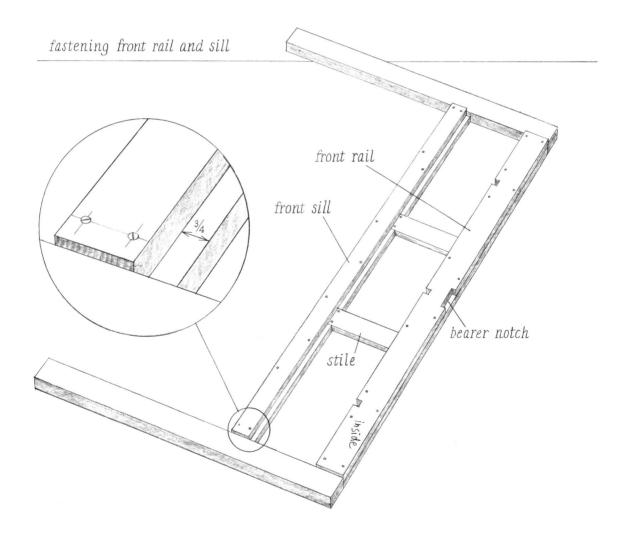

front rail

front sill

bearer notch

stile

inside

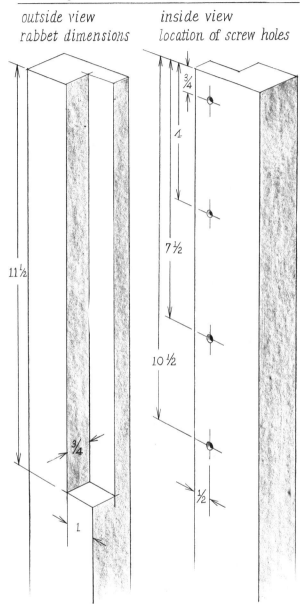

back legs:

*outside view
rabbet dimensions*

*inside view
location of screw holes*

11½

¾

¾

1

1

7½

10½

½

BACK UNIT

Cut the back legs, adding 2 inches to the length for waste. Plane them to uniform thickness and width. Use a jack or jointer plane to dress all four sides square and smooth. Lay out and cut the stopped rabbets for the backboard (see *Making Joints*, p. 87) to the dimensions given in the illustration. Drill and countersink the 4 screw holes *from the inside* of each leg in the locations shown. Then use the miter box and backsaw to cut off the surplus 1 inch of waste from the tops and bottoms of the legs, making sure they are exactly the same length as the front ones.

It is important to make the back unit exactly the same length as the front unit. To do this, lay the front unit down flat on 2 x 4 blocks. Clamp the back legs on top of the front legs, aligning them flush on the edges and at the top. Then measure the distance between the rab-

bets as shown. Use this measurement to cut and trim the backboard to exact length. Carefully plane both its ends square with the block plane (see *Woodworking Practices,* p. 29). The squareness of these joints determines whether the back legs are straight, toed-in, or splayed out. With the clamps still on, lay the backboard into the rabbets, shaving one end if necessary to get a good, snug fit.

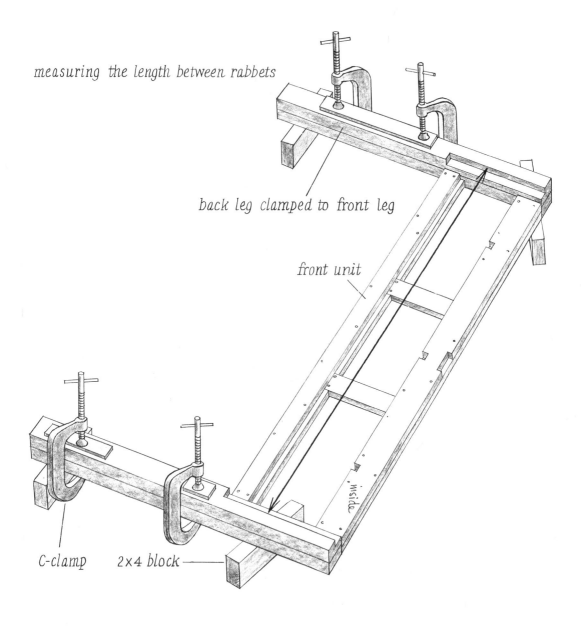

measuring the length between rabbets

back leg clamped to front leg

front unit

inside

C-clamp   *2×4 block*

fitting the backboard into the rabbets

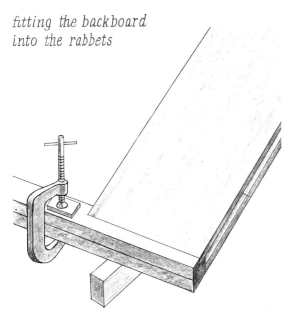

fastening the backboard with dowel pins

¼-inch holes 1" deep

1 ³/8

½

backboard

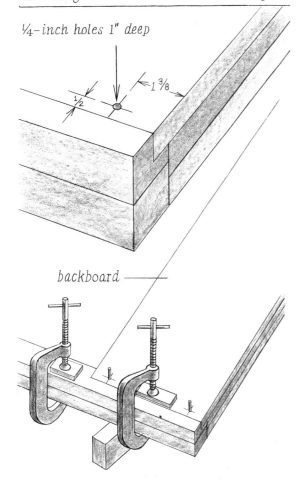

ASSEMBLING THE BACK UNIT

Put an additional clamp on each end of the backboard as shown, to hold it tight into the rabbets. Then drill 4 dowel pinholes—2 at each end—in the locations shown. Cut 4 dowel pins 1/4 inch in diameter and 1 1/8 inches long. Slightly taper their entering ends so they will drive more easily. Use a wooden matchstick to twirl glue into the pinholes. Coat the walls with glue, but don't let it puddle in the bottom of the holes. Then drive the pins. Wipe off any excess glue with a damp sponge.

As quickly as possible, remove the clamps and stand the back unit on its feet leaning against the bench, its inside facing you. Drive the 8 screws—4 at each end—from the inside, through the legs and into the backboard. Set the work aside to dry overnight. Then trim the dowel pins flush (see *Making Joints*, p. 79).

fastening back rail and sill

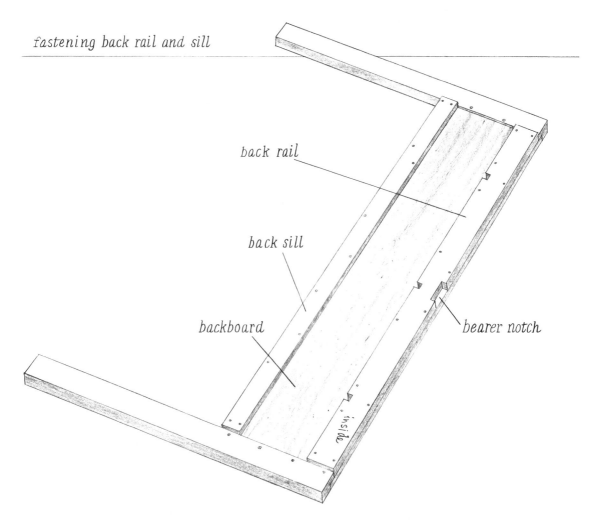

back rail

back sill

backboard

bearer notch

inside

Next, fasten the back rail to the backboard flush at the top and with the bearer notch on top. Then fasten the back sill in place, flush along the lower edge of the backboard.

END UNITS

Cut the two ends to size, making sure that the wood grain runs horizontally with the short dimension, not up and down. Use the block plane and the square to get their ends smooth and square. Do not sandpaper these end-grain surfaces: the outer edges must be clean and sharp in order to make a tight seam with the legs.

squaring the ends

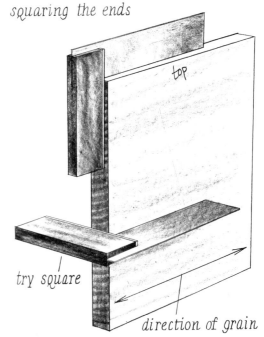

top

try square

direction of grain

squaring the cleats

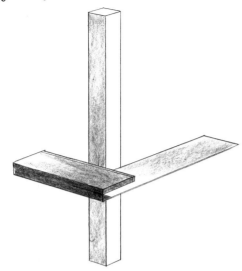

Next, cut the four end cleats to size. It is especially important to make the long sides of the cleats square, so that when the end units are attached to the front and back units, the corners of the sideboard will also be square. Drill and countersink the screw holes as shown. Spread a thin, even coat of glue on each cleat. Clamp them in position on the sideboard end pieces, then drive the screws. Wipe off any excess glue with a damp sponge.

checking a finished end unit with the square

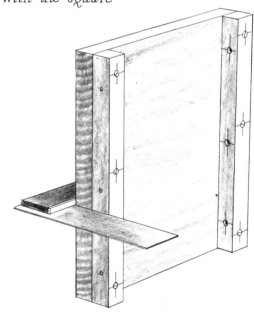

end cleats / *location of screw holes*

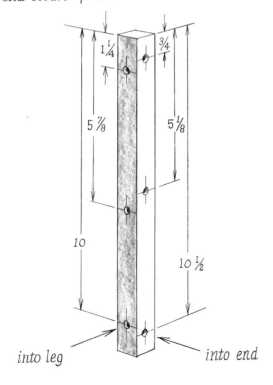

$1\frac{1}{4}$ $\frac{3}{4}$

$5\frac{7}{8}$ $5\frac{1}{8}$

10 $10\frac{1}{2}$

into leg *into end*

Sideboard

ASSEMBLING THE FRAME

Lay the front unit facedown on boards on a pair of sawhorses. Glue the cleat-side of one end unit and stand it on the front unit, flush with the leg and with the top as shown. Clamp it in place and drive the screws through the cleat into the leg. Immediately wipe off any excess glue with a damp sponge. Fasten the other end unit in place in the same way. Leave the work to dry overnight.

Set the front unit on the floor and spread glue on the other end cleats. Working quickly, lay the back unit facedown on the sawhorses. Pick up the front unit, turn it over, and lay it on top of the back unit, making sure that everything is flush at the ends and at the top. Then wedge two clamp boards at each end as shown in the illustration, check the alignment again, and drive the screws through the cleats and into the legs. Clean off any excess glue with a damp sponge, and put the work aside to dry overnight.

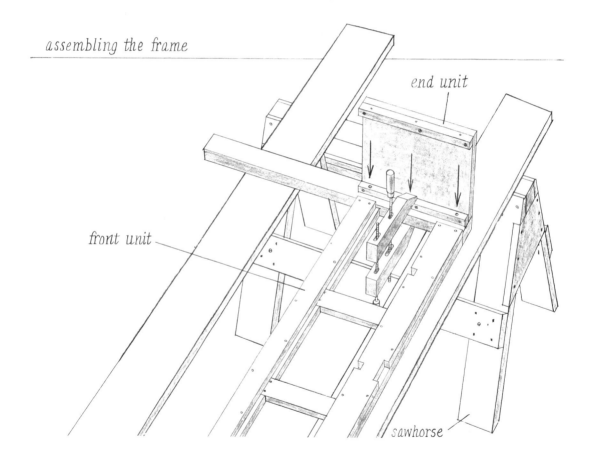

assembling the frame

end unit

front unit

sawhorse

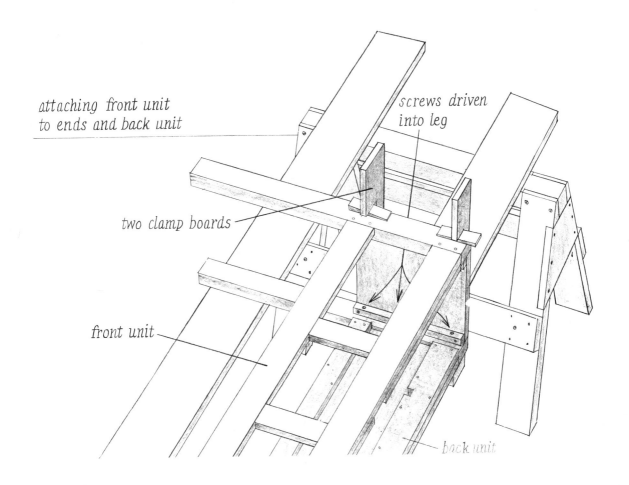

attaching front unit
to ends and back unit

screws driven
into leg

two clamp boards

front unit

back unit

SIDE RUNNERS AND GUIDES

These are made up as units and installed on the left and right sides of the sideboard. Cut the side runners to size and cut the notches front and back (see *Making Joints,* p. 80) to the dimensions given in the illustration. Drill and countersink the screw holes. Then cut the guides to size, drill and countersink the screw holes, and fasten them to the tops of the runners as shown.

To install these units, stand the sideboard on its legs and lay each unit in position, resting on the front and back sills and with the notches fitting around the inside corners of the front and back legs. Fasten each unit with 4 screws—2 through the guides into the end cleats, and 2 down through the runners into the sills.

side runners and guides

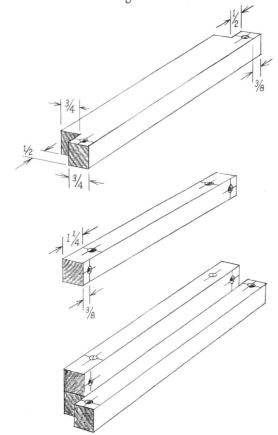

DOUBLE RUNNERS AND GUIDES

These are also made up as two units and fastened to the front and back sills. Cut the runners and guides to size and drill and countersink the screw holes. Align the guides on the runners and screw them in place as shown in the illustration.

To install one of these units, lay it in place resting on the front and back sills. Align the front end of the unit so that the edges of the guides are flush with the edges of the stile. Drive one screw through the front end of the runner down into the sill. Then adjust the back end of the unit so that the distance between this double guide and the side guide is the same front and back, thus allowing the drawer to slide without pinching. Drive one screw through the back of the runner into the back sill. Check the measurement between guides again, then drive the rest of the screws. Install the other unit in the same way. Then turn the sideboard bottom-side up.

double runners and guides

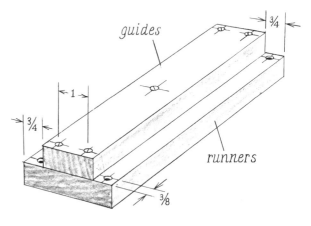

installing the runners and guides

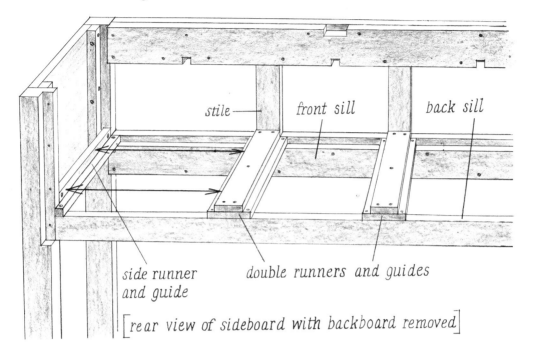

stile

front sill

back sill

side runner
and guide

double runners and guides

[rear view of sideboard with backboard removed]

DRAWER KICKERS

Cut the three kickers the same length as the double runners just installed. Plane and sand their edges smooth. Drill and countersink the screw holes. Fit the kickers down into the notches and fasten them in place with a single screw at each end. Stand the sideboard on its legs.

installing the drawer kickers :
sideboard bottom-side up

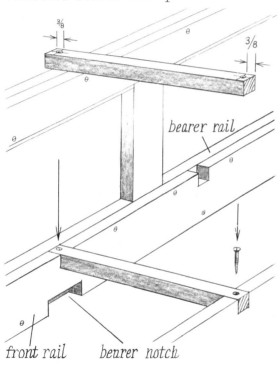

front rail   bearer notch

bearer rail

BEARER

Cut the bearer to size, first measuring from front to back in the notches of the front and back rails to determine its exact length. Drill and countersink 2 screw holes in each end from the top side, and 2 holes from the underside, as shown in the illustration. Fasten the bearer in place by driving screws into the notches. The other 2 holes will be used when the tabletop is attached to the frame.

installing the bearer

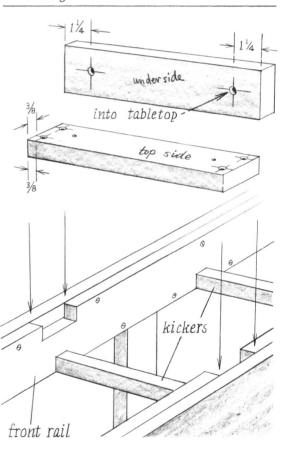

underside

into tabletop

top side

kickers

front rail

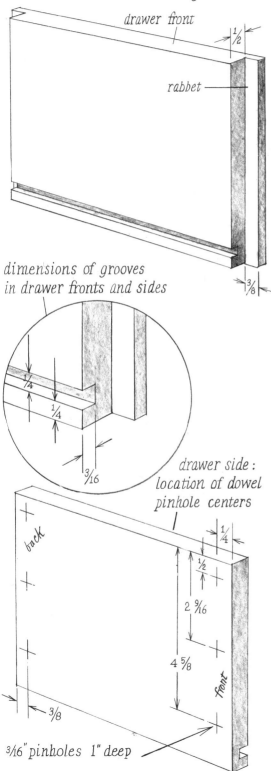

drawer fronts and sides:
dimensions for rabbets and grooves

drawer front

rabbet

$\frac{1}{2}$

$\frac{3}{8}$

dimensions of grooves
in drawer fronts and sides

$\frac{1}{4}$

$\frac{1}{4}$

$\frac{3}{16}$

drawer side:
location of dowel
pinhole centers

back

front

$\frac{1}{4}$

$\frac{1}{2}$

$2\frac{9}{16}$

$4\frac{5}{8}$

$\frac{3}{8}$

$\frac{3}{16}''$ pinholes 1" deep

DRAWERS

The drawers are joined with dowel pins at both the front and the back. Use the dimensions in the illustrations to lay out the rabbets in the drawer fronts, and to locate the grooves in the drawer fronts and sides. Also lay out the positions of the dowel pinhole centers in the drawer sides to the dimensions given. Then build and fit the drawers according to the procedures described in *Drawer Construction*, page 112. Note that there are no grooves in the drawer backs. The bottoms are simply nailed to their under edges. Cut the drawer bottoms to fit, and sand their inside surfaces to final smoothness (see *Sanding*, p. 132) before assembling the drawers.

DRAWER PULLS AND STOPS

Lay out the position of the drawer pulls centered both ways on the drawer fronts. Drill the screw holes and attach the pulls (see *Drawer Construction*, p. 120).

Make up the six drawer stops, with the wood grain following the long dimension. Drill and countersink the screw holes as shown in the illustration. Then one at a time push the drawers into the sideboard so that their fronts are flush with the outside edge of the drawer rail. Without moving the drawer, make a pencil mark on each runner at the back of the drawer. Slide the drawer out, align the stops with the pencil marks, and screw the stops to the sides of the runners.

TABLETOP

Cut the single-board top to rough size and use a jack or jointer plane to trim the long edges to make the width a uniform 12 1/4 inches (see *Making Joints*, p. 47). To trim the tabletop to exact length, hold the carpenter's square against one edge of the board and draw a pencil line across one end. Use a fine-toothed crosscut saw (12 pt. or 14 pt.) to trim off the surplus wood to the line. Then smooth the end-grain saw cut with the block plane. Measure the finished length from this good end, square a line across as before, and trim off and plane it smooth in the same way (see *Making Joints*, p. 48). Sand the ends of the tabletop (end grain) to final smoothness (see *Woodworking Practices*, p. 40,

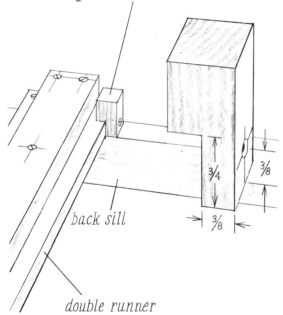

drawer stop fastened to side of runner

back sill

3/4

3/8

3/8

double runner

attaching cleats to the tabletop

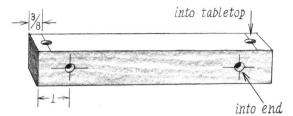

into tabletop

$\frac{3}{8}$

into end

$\leftarrow 1 \rightarrow$

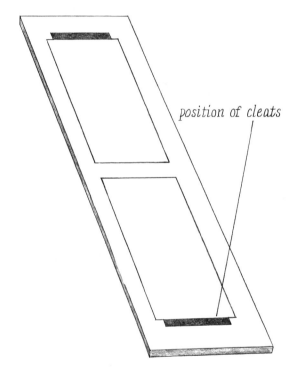

position of cleats

and *Sanding*, p. 132). Make the tabletop cleats and drill and countersink the screw holes in the locations shown in the illustration.

To attach the tabletop to the sideboard frame, lay the tabletop facedown. Set the frame bottom-side up on top of it and adjust its position so that there is a uniform amount of overhang at both ends, and the frame and tabletop are flush along the back. Then mark the position of the tabletop cleats on the tabletop by tracing a line around the inside of the frame. Remove the frame, align the cleats inside these marks, and screw them in place. Again set the frame bottom-side up, and down over the cleats. Drive 2 screws through each cleat into the side rails, and 2 screws through the bearer into the tabletop. Stand the sideboard on its legs and put in the drawers.

Index

Actual dimensions, 15
Board foot, 14
Clamp board, making, 35
Cleats, 45
Countersinking, 39
Door button, making, 128-129
Doorknobs, installing, 129
    hardware sources, 121
Door latch, installing, 199
    hardware sources, 121
Door, hanging, 122-129
    hardware sources, 121
Dovetail gauge, 52
Dowel, 16
Drawbore pins, 72, 78-79
Drawer
    construction, 112-121
    hardware sources, 121
    installing pull, 120-121
    making pullout stops, 119-120
    sealing inside of, 136
Finishes, 142-151
    paint, 149-151
    penetrating-resin oils, 147-149
    polyurethane varnish, 142-146
    varnish, 142-146

Finishing, 130-151
    paint, 149-151
    penetrating-resin oils, 147-149
    polyurethane varnish, 142-146
    staining, 138-142
    surface preparation, 131-136
    varnish, 142-146
Furniture hardware
    door button, 128-129
    doorknobs, 129
    door latch, 199
    drawer pull, 120-121
    hinges, 122-128
    sources of, 121
Furniture projects
    New York Hutch, 155
    Armoire, 169
    Corner Cupboard, 183
    Slant-back Dresser, 201
    Pine Dressing Table, 219
    One-drawer Stand, 235
    Breadboard-top Table, 247
    Pencil-post Bed, 257
    Writing Table, 273
    Blanket Chest, 291
    Sideboard, 303

Furniture square, 15
Glue, 43-44
Gluing, 44-45
Hanging doors, 122-129
Hinges, installing, 122-128
   hardware sources, 121
   pintle, 292, 298-300
Jointing, 28
Joints
   butt, 46-51
   dovetail, 52-59
   groove, 60-62
   halved, 62-66
   housed, 66-69
   mitered, 69-71
   mortise and tenon, 72-79
   notch, 80-82
   rabbet, 83-87
   tongue and groove, 88-92
Lathebox, making, 94-97
Lumber
   buying, 20
   manufacturing, 11-13
   sources, 23-26
   storing, 21-22
Mitering jig, 197
Molding, 16, 167, 180-181, 197
Nailing lines, 36
Nails, 42-43
Nominal dimensions, 15
Octagonal shaping, 102-105
   Pencil-post Bed, 265-269
Paint, 149-151
   primer coat, 136, 149
Paste wood filler, 138
Patterns, 31
Penetrating-resin oils, 147-149
   coloring, 148-149
Pilot hole depth gauge, 38
Pilot holes, 37
Planing end grain, 29-30
Planing, surface, 28

Plywood, 16
Polyurethane varnish, 142-146
Primer coat, 136, 149
Turned legs, 94-111
   lathebox for, 94-97
   octagonal shaping, 102-105
   round turning, 97-107
   shaping posts, *Pencil-post Bed,* 265-269
   square-tapering: four sides, 110-111
   square-tapering: two sides, 108-109
Tack rag, 135-136
Staining, 138-142
   penetrating oil stain, 140
   pigmented oil wiping stain, 139
   water stains, 140
Square-tapering
   four sides, 110-111
   two sides, 108-109
Sanding, 132-135
   end grain, 40-41
   sandpaper chart, 134
Screws, 43
Shellac wash coat, 136
Round turning, 97-107
Raising the grain, 135
Universal Tinting Colors, 148-149
Varnishes, 142-146
Wood species, 17-19
   beech, 18
   birch, 18
   butternut, 19
   cherry, 18
   mahogany, 18
   red maple, 18
   sugar maple, 17
   Northern red oak, 18
   white oak, 18
   Eastern white pine, 19
   Idaho pine, 19
   black walnut, 19
Wood sealers, 136-138
   shellac wash coat, 136